The
PSALMS

The Psalms
Author, Don Kelso
Copyright 2005 Word Of Life
10 Digit ISBN 1-885273-19-3
13 Digit ISBN 978-1-885273-19-2
Second Printing

Scripture from King James Version

First Century Publishing
PO Box 130
Delmar, NY 12054
1.800.578.6060
www.firstcenturypublishing.com

The
PSALMS

By
Don Kelso

Dedication

Being mindful of the directives
in Deuteronomy 4:9, Psalm 78:4-7, and 2 Timothy 2:2
and recalling the words of our Lord Jesus Christ on Resurrection Day
as recorded in Luke 24:44,
I dedicate this work to my ten grandchildren-

Renee, Bryan, Carrie, David, John, Michelle, Joshua, Jessica, Jeffrey
and Kelsey.

"Children's children are the crown of old men..." Proverbs 17:6

Acknowledgements

Acknowledgements and thanks are due to the many people who provided both the physical labor and the financial support to make the publication of this book possible.

Special thanks to the following ladies—

Martha Jensen, beloved friend of many years, transcribed my longhand scribbling into readable type.

My dear daughter, **Denise Loock**, edited the entire original text and transferred it onto floppy disks so that it would be easily accessible and reproducible.

Barbara Ziemer, diligent fellow-worker, performed the tedious task of collating and then binding the individual pages of the manuscript into booklet form so that preliminary, partial printings could be distributed to friends.

My faithful wife, **Dot**, gave the necessary prayer support and the encouragement through the many hours of writing and proofreading.

About the Author
By Denise Kelso Loock

My Father, Don Kelso received Christ as his savior when he was 35 years old. On an autumn afternoon in 1958, Dad's lawyer, Jim Welch, presented the gospel to him. And right there, in Judge Welch's office, he prayed the prayer of salvation.

The next afternoon, as Dad was eating a quick lunch at his desk, a chiropractor, whose office was just down the street from Dad's office building, paid the new Christian a visit. As he entered the office, Dr. Walter Sligh said, "My friend, Jim Welch, told me something happened to you yesterday."

Dad responded by reciting his testimony. Dr. Sligh then handed him a New Testament and challenged him with these words: "Read this today and do not fail to read it everyday until you meet the Lord." Dad did. And so began his insatiable desire for God's Word. Within a couple of years, Dad was teaching Sunday School in his church. Later, his Bible teaching ministry expanded to home Bible studies, Christian Business Men's Committee (CBMC) retreats, and eventually to Bible Institutes and Bible Conference Centers around the world. To date, Dad has taught the Bible in twenty-four countries across the six inhabited continents. He still studies his Bible every morning before most people are awake. For forty-seven years, his daily walk with God has exemplified the teachings of Psalm 119. He has hidden God's Word in his heart (v. 11), God has opened Dad's eyes to His truths (v. 18), His testimonies have been Dad's meditation (v. 99), and he has shared "wondrous things out of [God's] law" (v. 18) with thousands of people all over the world.

Don and Dot, his wife of 60 years, reside in Hillsborough, New Jersey.

Foreword

Mr. Don R. Kelso, whom I lovingly call Mr. "K", was not only used by God to bring me to Word of Life Island where I trusted Christ as my Savior, but to instill within me a deep hunger and thirst for the Word of God. It was also Mr. "K" who channeled me towards the mission field to share the Gospel of Christ. I will never forget as a teenager the Monday afternoons I would spend in his home where he not only taught me the Word of God but also awakened my heart to study God's Holy Word. His great hunger for the Word and exceptional insight into the Word have been the keys to his faithful communication to thousands of his Bible students around the world.

His work on the Psalms is just an example of the insight God has given to him. I know you will be blessed as you take a look into the Book with Mr. "K." You will find his commentary can be used as a devotional, a quiet time meditation or a longer Bible study as you consider the cross references and their context.

My prayer is that your heart will be set aflame to love the God of the Word as you study this portion of God's Word in the Psalms.

I will always remain grateful to God for placing Mr. "K" in my life.

Abounding in His Grace,

Joe Jordan
Executive Director
Word of Life Fellowship

Introduction

Our English word psalms derives from a Greek word denoting "poems sung to the accompaniment of string instruments." The English translation of the Hebrew title is "Book of Praises." Actually, Psalms consists of five books-each ending with a doxology. The superscriptions in the Hebrew text ascribe authorship of seventy-three psalms to David and twenty-seven to various other writers. Fifty psalms are anonymous. However, New Testament references and textual content indicate Davidic authorship of some of those fifty psalms. Truly, David, the son of Jesse, was "raised up on high, the anointed of the God of Jacob" to be not only the king but also "the sweet psalmist of Israel" (2 Sam. 23:1).

The Psalms contain praise, petition, and prophecy as well as perspective on the past history of God's people. A number of them are songs about the creation, glorifying the Creator. Others extol the veracity and the power of God's Word. The prophetic psalms are especially intriguing. Sixteen of these are designated "messianic" because, in whole or in part, they foretell events concerning either the first or second coming of Christ. The words of the risen Christ Himself in Luke 24:27 and 24:44 should alert us to search for our Lord in every psalm.

Several scriptures let us know that the human authors were aware that they were writing under the power and in the wisdom of a Divine Author. (See 2 Sam. 23:2, Ps. 102:18, 19 and 1 Pet. 1:10-12.)

If you will find time to meditate on the words of Psalms, here are some promises for you. You will be fruitful and prosperous in all that you do (Ps. 1:2, 3). You will sleep well (Ps. 4:4, 8). Your soul will be satisfied (Ps. 63:5, 6). You will be glad in the Lord (Ps. 104:34). You will not sin against your God (Ps. 119:11), but you will have respect unto His ways (Ps. 119:15). You will be wiser than your enemies, and you will understand more than your teachers or your elders (Ps. 119:97-100).

Psalm 1

1. BLESSED *IS* the man that walketh not in the counsel of the ungodly, nor standeth in the way of sinners, nor sitteth in the seat of the scornful.
2. But his delight *is* in the law of the LORD, and in his law doth he meditate day and night.
3. And he shall be like a tree planted by the rivers of water, that bringeth forth his fruit in his season; his leaf also shall not wither; and whatsoever he doeth shall prosper.
4. The ungodly *are* not so: but *are* like the chaff which the wind driveth away.
5. Therefore the ungodly shall not stand in the judgment, nor sinners in the congregation of the righteous.
6. For the LORD knoweth the way of the righteous: but the way of the unglodly shall perish.

Commentary_____

Our very first psalm tells of two persons, two ways, and two destinies. The first individual is described as "blessed." His way is called righteous, and he is destined to "prosper." The second individual is called ungodly in his way, and he "shall perish."

Notice that there are three pursuits from which the blessed man refrains—having to do with his walk, where he stands, and with whom he sits. Instead, he engages himself in pursuits which cause whatsoever he does to "prosper."

How does a tree prosper? By engaging in frantic activity? Does it wave its branches forcefully so that it will bear much fruit? Of course not. It prospers by situating itself correctly and receiving the God-given provision. Likewise, the godly person earnestly desires the fruit-producing water of life and the fruit comes forth!

The blessed person is situated "in Christ" (Eph. 1:3) and is walking "in the Spirit" (Gal. 5:16). He is righteous because he is one with Christ who is the Way (Ps. 1:1), the Truth (Ps. 1:2) and the Life (Ps. 1:3).

The ungodly man is "in Adam" (1 Cor. 15:22) and his walk is "according to the course of this world" (Eph. 2:2). Therefore, he will perish!

Application_____

If I delight in the Word of God, I will meditate in the Word of God. If I don't meditate, it is evident that I am not delighted in His Word, and therefore should not expect to qualify for the promise—"whatsoever he doeth shall prosper."

Psalm 2

1. WHY DO the heathen rage, and the people imagine a vain thing?
2. The kings of the earth set themselves, and the rulers take counsel together, against the LORD, and against his anointed, *saying*,
3. Let us break their bands asunder, and cast away their cords from us.
4. He that sitteth in the heavens shall laugh: the Lord shall have them in derision.
5. Then shall he speak unto them in his wrath, and vex them in his sore displeasure.
6. Yet have I set my king upon my holy hill of Zion.
7. I will declare the decree: the LORD hath said unto me, Thou *art* my son; this day have I begotten thee.
8. Ask of me, and I shall give thee the heathen *for* thine inheritance, and the uttermost parts of the earth *for* thy possession.
9. Thou shall break them with a rod of iron; thou shall dash them in pieces like a potter's vessel.
10. Be wise now therefore, O ye kings: be instructed, ye judges of the earth.
11. Serve the LORD with fear, and rejoice with trembling.
12. Kiss the Son, lest he be angry, and ye perish *from* the way, when his wrath is kindled but a little. Blessed *are* all they that put their trust in him.

Commentary_____

Sixteen psalms are designated as "messianic." These, in whole or in part, contain prophetic references to the first or second coming of Christ. In addition, there is New Testament documentation of the messianic portion. Psalm 2 is quoted in Acts, Hebrews, and Revelation for a total of seven times. In Acts 4:25-26, the Apostle Peter quotes verses 1 and 2 in order to prove that the events surrounding the crucifixion of Christ were both foreknown by God and in accordance with His plans and purposes. In Peter's day, Psalm 2:2 was fulfilled in the events recorded in Matthew 26:3-4, Mark 3:6, Luke 23:12-13, and Acts 4:1.

Consider Psalm 2 as a drama on a world stage. In verses 1 and 2, the political and religious leaders are under the spotlight. In effect they say in verse 3, "We will not be controlled by God." They are swept off the stage in verse 4 by God the Father. In verse 6, God the Father announces that He has determined who will be King on Earth. In verse 7, God the Son takes center stage and gives forth a royal decree under the authority given by the Father. His total decree is a promise from the Father! In verse 10, while the spotlight remains on the Son, God the Holy Spirit sounds out advice and warning and offers salvation.

Application_____

According to the last words of Psalm 2, who will be blessed? If you have already trusted Him as Savior, do you now trust Him as absolute King of your life (Col. 2:6)?

Psalm 3

A Psalm of David, when he fled from Absalom his son.

1. LORD, HOW are they increased that trouble me! many *are* they that rise up against me.
2. Many *there be* which say of my soul, *There is* no help for him in God. Selah.
3. But thou, O LORD, *art* a shield for me; my glory, and the lifter up of mine head.
4. I cried unto the LORD with my voice, and he heard me out of his holy hill. Selah.
5. I laid me down and slept; I awaked: for the LORD sustained me.
6. I will not be afraid of ten thousands of people, that have set *themselves* against me round about.
7. Arise, O LORD; save me, O my God: for thou hast smitten all mine enemies *upon* the cheek bone; thou hast broken the teeth of the ungodly.
8. Salvation *belongeth* unto the LORD: thy blessing is upon thy people. Selah.

Commentary_____

Many of the psalms of David arose from his experiences. Psalm 3 was probably written on the first or second morning after his nighttime flight across the Jordan River when he was pursued by the armies of his son Absalom. (See 2 Sam. 17).

As David was reflecting upon the events of the previous night, he recorded the progress of his outlook from troubled (vs. 1, 2) to trusting (vs. 3, 4) to tranquil (v. 5). He awakened triumphant (vs. 6-8)! His recipe for transforming a troubled soul into a trusting soul was to turn his thoughts from "the many against me" to "the LORD my shield, my glory, and the lifter up of my head." The result is a tranquil soul that is able to lie down and sleep and then to awake with confidence restored. Although the battle lay ahead, the victory was already claimed.

The little Hebrew word *selah* is found in the Bible only in Psalms (71 times) and Habakkuk (3 times). Most Bible scholars see the word as a directive to the instrumental musicians accompanying the singing of the psalm. This would mean the word was not in the original composition. Other scholars say the root meaning is "always and forever." One commentator believes the thought conveyed to the reader is "you have just read eternal truth—pause and reflect upon it."

Application_____

How often have troubles arisen in your life that robbed you of sleep and tranquility? Not many of us have been in circumstances as dire as David's. Yet he testifies that this "recipe" worked for him!

Psalm 4

To the chief Musician on Neginoth. A Psalm of David.

1. HEAR ME when I call, O God of my righteousness: thou hast enlarged me *when I was* in distress; have mercy upon me, and hear my prayer.
2. O ye sons of men, how long *will ye turn* my glory into shame? *how long* will ye love vanity, *and* seek after leasing? Selah.
3. But know that the LORD hath set apart him that is godly for himself: the LORD will hear when I call unto him.
4. Stand in awe, and sin not: commune with your own heart upon your bed, and be still. Selah.
5. Offer the sacrifices of righteousness, and put your trust in the LORD.
6. *There be* many that say, Who will shew us *any* good? LORD, lift thou up the light of thy countenance upon us.
7. Thou hast put gladness in my heart, more than in the time *that* their corn and their wine increased.
8. I will both lay me down in peace, and sleep: for thou, LORD, only makest me dwell in safety.

Commentary_____

Since ancient times, Psalm 3 has been entitled "a morning psalm" and Psalm 4 "an evening psalm." Psalm 4 was probably penned as a result of the victory recorded in 2 Samuel 18:1-8 and before David learned of the death of Absalom (2 Sam. 18:9).

"O God of my righteousness"—David knew that he possessed no righteousness of his own and that a right relationship with God depended upon appropriating for himself God's own righteousness. When one is walking in divinely supplied righteousness, he has God's special attentiveness because "the LORD has set him apart" (v. 3). Absalom offered a vain sacrifice that was unacceptable to God (2 Sam. 15:12), whereas David understood the true significance of animal sacrifice. Compare Psalm 50:8-15 with Psalm 51:16-19.

When a person receives material gain such as a bountiful harvest (v. 7), there is gladness of heart. David wants us to know that there is available from the Lord an inner gladness of heart that transcends any elation obtained from material gain. The evidence of such gladness is peace and security and a good night's sleep! Our God supplies the best brand of sleeping pills!

Application_____

"The work of righteousness shall be peace: and the effect of righteousness, quietness and assurance forever" (Isa. 32:17). Whether it be peace among nations, peace within the family circle, or peace within the heart, there is no peace apart from righteousness because peace is a product of righteousness.

Psalm 5

To the chief musician upon Nehiloth. A Psalm of David.

1. GIVE EAR to my words, O LORD, consider my meditation.
2. Hearken unto the voice of my cry, my King, and my God: for unto thee will I pray.
3. My voice shalt thou hear in the morning, O LORD; in the morning will I direct *my prayer* unto thee, and will look up.
4. For thou *art* not a God that hath pleasure in wickedness: neither shall evil dwell with thee.
5. The foolish shall not stand in thy sight: thou hatest all workers of iniquity.
6. Thou shalt destroy them that speak leasing: the LORD will abhor the bloody and deceitful man.
7. But as for me, I will come *into* thy house in the multitude of thy mercy *and* in thy fear will I worship toward thy holy temple.
8. Lead me, O LORD, in thy righteousness because of mine enemies; make thy way straight before my face.
9. For *there is* no faithfulness in their mouth; their inward part *is* very wickedness; their throat *is* an open sepulchre; they flatter with their tongue.
10. Destroy thou them, O God; let them fall by their own counsels; cast them out in the multitude of their transgressions; for they have rebelled against thee.
11. But let all those who put their trust in thee rejoice: let them ever shout for joy, because thou defendest them: let them also that love thy name be joyful in thee.
12. For thou, LORD, wilt bless the righteous; with favour wilt thou compass him as *with* a shield.

Commentary_____

This psalm is a morning prayer for guidance throughout the day while living in a godless, hostile world. It has been suggested that it will be of particular relevance to the Jewish remnant during the Great Tribulation (Rom. 9:27). Certainly it is a good prayer for anyone of any age desiring to follow the right path in an adverse environment.

The "foolish" in verse 5 are not those who are simpletons or clowns but persons who possess an arrogant denial of God's right to exercise authority over His creatures (Ps. 14:1). Such are described in detail in Romans 3:10-18. There the apostle uses quotations from four psalms, including this one (v. 9), and also several passages from Isaiah to uncover the depth of human depravity.

The temple mentioned in verse 7 does not refer to the temple in Jerusalem, which was built after David's death, but to God's heavenly dwelling place. See Psalm 11:4 and Psalm 18:6.

The answer to the prayer in verse 10 will have final culmination at Armageddon as described in Revelation 19:11-21.

Notice in verse 11 that rejoicing doesn't arise from present favorable circumstances but from absolute trust in the defender and a love for His name (Lk. 6:22, 23; 1 Pet. 1:6).

Application_____

"Thou will bless and compass with a shield" (v. 12). What type of blessings do you want from God? According to Ephesians 1:3-7, we have already been "blessed" through being "chosen" (v. 4), "accepted" (v. 6), "redeemed" (v. 7), and "forgiven" (v. 7). Your sealing by the Holy Spirit (Eph. 1:13) is your "compassing with a shield." Do you also require material blessing?

Psalm 6

To the chief Musician on Neginoth upon Sheminith. A Psalm of David.

1. O LORD, rebuke me not in thine anger, neither chasten me in thy hot displeasure.
2. Have mercy upon me, O LORD; for I *am* weak: O LORD, heal me; for my bones are vexed.
3. My soul is also sore vexed: but thou, O LORD, how long?
4. Return, O LORD, deliver my soul: oh save me for thy mercies' sake.
5. For in death *there is* no remembrance of thee: in the grave who shall give thee thanks?
6. I am weary with my groaning; all the night make I my bed to swim; I water my couch with my tears.
7. Mine eye is consumed because of grief; it waxeth old because of all mine enemies.
8. Depart from me, all ye workers of iniquity; for the LORD hath heard the voice of my weeping.
9. The LORD hath heard my supplication; the LORD will receive my prayer.
10. Let all mine enemies be ashamed and sore vexed: let them return *and* be ashamed suddenly.

Commentary_____

From ancient times, seven of the psalms have been classified as "penitential." These seven express confession and sorrow for sins committed. Six of the seven are attributed to David and at least four are considered to have arisen from David's act of adultery with Bathsheba and his murder of Uriah (2 Sam. 11). When David was confronted with his sins by the prophet Nathan, he confessed (2 Sam. 12:13). Nathan told David that his sins were forgiven but prophesied that David would suffer grave consequences (2 Sam. 12:10-14). The fulfillment of these prophesied consequences are recorded in 2 Samuel 12:15--20:13.

In 2 Samuel 12:14, Nathan prophesied, "By this deed, you have given great occasion to the enemies of the LORD to blaspheme." This is the consequence that gave David grief of spirit and soul for the rest of his life.

David's penitential psalms can best be understood if read in the following sequence: first Psalm 38, then Psalm 6, next Psalm 51 and finally Psalm 32. This is likely the order in which they were penned over a period of weeks as he progressed from overwhelming remorse to a joyful realization of the blessedness of divine forgiveness. After reading this record of David's repentance and restoration, you will then understand why the LORD could call such a gross sinner as David, "a man after my own heart" (Acts 13:22).

Application_____

Every faithful servant of God will likely encounter a fellow Christian in deep remorse existing day to day with head bowed in shame and disgrace for sins already confessed and forgiven. Someone needs to show such a one how to get the "accuser" of the brethren off his back (Rev. 12:10). What better way than to show him the pathway trod by King David as recorded in God's Book!

Psalm 7:1-8

Shiggaion of David, which he sang unto the LORD, concerning the words of Cush the Benjamite.

1. O LORD my God, in thee do I put my trust: save me from all them that persecute me, and deliver me:
2. Lest he tear my soul like a lion, rending *it* in pieces, while *there is* none to deliver.
3. O LORD my God, if I have done this; if there be iniquity in my hands;
4. If I have rewarded evil unto him that was at peace with me; (yea, I have delivered him that without cause is mine enemy:)
5. Let the enemy persecute my soul, and take *it*; yea, let him tread down my life upon the earth, and lay mine honor in the dust. Selah.
6. Arise, O LORD, in thine anger, lift up thyself because of the rage of mine enemies: and awake for me *to* the judgment *that* thou hast commanded.
7. So shall the congregation of the people compass thee about: for their sakes therefore return thou on high.
8. The LORD shall judge the people: judge me, O LORD, according to my righteousness, and according to mine integrity *that is* in me.

Commentary_____

For a number of years between the anointing of David by Samuel (1 Sam. 16:13), and the death of King Saul (1 Sam. 31:6), David was relentlessly pursued, persecuted and falsely accused by Saul and his armies. Saul knew that David was the LORD's choice for king (1 Sam. 24:20), but he coveted the crown for his own son. During these years, David penned several psalms. The likely historical background for Psalm 7 is given in 1 Samuel 23-26.

Notice the superscription above the psalm. Since the translators didn't know the meaning of *Shiggaion*, they left it untranslated. Respected Hebrew scholars have various opinions about this word's meaning. The historical text doesn't mention a Benjamite named Cush. The name *Cush* is probably a reference to Saul, the Benjamite who persecuted (v. 1), pursued (v. 2) and falsely accused (v. 3) David.

In verses 3-5, David declares his innocence before the LORD. In verse 6, he pleads with the LORD to awaken unto His office of Judge and take action against David's enemies. In verse 7, he points out that his request is being made on behalf of the LORD's people. In verse 8, he quotes from Deuteronomy 32:36 in order to give a scriptural basis for his plea.

Application_____

Verse 2 reminds us that David's real enemy (and ours) is the Devil who "like a roaring lion walketh about seeking whom he may devour" (1 Pet. 5:8). In His own time, the Judge of the whole earth will rise up and judge both Satan and those who do his work (Mt. 25:41; Rev. 20:10). Just as Satan uses humans to do his work, so will the LORD use us in bringing Satan to judgment (Rom. 16:20).

Psalm 7: 9-17

9. Oh let the wickedness of the wicked come to an end; but establish the just: for the righteous God trieth the hearts and reins.

10. My defense *is* of God, which saveth the upright in heart.

11. God judgeth the righteous, and God is angry *with the wicked* every day.

12. If he turn not, he will whet his sword; he hath bent his bow, and made it ready.

13. He hath also prepared for him the instruments of death; he ordaineth his arrows against the persecutors.

14. Behold, he travaileth with iniquity, and hath conceived mischief, and brought forth falsehood.

15. He made a pit, and digged it, and is fallen into the ditch *which* he made.

16. His mischief shall return upon his own head, and his violent dealing shall come down upon his own pate.

17. I will praise the LORD according to his righteousness: and will sing praise to the name of the LORD most high.

Commentary_____

David longs for a time when wickedness will cease and righteous-ness will prevail. He also knows that only his God can accomplish this result. He expresses his confidence that the LORD has both the will and the ability to make things right.

When David is given the opportunity to avenge himself, he refuses to do so (1 Sam. 26:8-11). He knows that vengeance belongs to God alone (Deut. 32:35, Heb.10:30). Therefore he appeals to God for vindi-cation.

Having declared his confidence in God (v. 10), David uses this psalm to counsel others about God's attitude and actions concerning the righteous versus the wicked. Let the wicked be informed that "the righteous God" is fully aware of the thoughts and deeds of the wicked. God is angry with their wickedness and is fully prepared to take appro-priate action in His time.

In verse 14, David describes his adversary. In verse 15, he likens him to a huntsman who digs a camouflaged pit to catch prey and then falls into his own trap. See also Psalm 57:6, Proverbs 26:27 and Ecclesiastes 10:8. The fate of Haman (Est. 7:10) is a good scriptural example of a wicked man destroyed by his own evil "devices"
(Ps. 10:2).

Application_____

Notice in verse 17 of our psalm how David ends by offering praise and adoration to his God. He knows how to get God's ear so that God has a basis for preserving David in order to use him to perform God's purposes on Earth. David exalts the LORD regardless of his circum-stances. Again, this is the reason God is pleased to call David "a man after His own heart" (Acts 13:22).

Psalm 8

To the chief Musician upon Gittith, A Psalm of David.

1. O LORD our Lord, how excellent *is* thy name in all the earth! who hast set thy glory above the heavens.
2. Out of the mouth of babes and sucklings hast thou ordained strength because of thine enemies, that thou mightest still the enemy and the avenger.
3. When I consider thy heavens, the work of thy fingers, the moon and the stars, which thou hast ordained;
4. What is man, that thou are mindful of him? and the son of man, that thou visitest him?
5. For thou hast made him a little lower than the angels, and has crowned him with glory and honour.
6. Thou madest him to have dominion over the works of thy hands; thou hast put all *things* under his feet.
7. All sheep and oxen, yea, the beasts of the field;
8. The fowl of the air, and the fish of the sea, *and whatsoever* passeth through the paths of the seas.
9. O LORD our Lord, how excellent *is* thy name in all the earth!

Commentary

Has God indeed crowned man with glory and honor above all created things, including the angels? It is true that God has ordained that man shall have dominion "over all the earth" (Gen. 1:26; Ps. 8:6; Heb. 2:8). He has not retracted nor will He retract that ordinance. However, the human race, in Adam, forfeited that dominion to Satan. When the Son of Man, Christ Jesus, has all things "put under His feet" (Ps. 8:6; 1 Cor.15:25; Eph. 1:22), the dominion by man will far surpass that which was lost in Adam. The Man Christ Jesus shall be exalted "far above all principality, and power and might, and dominion" (Eph. 1:21). We who are "joint heirs with Christ" shall be "glorified together" with Him (Rom. 8:17).

Psalm 8 is the second of the Messianic Psalms. (See commentary on Psalm 2). Messianic Psalms can be fully appreciated only when Jesus Christ is the focal point. Verse 2 was quoted by Christ on the day of the "triumphal entry" (Matt. 21:16). Verses 4--6 are quoted in Hebrews 2:6-8, with Hebrews 2:9 explaining that the reference is to Jesus. Above, we pointed to the quotations from verse 6 in 1 Corinthians and Ephesians.

"O LORD (*Yahweh*), our Lord (*Adonai*) how excellent is thy name in all the earth!" The first and last lines of Psalm 8 are the same for emphasis. *Yahweh* (*Jehovah*) is God as He deigns to reach down to man. *Adonai* is God as man responds. Jesus is both God reaching down to us and our access to God.

Application

"—we would see Jesus" (Jn. 12:21). Let us look for the person and ministry of Christ in every psalm—especially in the Messianic Psalms. Read what Jesus Himself said on His resurrection day concerning His presence in the Psalms (Lk. 24:44).

Psalm 9:1-10

To the chief Musician upon Muthlabben, A Psalm of David.

1. I WILL praise *thee*, O LORD, with my whole heart; I will shew forth all thy marvelous works.
2. I will be glad and rejoice in thee: I will sing praise to thy name, O thou most High.
3. When mine enemies are turned back, they shall fall and perish at thy presence.
4. For thou hast maintained my right and my cause; thou satest in the throne judging right.
5. Thou hast rebuked the heathen, thou hast destroyed the wicked, thou hast put out their name for ever and ever.
6. O thou enemy, destructions are come to a perpetual end: and thou hast destroyed cities; their memorial is perished with them.
7. But the LORD shall endure for ever: he hath prepared his throne for judgment.
8. And he shall judge the world in righteousness, he shall minister judgment to the people in uprightness.
9. The LORD also will be a refuge for the oppressed, a refuge in times of trouble.
10. And they that know thy name will put their trust in thee: for thou, LORD, hast not forsaken them that seek thee.

Commentary_____

Because of structure and content, scholars have long deduced that Psalms 9 and 10 were originally one acrostic poem of 22 four-line stanzas. Each line of the first stanza began with *Aleph,* the first letter, and so on through the 22 letters of the Hebrew alphabet. When the psalm was divided, probably for liturgical purposes, the stanzas for some Hebrew letters were omitted. However, we can be certain that the Holy Spirit has preserved for us that which is needful. His faithfulness is to all generations (Ps. 33:11; 100:5; 119:89, 90).

King David declares his determination to render wholehearted praise to the LORD and to yield body, soul, and spirit to the LORD's marvelous works (v. 1). He will joyfully praise the Most High (v. 2) because of past victories (vv. 3-6). In verse 7, he acknowledges that the LORD has heard and will continue to hear the plea he made in Psalm 7:6. In verses 8 and 9, David looks forward to the time, later prophesied in Isaiah 11:1-5, when the righteous Judge shall sit upon His throne at Jerusalem.

Meanwhile, God's people from David's day until our day rested and continue to rest in the promises of verses 9 and 10. Think of the comfort this psalm will be to the oppressed people waiting for Messiah's deliverance during the Great Tribulation.

Application_____

Notice the order of the four "I wills" in the first two verses of Psalm 9. A singing heart comes from one who is glad and rejoicing. There is nothing in this world that gladdens a heart more than the realization that God is using one's life to show forth His marvelous works. This privilege is reserved for those who are "wholehearted" in their praise to the Lord.

Psalm 9:11-20

11. Sing praises to the LORD, which dwelleth in Zion: declare among the people his doings.
12. When he maketh inquisition for blood, he remembereth them: he forgetteth not the cry of the humble.
13. Have mercy upon me, O LORD; consider my trouble *which I suffer* of them that hate me, thou that liftest me up from the gates of death:
14. That I may shew forth all thy praise in the gates of the daughter of Zion: I will rejoice in thy salvation.
15. The heathen are sunk down in the pit *that* they made: in the net which they hid is their own foot taken.
16. The LORD is known *by* the judgment *which* he executeth: the wicked is snared in the work of his own hands. Higgaion. Selah.
17. The wicked shall be turned into hell, *and* all the nations that forget God.
18. For the needy shall not alway be forgotten: the expectation of the poor shall *not* perish for ever.
19. Arise, O LORD; let not man prevail: let the heathen be judged in thy sight.
20. Put them in fear, O LORD: *that* the nations may know themselves *to be but* men. Selah.

Commentary_____

The name Zion is found thirty-seven times in the Psalms. One cannot understand the full significance of some psalms without knowing the significance of Zion. It is named at least 150 times in the Old Testament and 7 times in the New Testament. Historically, Zion was that particular fortress hill on which King David built his palace. After the Temple was built, it became a designation for the city of Jerusalem, particularly as that city was the place of gathering for the faithful who came to observe the feasts three times each year. Figuratively, Zion is that place from which God's true government emanates.

Psalm 9 declares at least five awesome truths about the LORD (*Yahweh*). First, He shall endure forever (v. 7). Second, He has prepared a throne for judgment (v. 7). Third, He shall judge the world in righteousness (v. 8). Fourth, He will be a refuge for the oppressed in times of trouble (v. 9). Fifth, He is known by the judgment he executes (v. 16).

As a result of the five truths above, what will happen to the wicked enemies of God's people? They shall fall and perish (v. 3). Their names shall be blotted out forever (v. 5). They shall sink in the pit that they made (v. 15). They shall be snared in the work of their own hands (v. 16). They shall know themselves to be but men (v. 20).

Therefore, what should *Yahweh's* people do? Put their trust in Him (v.10). Seek Him (v. 10). Sing His praises (v. 11). Declare His doings (v. 11). Rejoice in His salvation (v. 14).

Application_____

"For whatsoever things were written aforetimes were written for our learning, that we, through patience and comfort of the scriptures, might have hope" (Rom. 15:4). To what extent do you think God may have had you in mind when He had the above truths put in writing thousands of years ago?

Psalms 10:1-11

1. WHY STANDEST thou afar off, O LORD? *why* hidest thou *thyself* in times of trouble?
2. The wicked in *his* pride doth persecute the poor: let them be taken in the devices that they have imagined.
3. For the wicked boasteth of his heart's desire, and blesseth the covetous, *whom* the LORD abhorreth.
4. The wicked, through the pride of his countenance, will not seek *after God*. God *is* not in all his thoughts.
5. His ways are always grievous; thy judgments *are* far above out of his sight: *as for* all his enemies, he puffeth at them.
6. He hath said in his heart, I shall not be moved: for *I shall* never *be* in adversity.
7. His mouth is full of cursing and deceit and fraud: under his tongue *is* mischief and vanity.
8. He sitteth in the lurking places of the villages: in the secret places doth he murder the innocent: his eyes are privily set against the poor.
9. He lieth in wait secretly as a lion in his den: he lieth in wait to catch the poor: he doth catch the poor, when he draweth him into his net.
10. He croucheth, *and* humbleth himself, that the poor may fall by his strong ones.
11. He hath said in his heart, God hath forgotten: he hideth his face; he will never see *it*.

Commentary_____

In both Psalm 9 and Psalm 10, the psalmist is observing the wicked and God's judgment of wickedness. Why is it then that in Psalm 9 there is singing, praising and rejoicing while in Psalm 10 there is somber consternation? In Psalm 9, although the psalmist observes the wicked, his eyes are focused upon the Judge of all the earth. In Psalm 10, although he is aware of the Judge, his eyes are focused upon the unjudged wicked. That's the difference between singing and somberness whether one is living in David's day or ours. On the one hand, God seems to be "dwelling in Zion" (9:11); on the other hand, He seems to be "hiding afar off" (10:1).

A fuller explanation involves the identity of the wicked ones under King David's observation. Those in Psalm 9 are inhabitants of the surrounding heathen nations. David's armies are being used by God to bring judgment upon the wickedness of those nations (9:15). In Psalm 10 it appears that David's concern is about the proud oppressors of the poor within his own realm. He is puzzled as to why God is bringing judgment to the wicked ones outside his realm and appears to be unconcerned about the wickedness within his realm.

"God is not in all his thoughts" (Ps. 10:4). "The LORD knows the thoughts of man" (Ps. 94:11). "They know not the thoughts of the LORD" (Mic. 4:12). Although man may not want to think about God, that doesn't keep God from knowing the thoughts of man. It just prevents man from knowing how God thinks. How comforting for the believer to know that His thoughts are "us-ward" (Ps.40:5).

Application_____

The Bible is clear concerning the fact that God knows our thoughts (Ps. 139:2; Lk. 9:47). The unspiritual person resents this as an invasion of his privacy. The spiritual person is comforted that God knows and still cares. I wonder how pleased God is with my thought life!

Psalm 10:12-18

12. Arise, O LORD; O God, lift up thine hand: forget not the humble.
13. Wherefore doth the wicked contemn God? he hath said in his heart, Thou wilt not require *it*.
14. Thou hast seen *it;* for thou beholdest mischief and spite, to requite *it* with thy hand: the poor committeth himself unto thee; thou art the helper of the fatherless.
15. Break thou the arm of the wicked and the evil *man:* seek out his wickedness *till* thou find none.
16. The LORD *is* King for ever and ever: the heathen are perished out of his land.
17. LORD, thou hast heard the desire of the humble: thou wilt prepare their heart, thou will cause thine ear to hear:
18. To judge the fatherless and the oppressed, that the man of the earth may no more oppress.

Commentary_____

We learned in Psalm 9 that the psalmist is certain that God will
judge wickedness. However, in 10:1 he expresses impatience with
God's timing. In verses 2 through 11, he rehearses to God all the
reasons it is time for God to act. In verses 12-15 he is saying, "God,
you are forgetting that the lowly ones are counting on you, so please
get busy with your judging!" The psalmist knows that God is omniscient (v. 14). He knows that God is able (v. 15). So why is God waiting to act?

The psalmist's problem is the same as our problem concerning
many of our petitions. We are looking at circumstances from our perspective instead of God's perspective. The root problem is that we
have not spent enough time meditating upon God's Word. That's
where we'll find God's viewpoint. It is interesting to note that the first
three recorded prayers in the Bible are all petitions by Abraham, "the
Friend of God." In each case the answer was "no!"
(Gen. 15:3, 17:18, 18:23). Abraham didn't know God's viewpoint.

Thankfully, David ended his prayer well (vv. 16-18). He simply
recounted to God that which he knew to be true about God concerning the problem. As a result, God measured to him enough faith to
be at rest (Ps. 37:5-7).

Application_____

Is God causing you to wait concerning some of your anxious petitions? You know that God is omniscient. Therefore, He knows the correct timing. You know that He is omnipotent. Therefore, He is able to
do it when the time is right. Rest and rejoice in that knowledge!

Psalm 11

To the chief Musician. *A Psalm* **of David**

1. IN THE LORD put I my trust: how say ye to my soul, Flee *as* a bird to your mountain?
2. For, lo, the wicked bend *their* bow, they make ready their arrow upon the string, that they may privily shoot at the upright in heart.
3. If the foundations be destroyed, what can the righteous do?
4. The LORD *is* in his holy temple, the LORD'S throne *is* in heaven: his eyes behold, his eyelids try, the children of men.
5. The LORD trieth the righteous: but the wicked and him that loveth violence his soul hateth.
6. Upon the wicked he shall rain snares, fire and brimstone, and an horrible tempest: *this shall be* the portion of their cup.
7. For the righteous LORD loveth righteousness; his countenance doth behold the upright.

Commentary

Psalm 11 likely arises from the historical events recorded in 1 Samuel 15-17. In direct opposition to God's known will, the people of Israel had insisted on having a king "that we also may be like all the nations" (1 Sam. 8:20). Now the harvest had failed and the people were hiding in caves, thickets, rocks, holes and pits for fear of the invading Philistines (1 Sam. 13:6). The king was rejected by God because of disobedience (13:13; 15:19; 16:14). King Saul had become a sniveling coward and the army had fled before the Philistines (17:24). The King and the people were "dismayed and greatly afraid" (17:11).

In Psalm 11, David hears, "flee to the mountains! Wickedness is winning over righteousness! The foundations of the nation are destroyed! What is there to do but flee?" David's reaction: My trust is in the LORD. He is on the throne in a place where the enemy cannot reach. He is intently watching the scene concerning His people on earth. He is holy and looks upon His people as holy because He has set them apart for His purposes. He is in control and is testing His people. He will care for them and will rain destruction upon the wicked whom He hates.

Application

If you are a realist, you recognize that the foundations of the social order in which you live are crumbling. The Bible predicts that the political, religious, military, educational and cultural orders of this present world will surely be destroyed. So "what can the righteous do?" Answer—place complete reliance upon the all-sufficient God of the Universe personified in the Lord Jesus Christ who loves you and gave Himself for you. "I have overcome the world" (Jn 16:33).

Psalm 12

To the chief Musician upon Sheminith. A Psalm of David.

1. HELP, LORD; for the godly man ceaseth; for the faithful fail from among the children of men.
2. They speak vanity every one with his neighbour: *with* flattering lips *and* with a double heart do they speak.
3. The LORD shall cut off all flattering lips, *and* the tongue that speaketh proud things:
4. Who have said, With our tongue will we prevail; our lips *are* our own: who *is* lord over us?
5. For the oppression of the poor, for the sighing of the needy, now will I arise, saith the LORD; I will set *him* in safety *from him that* puffeth at him.
6. The words of the LORD *are* pure words: *as* silver tried in a furnace of earth, purified seven times.
7. Thou shall keep them, O LORD, thou shalt preserve them from this generation for ever.
8. The wicked walk on every side, when the vilest men are exalted.

Commentary_____

Psalm 12 consists of four two-verse stanzas. The first two stanzas tell how sinful man uses words to oppress others and defy the LORD. In answer to the plea in verse 1, God reveals what He will ultimately do about the situation. In verses 5-8 He gives words of assurance to the oppressed, poor, and needy. For all generations, the LORD will preserve both His Words and the oppressed. This promise is true even though "the wicked walk on every side" and "the vilest men are exalted."

To flatter is to praise or compliment in order to receive a favorable reaction, without regard for veracity. Most people employ flattery to some degree. We may not flatter for socially evil motives such as occupational advancement, political support or sexual favor. Maybe we flatter simply because we want to be considered "nice." If you want to know what God thinks of flattery, look up the word in its noun, verb and adjective forms in a good concordance.

Many numbers such as *seven* (v. 6) are frequently used in a figurative sense in Scripture. The figurative meaning for *seven* is "complete" or "to the fullest extent" (Dan. 3:19). Sometimes the number is to be interpreted literally but also has a figurative connotation (2 Ki. 5:14, 8:1). The discerning reader will understand that figurative connotation by the context.

Application_____

Only by diligent study of the Bible can we know how to use words in a way that is pleasing to the Lord (2 Tim. 2:15-17). If we rely upon our society's educational process, we will surely use words to our temporal and eternal detriment (1 Tim. 6:20, 21).

Psalm 13

To the chief Musician. A Psalm of David.

1. HOW LONG wilt thou forget me, O LORD? for ever? how long wilt thou hide thy face from me?
2. How long shall I take counsel in my soul, *having* sorrow in my heart daily? how long shall mine enemy be exalted over me?
3. Consider *and* hear me, O LORD my God: lighten mine eyes, lest I sleep the *sleep of* death;
4. Lest mine enemy say, I have prevailed against him; and those that trouble me rejoice when I am moved.
5. But I have trusted in thy mercy; my heart shall rejoice in thy salvation.
6. I will sing unto the LORD, because he hath dealt bountifully with me.

Commentary_____

Most likely twelve to fourteen years passed between the time David was anointed king by Samuel (1 Sam. 16:13) and the day he began to reign at age thirty (2 Sam. 5:4). After slaying Goliath, David was a part of King Saul's court for several years. When Saul saw that David was more popular than he was, Saul tried to kill David in several ways. David escaped and was a fugitive for a number of years. Several times he despaired of his life until he recalled God's promise to make him king. When his trust overcame his fear, he would write a psalm. This is one that arose from that experience. It was probably penned during the latter years of his flight after he had tried several devious devices to survive (1 Sam. 21:10-15; 27:5-12).

At times it really seemed to David that his LORD had forgotten him (v. 1). During those times he would counsel himself and use his own ingenuity to solve his problems. This brought nothing but sorrow (v. 2). So he pled with God, using both of the most prevalent names for God (*Elohim and Yahweh*). He begged for enlightenment (v. 3). Then he reasoned with God, saying how the enemy would be the one to benefit by David's death (v. 4). The LORD answered by measuring to David sufficient faith to trust (v. 5; Rom. 12:3). Despite his dire circumstances, David was able to rejoice in the salvation God had promised. His faith produced singing for David and this psalm for us.

Application_____

Think of all the occasions throughout history on which God's people have needed and used this psalm of David's faith for strength in their times of weakness. Think of all the people who have sunk in the mire of despondency because they haven't spent enough time in the Word to know this psalm is available.

Psalm 14

To the chief Musician. *A Psalm* **of David.**

1. THE FOOL hath said in his heart *There is* no God. They are corrupt, they have done abominable works, *there is* none that doeth good.
2. The LORD looked down from heaven upon the children of men, to see if there were any that did understand, *and* seek God.
3. They are all gone aside, they are *all* together become filthy: *there is* none that doeth good, no, not one.
4. Have all the workers of iniquity no knowledge? who eat up my people *as* they eat bread and call not upon the LORD.
5. There were they in great fear: for God *is* in the generation of the righteous.
6. Ye have shamed the counsel of the poor, because the LORD *is* his refuge.
7. Oh that the salvation of Israel *were come* out of Zion! when the LORD bringeth back the captivity of his people, Jacob shall rejoice, *and* Israel shall be glad.

Commentary_____

Psalm 14 is repeated as Psalm 53 with some variation and is quoted in Romans 3:10-12 to show the condition of the unregenerate human heart.

"—said in his heart." In Bible terminology, sins of thought and conduct are "heart errors." Israel wandered in the desert instead of possessing the land of abundance because they "erred in their hearts " (Ps. 95:10; Heb. 3:10). Jesus said all of the gross sins listed in Mark 7:21-22 came from the heart. Pharaoh (Ex. 9:34), Ananias (Acts 5:4), and Simon the Sorcerer (Acts 8:21) all had "heart" problems.

"The LORD looked down from heaven—." In Scripture, often the LORD looks down from heaven to bring judgment to sinful man—for example, the flood (Gen. 6:5), the confusion of languages (Gen. 11:5), and the destruction of Sodom and Gomorrah (Gen. 18:21). When the LORD comes down from heaven, usually it is to show mercy and bring deliverance. See Exodus 3:8, 19:20, 20:20, 34:5 and John 6:33, 38, 51. Also note Acts 7:34.

Verse 7 looks forward to the Millennium when God's people in Israel will live in blessedness under the rule of their Messiah. God changed *Jacob's* name to Israel in Genesis 32:28. The name Jacob is used to designate all of the literal descendants of the patriarch Jacob, son of Isaac, son of Abraham. *Israel* (meaning "Prince of God" or "God's ruler") designates the nation of people that derived from Jacob's twelve sons. So in a sense the terms can be synonymous.

Application_____

One day we will rejoice and be glad along with God's special nation as we join in the benefits of the reign of Jesus Christ on Earth. Looking forward in joyous anticipation, let us not be weary in well doing (Gal. 6:9).

Psalm 15

A Psalm of David.

1. LORD, WHO shall abide in thy tabernacle? who shall dwell in thy holy hill?
2. He that walketh uprightly, and worketh righteousness, and speaketh the truth in his heart.
3. *He that* backbiteth not with his tongue, nor doeth evil to his neighbor, nor taketh up a reproach against his neighbor.
4. In whose eyes a vile person is contemned; but he honoureth them that fear the LORD. *He that* sweareth to *his own* hurt, and changeth not.
5. *He that* putteth not out his money to usury, nor taketh reward against the innocent. He that doeth these *things* shall never be moved.

Commentary_____

The subject matter of Psalm 14 involves the conduct of those who have no "heart for God." In contrast Psalm 15 tells how an individual lives who has a genuine "heart for God."

The question in the first verse of Psalm 15 is not asking what is required to attain a place in heaven. It is asking how one conducts himself here on Earth as a proper member of the household of God. In order to have moment by moment fellowship with a holy God, one needs an upright walk, righteous works, and truthful words (v. 2). Verses 3 through 5 expand upon the walk, works, and words theme but in inverse order. There are eight practical examples.

The surest way to do evil to a neighbor or reproach a friend is to use the tongue against him. The result is not only the loss of a good neighbor but also broken fellowship with God. Good works and a proper walk involve keeping promises regardless of cost (v. 4).

Disunity and discord within the household of faith frequently involve financial matters (v. 5). According to 1 Corinthians 6:7, we should be willing to be defrauded financially by a brother in Christ rather than to seek legal remedies (Eph. 4:2, 3).

The last line of verse 5 is a promise from God that one who lives by these principles will not be toppled from his foundation of faith in God's Word.

Application_____

It is amazing that words written 3,000 years ago could be completely applicable in the modern hi-tech world. It should cause the person who has "a heart for God" to cry from within, "Surely these are God-words and not man-words. Only an eternal omniscient God could see my time and know how to meet my needs."

Psalm 16

Michtam of David.

1. PRESERVE ME, O God: for in thee do I put my trust.
2. O *my soul*, thou hast said unto the LORD, Thou *art* my Lord: my goodness *extendeth* not to thee;
3. *But* to the saints that *are* in the earth, and *to* the excellent, in whom *is* all my delight.
4. Their sorrows shall be multiplied *that* hasten *after* another *god:* their drink offerings of blood will I not offer, nor take up their names into my lips.
5. The Lord *is* the portion of mine inheritance and of my cup: thou maintainest my lot.
6. The lines are fallen unto me in pleasant *places;* yea, I have a goodly heritage.
7. I will bless the LORD, who hath given me counsel: my reins also instruct me in the night seasons.
8. I have set the LORD always before me: because *he is* at my right hand, I shall not be moved.
9. Therefore my heart is glad, and my glory rejoiceth: my flesh also shall rest in hope.
10. For thou wilt not leave my soul in hell; neither wilt thou suffer thine Holy One to see corruption.
11. Thou wilt shew me the path of life: in thy presence *is* fulness of joy; at thy right hand *there are* pleasures for evermore.

Commentary_____

David introduces this Messianic Psalm by invoking the three most frequent Old Testament names for God—*Elohim* (God), *Yahweh* or *Jehovah* (LORD), and *Adonai* (Lord).

For those who enjoy alliteration, here is an outline for verses 1 through 7:

v. 1 secure in the Lord
v. 2 surrendered to the Lord
v. 3 separated unto the Lord's people
v. 4 separated from the world's people
v. 5 sustained by the Lord
v. 6 satisfied in the Lord
v. 7 supported by the Lord

Verses 8 through 11 comprise the Messianic portion of the psalm. In the first sermon preached after the birth of the church on the day of Pentecost, the Apostle Peter used this psalm to prove that the resurrection of Jesus Christ, as well as His death on the cross, was "according to the Scriptures" (1 Cor. 15:4). Verses 8-11 are quoted in Acts 2:25-28. The Spirit's own interpretation follows in Acts 2:29-31. In view of the results of the preaching of this sermon (Acts 2:41), we will do well to look there for an understanding of the Messianic portion of the psalm.

In Acts 13:35 the Apostle Paul quotes Psalm 16:10 to prove that Jesus conquered death and was alive on the resurrection side of death in His resurrected body. Read Paul's exposition of the verse in Acts 13:36-39.

Application_____

Count the number of verses in Peter's sermon (Acts 2:22-36) to discover how effectively the saving gospel message can be presented in a few words. He didn't try to explain the gospel; he simply proclaimed the gospel. The "power of God unto salvation" is in the message—not in the explanation of the message (Rom. 1:16; 1 Cor. 15:1).

Psalm 17:1-7

A Prayer of David.

1. HEAR THE right, O LORD, attend unto my cry, give ear unto my prayer, *that goeth* not out of feigned lips.
2. Let my sentence come forth from thy presence; let thine eyes behold the things that are equal.
3. Thou hast proved mine heart; thou hast visited *me* in the night; thou hast tried me, *and* shalt find nothing; I am purposed *that* my mouth shall not transgress.
4. Concerning the works of men, by the word of thy lips I have kept *me from* the paths of the destroyer.
5. Hold up my goings in thy paths, *that* my footsteps slip not.
6. I have called upon thee, for thou wilt hear me, O God: incline thine ear unto me, *and hear* my speech.
7. Shew thy marvellous lovingkindness, O thou that savest by thy right hand them which put their trust *in thee* from those that rise up *against them*.

Commentary_____

Many of the psalms, or portions thereof, are in the form of prayers. Psalm 17 is one of five that are specifically entitled "a prayer." A probable historical setting for this psalm involves David's perilous situation as recorded in 1 Samuel 23: 25, 26.

At that time, through depending upon the LORD during his many trials and testings, David had come to know his God intimately. He knew that the LORD hears the cry of one calling from a sincere heart having a just cause (v. 1). He knew God vindicates the innocent and makes right the things that are uneven (v. 2). David was confident that he was not undergoing punishment by God for sinful words and conduct (v. 3). He had avoided association with men of evil purposes by heeding God's Word (v. 4). He was looking to God for direction so that he would not slip in his walk (v. 5).

David was having difficulty reconciling his dire situation with that which he knew to be true concerning the character and purposes of his God. He had experienced miraculous deliverance in past perils. In verses 6 and 7, he is earnestly pleading with God to demonstrate His power and His lovingkindness. The basis of his plea is that his heart attitude and his conduct entitle him to God's action on his behalf.

Application_____

There comes into the life of every believer those times when our situation doesn't appear to mesh with our understanding of God's love for us and His watch-care over us. Applying scriptures like Psalm 139:23-24 and studying Psalm 17 should be helpful in building a firm confidence as we trust our God.

Psalm 17:8-15

8. Keep me as the apple of the eye, hide me under the shadow of thy wings,

9. From the wicked that oppress me, *from* my deadly enemies, *who* compass me about.

10. They are inclosed in their own fat: with their mouth they speak proudly.

11. They have now compassed us in our steps: they have set their eyes bowing down to the earth;

12. Like as a lion *that* is greedy of his prey, and as it were a young lion lurking in secret places.

13. Arise, O LORD, disappoint him, cast him down: deliver my soul from the wicked, *which is* thy sword:

14. From men *which are* thy hand, O LORD, from men of the world, *which have* their portion in *this* life, and whose belly thou fillest with thy hid *treasure*: they are full of children, and leave the rest of their *substance* to their babes.

15. As for me, I will behold thy face in righteousness: I shall be satisfied, when I awake, with thy likeness.

Commentary

"The apple of the eye" is figurative for that which is dearest and most needful of safe-guarding (Deut. 32:10; Pr. 7:2; Lam. 2:18; Zech. 2:8). "Under the shadow of thy wings" denotes the place of optimum safety (Ps. 36:7, 57:1, 61:4, 63:7, 91:1-4).

David's enemies are described as "wicked," oppressive, and "deadly." They have fleshly appetites and speak boastfully. They are like a crouching lion "greedy" for prey (vv. 9-12).

In verse 13, David calls upon the LORD to deprive the lion of his prey. In verse 14, the wicked are said to live only for this life, gathering treasures in order to accumulate wealth for their children.

Verse 15 gives us insight into that which Old Testament saints understood concerning life beyond the grave. This verse, along with Job 19:25-27 and Isaiah 26:19, verifies that they looked for bodily resurrection, which would bring ultimate satisfaction in the presence of the LORD. Parallel New Testament passages include 1 Corinthians 13:12 and 1 John 3:2.

Trust in an eternal God gave David an eternal perspective on life in contrast to the temporal perspective of his enemies. The extent to which we live day to day with an eternal perspective is the extent to which we will experience moment-by-moment victory over circumstances.

Application

Looking back over the psalm, we see that the LORD searches the heart (v. 3), saves the trusting (v. 7), shelters His dear ones (v. 8), shields from the adversary (v. 9), and satisfies forever (v. 15). We should keep in mind that the Spirit had in view the needs of all who would need David's words throughout the centuries.

Psalm 18:1-12

To the chief Musician, *A Psalm* of David, the servant of the LORD, who spake unto the LORD the words of this song in the day *that* the LORD delivered him from the hand of all his enemies, and from the hand of Saul: And he said,

1. I WILL love thee, O LORD, my strength.
2. The LORD *is* my rock, and my fortress, and my deliverer; my God, my strength, in whom I will trust; my buckler, and the horn of my salvation, *and* my high tower.
3. I will call upon the LORD, *who is worthy* to be praised: so shall I be saved from mine enemies.
4. The sorrows of death compassed me, and the floods of ungodly men made me afraid.
5. The sorrows of hell compassed me about: the snares of death prevented me.
6. In my distress I called upon the LORD, and cried unto my God: he heard my voice out of his temple, and my cry came before him, *even* into his ears.
7. Then the earth shook and trembled; the foundations also of the hills moved and were shaken, because he was wroth.
8. There went up a smoke out of his nostrils, and fire out of his mouth devoured: coals were kindled by it.
9. He bowed the heavens also, and came down: and darkness *was* under his feet.
10. And he rode upon a cherub, and did fly: yea, he did fly upon the wings of the wind.
11. He made darkness his secret place; his pavilion round about him *were* dark waters *and* thick clouds of the skies.
12. At the brightness *that was* before him his thick clouds passed, hail *stones* and coals of fire.

Commentary_____

Psalm 18 is also recorded in 2 Samuel as chapter 22 with a few variations. For instance, the superscription of Psalm 18 is verse 1 of 2 Samuel 22. The historical setting for the psalm is the height of David's kingdom. Verses 1-12 involve praise and thanksgiving to God for the extent to which He will go to deliver His own. In this psalm David acknowledges that all of the glory and honor for his success belongs to his God.

In verse 2, the psalmist proclaims His LORD by using two of His names, two descriptive nouns and *five* metaphors. Because of the widespread use in the Scriptures of the word *horn* in an obviously figurative manner, it particularly catches our attention here since it is used as a metaphor for God.

In Deuteronomy 33:17, the descendants of Joseph are said to have "horns like the horns of a wild ox" with which they will push other people. In her prayer, of praise and adoration, Hannah thanks the LORD for giving her a horn to use against her adversary (1 Sam. 2:1). At the end of her prayer, Hannah prophesies that the Messiah will possess an exalted horn (v. 10). In Luke 1:69, Zechariah calls the coming Messiah Israel's "horn of salvation." That prophecy will ultimately be fulfilled at Armageddon. Even though Antichrist will be the most powerful ruler in human history, God calls him a "little horn" (Dan. 7:8) because compared to the "horn of salvation," that is what the Antichrist will be. In Scripture, when one is said to have a horn or to be a horn, he has a usable advantage over his adversary just as a horned animal has an advantage over a hornless one.

Application_____

"All the horns of the wicked also will I cut off, but the horns of the righteous shall be exalted" (Ps. 75:10). Have you ever thanked God for giving you "horns" of righteousness?

Psalm 18:13-24

13. The LORD also thundered in the heavens, and the Highest gave his voice; hail *stones* and coals of fire.
14. Yea, he sent out his arrows, and scattered them; and he shot out lightnings, and discomfited them.
15. Then the channels of waters were seen, and the foundations of the world were discovered at thy rebuke, O LORD, at the blast of the breath of thy nostrils.
16. He sent from above, he took me, he drew me out of many waters.
17. He delivered me from my strong enemy, and from them which hated me: for they were too strong for me.
18. They prevented me in the day of my calamity: but the LORD was my stay.
19. He brought me forth also into a large place; he delivered me, because he delighted in me.
20. The LORD rewarded me according to my righteousness; according to the cleanness of my hands hath he recompensed me.
21. For I have kept the ways of the LORD, and have not wickedly departed from my God.
22. For all his judgments *were* before me, and I did not put away his statutes from me.
23. I was also upright before him, and I kept myself from mine iniquity.
24. Therefore hath the LORD recompensed me according to my righteousness, according to the cleanness of my hands in his eyesight.

Commentary_____

"The LORD also thundered"—*Yahwe*h manifested Himself in judgment. "The Highest (usually translated Most High) gave his voice" (Ps. 29:3-5). "The Most High God, possessor of Heaven and Earth" (Gen. 14:22) is the LORD's title as the Supreme Ruler of the Universe.

The many waters of verse 16 are the "strong enemy" and "those who hate me" of verse 17 (Ps. 93:4, 144:7). Do you think there might also be a prophetic implication in regards to the nation of Israel? Did God also have the "flood" of Revelation 12:15 and the "many waters" of Revelation 17:1 and 17:15 in view? This could explain some of the language of verses 7-15, which appears to be more applicable to end times than to David's time. Keep in mind the following:

1) Prophets knew they were saying much that was for future hearers (Ps. 102:18; 1 Peter 1:11, 12).
2) Much prophecy is written in the past tense. From God's point of view, future events are as certain as if they had already transpired.

What David experienced in verses 16-19 could also apply to your own salvation. Notice God's salvation is not just for the purpose of saving you from Hell. When He delivers "out of," He also takes "into" (Ex. 3:8). As you read verses 20-24, think in terms of your own Christian walk in relationship to the judgment seat of Christ (2 Cor. 5:10).

Application_____

The practical value of Bible study comes from applying the passage under consideration to our daily conduct. In a manner of speaking, we must learn to place ourselves into the situation presented and find a way of applying the words to our hour-by-hour Christian walk. Can you do this with verse 24?

Psalm 18:25-36

25. With the merciful thou wilt shew thyself merciful; with an upright man thou wilt shew thyself upright;
26. With the pure thou wilt shew thyself pure; and with the froward thou wilt shew thyself froward.
27. For thou wilt save the afflicted people; but wilt bring down high looks.
28. For thou wilt light my candle: the LORD my God will enlighten my darkness.
29. For by thee I have run through a troop; and by my God have I leaped over a wall.
30. *As for* God, his way *is* perfect: the word of the LORD is tried: he *is* a buckler to all those that trust in him.
31. For who *is* God save the LORD? or who *is* a rock save our God?
32. *It is* God that girdeth me with strength, and maketh my way perfect.
33. He maketh my feet like hinds' *feet*, and setteth me upon my high places.
34. He teacheth my hands to war, so that a bow of steel is broken by mine arms.
35. Thou hast also given me the shield of thy salvation: and thy right hand hath holden me up, and thy gentleness hath made me great.
36. Thou hast enlarged my steps under me, that my feet did not slip.

Commentary_____

David's desire was to be merciful and upright (v. 25) as well as pure (v. 26) and humble (v. 27). Therefore, the LORD delighted in him and brought deliverance from his enemies (v. 19). God was pleased to give him the light of the LORD for his walk in a world of darkness (v. 28). David gave all the credit for his victories to his God (v. 29) and never missed an opportunity to extol God and His Word (v. 30).

The word *rock* is the translation of two Hebrew words. Both are used as metaphors for God in Psalm 18. *Sela* in verse 2 means a rocky protrusion like a crag. *Tsoor* in verse 31 means a rocky mass like a boulder. Both words are used in Deuteronomy 32:13.

The verb "gird" (vv. 32 and 39) and the corresponding noun "girdle" are used both literally and figuratively in both Testaments of older English versions. Modern versions experience difficulty finding suitable synonyms for these archaic words (Ps. 109:18, Eph. 6:14, 1 Pet.1:13) and still preserve the word's figurative and literal meaning. In Bible times, a girdle was a necessary adjunct to male apparel. It was similar to a sash worn around the waist. When at rest, a man loosened his girdle. In order to work, run or fight he tied the girdle tightly around his waist. Figuratively, to gird oneself is to prepare for action! See 1 Kings 18:46 and Luke 12:35-37.

In verses 30 and 31 David exalts His God and then in verses 32-36, he recounts what God has accomplished for him and in him.

Application_____

Because the way of God is perfect and the word of God is proven, we can trust in Him (v. 30). If we are fearful in any circumstance of life, it is because we are deficient in trust not because the provision is insufficient! How do we correct our deficiency? We must simply recount His faithfulness in past experiences.

Psalm 18:37-50

37. I have pursued mine enemies, and overtaken them: neither did I turn again till they were consumed.
38. I have wounded them that they were not able to rise: they are fallen under my feet.
39. For thou hast girded me with strength unto the battle: thou hast subdued under me those that rose up against me.
40. Thou hast also given me the necks of mine enemies; that I might destroy them that hate me.
41. They cried, but *there was* none to save *them: even* unto the LORD, but he answered them not.
42. Then did I beat them small as the dust before the wind: I did cast them out as the dirt in the streets.
43. Thou hast delivered me from the strivings of the people; *and* thou hast made me the head of the heathen: a people *whom* I have not known shall serve me.
44. As soon as they hear of me, they shall obey me: the strangers shall submit themselves unto me.
45. The strangers shall fade away, and be afraid out of their close places.
46. The LORD liveth; and blessed *be* my rock; and let the God of my salvation be exalted.
47. *It is* God that avengeth me, and subdueth the people under me.
48. He delivereth me from mine enemies: yea, thou liftest me up above those that rise up against me: thou hast delivered me from the violent man.
49. Therefore will I give thanks unto thee, O LORD, among the heathen, and sing praises unto thy name.
50. Great deliverance giveth he to his king; and sheweth mercy to his anointed, to David, and to his seed for evermore.

Commentary_____

The historical background for Psalm 18:37-42 is found in 1 Chronicles 18 and 19 as well as in the parallel passages of 2 Samuel. These verses rehearse the conquest of the enemies of David's conquering armies. In verse 43, David gives God credit for both ending the years of strife within his own country and his exaltation as ruler over the surrounding nations. In verses 44 and 45, he tells of the submission of other peoples and of their obeisance to him.

One wonders to what extend David presently has knowledge of the thousands of believers who today sing the words of verse 46 as a praise chorus to the LORD whom he served 3,000 years ago! Maybe such singing and praising is the beginning of what was on the mind of Jesus as he faced the cross (Hebrews 12:2).

When David was pursued by King Saul, he had two clear opportunities to slay his persecutor. He chose to let God be his avenger. Now he is praising God not only for deliverance but also for his exaltation (vv. 47, 48).

In Romans 15:4, the Apostle Paul assures us that the Old Testament was written for us. Then in Romans 15:9-12, the Apostle uses five Old Testament passages to prove that the Holy Spirit not only had Gentiles in mind when He authored the Scriptures but also that they have always been included in God's plans. Verse 49 is the first of those five passages.

Verse 50 looks forward to the greater David, Messiah, and points out the eternality of God's plans concerning David.

Application_____

Look carefully at Romans 15:4 and then consider how you can derive learning, patience, comfort and hope from the truths in Psalm 18.

Psalm 19

To the chief Musician, A Psalm of David.

1. THE HEAVENS declare the glory of God; and the firmament sheweth his handiwork.
2. Day unto day uttereth speech, and night unto night sheweth knowledge.
3. *There is* no speech nor language, *where* their voice is not heard.
4. Their line is gone out through all the earth, and their words to the end of the world. In them hath he set a tabernacle for the sun,
5. Which *is* as a bridegroom coming out of his chamber, *and* rejoiceth as a strong man to run a race.
6. His going forth *is* from the end of the heaven, and his circuit unto the ends of it: and there is nothing hid from the heat thereof.
7. The law of the LORD *is* perfect, converting the soul: the testimony of the LORD *is* sure, making wise the simple.
8. The statutes of the LORD *are* right, rejoicing the heart: the commandment of the LORD *is* pure, enlightening the eyes.
9. The fear of the LORD *is* clean, enduring for ever: the judgments of the LORD *are* true *and* righteous altogether.
10. More to be desired *are they* than gold, yea, than much fine gold: sweeter also than honey and the honeycomb.
11. Moreover by them is thy servant warned: *and* in keeping of them *there is* great reward.
12. Who can understand *his* errors? cleanse thou me from secret *faults.*
13. Keep back thy servant also from presumptuous *sins;* let them not have dominion over me: then shall I be upright, and I shall be innocent from the great transgression.
14. Let the words of my mouth, and the meditations of my heart, be acceptable in thy sight, O LORD, my strength, and my redeemer.

Commentary

We might paraphrase verses 1-6 in this manner: God, through His creation, has without words, spoken to every human being that has ever lived in such a way that a response is required. The divine interpretation of thes verses is found in Romans 1:18-20.

In verses 7 and 8, the Word of God is designated in four different terms. His law in this context is His instruction in regard to sin and righteousness. His testimony is what He has to say about His own nature and purposes. His statutes are rules of conduct. His commandments are authoritative directives. Notice the four adjectives by which His Word is described—"perfect," "sure," "right," and "pure." In the same two verses, He tells us what His Word will do – "convert the soul," "make wise the simple," "rejoice the heart" and "enlighten the eyes."

Fear and love are two necessary and complimentary attitudes toward God. Love prevents fear from being shrinking servility. Fear keeps love from becoming mawkish or presumptuous familiarity. The relationship should be like that of a child toward a tender, loving parent who is also a consistent and effective disciplinarian.

When the Bible speaks of rewards, it uses superlatives (v. 11). See Genesis 15:1 and Luke 6:23, 35. God's system of testings and rewards is very important to Him. Christians in general know far too little about the subject.

In the Old Testament there were no sacrifices for presumptuous sins – only judgment (Num. 15:30, Deut. 17:12). In the New Testament they are called willful sins (Heb. 10:26) and sin unto death (1 Jn. 5:16).

Application

This world desperately needs something "perfect," something "sure," something "right," and something "pure." The people of this world need someone willing to dedicate a life to the task of delivering to them this "something"—the Word of God.

Psalm 20

To the chief Musician, A Psalm of David.

1. THE LORD hear thee in the day of trouble; the name of the God of Jacob defend thee;
2. Send thee help from the sanctuary, and strengthen thee out of Zion;
3. Remember all thy offerings, and accept thy burnt sacrifice; Selah.
4. Grant thee according to thine own heart, and fulfil all thy counsel.
5. We will rejoice in thy salvation, and in the name of our God we will set up *our* banners: the LORD fulfil all thy petitions.
6. Now know I that the LORD saveth his anointed; he will hear him from his holy heaven with the saving strength of his right hand.
7. Some *trust* in chariots, and some in horses: but we will remember the name of the LORD our God.
8. They are brought down and fallen: but we are risen, and stand upright.
9. Save, LORD: let the king hear us when we call.

Commentary_____

The setting for Psalm 20 is Jerusalem as King David and his general Joab are preparing to face superior enemy forces in battle. The occasion is thought to be the one recorded in 2 Samuel 10 and 1 Chronicles 19. The Ammonites had joined with the Syrians to overthrow David's rule. They hired thousands of chariots and foot soldiers against David. As was David's custom before going into battle, he called his people to worship and sacrifice.

The petition of verses 1-5 was probably sung by Levites responsible for worship procedures. "The God of Jacob defend thee"– the words of Jacob in Genesis 35:3 were no doubt the inspiration for their prayer. This petition exudes an aura of faith and anticipation. They are confident that the LORD will perform for them as He did for their patriarch.

In verses 6-8, the king himself or someone on his behalf responds in faith to the petition: "Now I know. . . He will hear. . . ." There is total reliance—no shadow of doubt, no "wavering" (Jas. 1:6).

"Some trust in chariots. . . ." Pharaoh trusted in his 600 chariots (Ex. 14:7). Moses had no chariots, but trusted solely in the LORD (Ex. 14:13). "Thus the LORD saved Israel that day out of the hand of the Egyptians. . ." (Ex. 14:30).

Notice in verse 8 that victory is appropriated before the battle begins.

Application_____

The petitions recorded in the Bible are short and to the point. Look at the first two Bible prayers that received affirmative answers – the prayer by Abraham's servant (Gen. 24:12-14) and the prayer by Jacob (Gen. 32:9-12). Both received immediate and precise answers! What can we learn from those two prayers?

Psalm 21

To the chief Musician, A Psalm of David.

1. THE KING shall joy in thy strength, O LORD; and in thy salvation how greatly shall he rejoice!
2. Thou hast given him his heart's desire, and hast not withholden the request of his lips. Selah.
3. For thou preventest him with the blessings of goodness: thou settest a crown of pure gold on his head.
4. He asked life of thee, *and* thou gavest *it* him, *even* length of days for ever and ever.
5. His glory *is* great in thy salvation: honour and majesty hast thou laid upon him.
6. For thou hast made him most blessed for ever: thou hast made him exceeding glad with thy countenance.
7. For the king trusteth in the LORD, and through the mercy of the most High he shall not be moved.
8. Thine hand shall find out all thine enemies: thy right hand shall find out those that hate thee.
9. Thou shalt make them as a fiery oven in the time of thine anger: the LORD shall swallow them up in his wrath, and the fire shall devour them.
10. Their fruit shalt thou destroy from the earth, and their seed from among the children of men.
11. For they intended evil against thee: they imagined a mischievous device, *which* they are not able *to perform*.
12. Therefore shalt thou make them turn their back, *when* thou shalt make ready *thine arrows* upon thy strings against the face of them.
13. Be thou exalted, LORD, in thine own strength: *so* will we sing and praise thy power.

Commentary_____

Students of the Psalms have long noted the connection between Psalms 20 and 21. Psalm 20 is a confident petition in anticipation of victory. Compare 20:2 with 21:6; 20:4 with 21:2 and 20:7 with 21:7.

The old English word *preventest* (v. 3) is from two Latin words meaning "come before." The word now has a different connotation than it did when the King James Version was produced. See Psalm 88:13, Psalm 119:147, and 1 Thessalonians 4:15.

"A crown of pure gold"—by way of application we read this in anticipation of the crown of victory awaiting us (2 Tim. 4:8) at the Lord's return (Rev. 22:12). Our desire for crowns is not to wear them but to have our part in the wondrous celebration of Revelation 4:9-11.

From our study of Psalm 17, we know that David looked forward to eternal life in a resurrection body. He would be the recipient of his LORD's blessings forever! Notice that his sole ground for receiving God's blessings, both temporal and eternal, is "the king trusteth in the LORD" (v. 7).

Verses 8-12 look forward to future battles and future victories. David's confidence for success is based on the knowledge that his enemies are the LORD's enemies and his battles are therefore the LORD's battles.

Application_____

This psalm begins and ends with rejoicing in the Lord's strength. Are you aware of the difference between attempting to attain joy in your own strength and manifesting joy through singing and praising in the strength and power of the Lord? The one leads to frustration. The other exalts the Lord and delights the soul.

Psalm 22:1-11

To the chief Musician upon Aijeleth Shahar, A Psalm of David.

1. MY GOD, my God, why hast thou forsaken me? *why art thou so* far from helping me, *and from* the words of my roaring?
2. O my God, I cry in the daytime, but thou hearest not; and in the night season, and am not silent.
3. But thou *art* holy, *O thou* that inhabitest the praises of Israel.
4. Our fathers trusted in thee: they trusted, and thou didst deliver them.
5. They cried unto thee, and were delivered: they trusted in thee, and were not confounded.
6. But I *am* a worm, and no man; a reproach of men, and despised of the people.
7. All they that see me laugh me to scorn: they shoot out the lip, they shake the head, *saying,*
8. He trusted on the LORD *that* he would deliver him: let him deliver him, seeing he delighted in him.
9. But thou *art* he that took me out of the womb: thou didst make me hope *when I was* upon my mother's breasts.
10. I was cast upon thee from the womb: thou *art* my God from my mother's belly.
11. Be not far from me; for trouble *is* near; for *there is* none to help.

Commentary_____

"Christ died for our sins according to the scriptures" (1 Cor. 15:3). Certainly, today's reading consists of scriptures according to which Christ died! The Holy Spirit is the author (2 Sam. 23:2). David is the prophet (Acts 4:25). The precise fulfillment is recorded in Matthew 27:39-49 and to a lesser extent in the other three Gospels.

It is not necessary to search for events in David's life which parallel these details. For His own purposes, the omniscient Spirit wanted to tell what would transpire a thousand years later in history. Specifically, He is revealing the heart sufferings that our Savior endured while hanging on the cross. Verses 1-5 speak of His heart sufferings due to His abandonment by God. We are not being informed that the Father-Son relationship was severed. We know this was not the case because of the first (Lk. 23:34) and the seventh (Lk. 23:46) utterances by Christ from the cross. The answer to the question in verse 1 is found in verse 3. The human sin-bearer was forsaken by a Holy God who could not look upon the exceeding sinfulness of the sins laid upon the sinless offering (2 Cor. 5:21).

The "daytime" and "night" of verse 2 correspond to the three hours of light and three hours of darkness during the crucifixion. Verses 6-11 describe the heart sufferings of Christ due to spurning by his fellow man. The emphasis is upon Christ's human characteristics.

Application_____

If you really want to think about what transpired in the mind of your own Savior as he bore your sins on the cross, meditate long and diligently upon this scripture portion. As you indicate a genuine interest, the indwelling Holy Spirit will awaken your understanding of that which is written here.

Psalm 22:12-21

12. Many bulls have compassed me: strong *bulls* of Bashan have beset me round.

13. They gaped upon me *with* their mouths, *as* a ravening and a roaring lion.

14. I am poured out like water, and all my bones are out of joint: my heart is like wax; it is melted in the midst of my bowels.

15. My strength is dried up like a potsherd; and my tongue cleaveth to my jaws; and thou hast brought me into the dust of death.

16. For dogs have compassed me: the assembly of the wicked have inclosed me: they pierced my hands and my feet.

17. I may tell all my bones: they look *and* stare upon me.

18. They part my garments among them, and cast lots upon my vesture.

19. But be thou not far from me, O LORD: O my strength, haste thee to help me.

20. Deliver my soul from the sword; my darling from the power of the dog.

21. Save me from the lion's mouth: for thou hast heard me from the horns of the unicorns.

Commentary_____

Ferocious bulls, predatory lions and scavenger dogs figuratively describe the spectators at our Lord's crucifixion. Careful review of the symbolic use of these animals elsewhere in Scripture leads us to conclude the following: the bulls represent the Roman military presence; the lion (v. 21) is both Satan and his agents (v. 13); the unicorn (wild ox) represents the political and religious powers that conspired to put Christ on the cross; and the dogs are the basest elements of human society who came to gawk and mock.

Verses 14-17 graphically describe the suffering of a human individual dying while nailed to a cross. This is particularly striking when we consider that the detailed account of Christ's physical suffering is given here, hundreds of years before death by crucifixion was ever practiced.

Matthew 27:35 records the precise fulfillment of verse 18. Any possibility that the crucifixion of Christ was staged by his followers in order to conform to scriptures is precluded by this incident.

Verses 19-21 prophesy a petition, which will be honored as described in the rest of the psalm. Actually, the psalm should be read at one sitting because God is not pleased to recount the horror of the crucifixion without immediately following it with the proclamation of the victorious resurrection.

Application_____

Never leave Christ on the cross! That is a grave fault of false religionists. "Death is swallowed up in victory" (1 Cor. 15:54). The cross and the tomb are empty! Christ is risen and glorified! Proclaim it loudly and frequently!

Psalm 22:22-31

22. I will declare thy name unto my brethren: in the midst of the congregation will I praise thee.
23. Ye that fear the LORD, praise him; all ye the seed of Jacob, glorify him; and fear him, all ye the seed of Israel.
24. For he hath not despised nor abhorred the affliction of the afflicted; neither hath he hid his face from him; but when he cried unto him, he heard.
25. My praise *shall be* of thee in the great congregation: I will pay my vows before them that fear him.
26. The meek shall eat and be satisfied: they shall praise the LORD that seek him: your heart shall live for ever.
27. All the ends of the world shall remember and turn unto the LORD: and all the kindreds of the nations shall worship before thee.
28. For the kingdom *is* the LORD'S: and he *is* the governor among the nations.
29. All *they that be* fat upon earth shall eat and worship: all they that go down to the dust shall bow before him: and none can keep alive his own soul.
30. A seed shall serve him; it shall be accounted to the Lord for a generation.
31. They shall come, and shall declare his righteousness unto a people that shall be born, that he hath done *this*.

Commentary_____

At verse 22 the psalm proceeds from the crucifixion to the resurrection. The words of this verse are attributed to the risen Jesus in Hebrews 2:12. The Holy Spirit used David as a prophet to tell what Jesus would say a thousand years in the future concerning His relationship to His followers. Notice how the relationship develops in the Gospel of John from Master to Friend to Brother. When we yield our lives to His call, the relationship is Master and servant (Jn. 13:13-16). When we show forth our love for Him as He has shown His love for us, we become His friends (Jn. 15:12-15). The ultimate relationship is brotherhood in the family of His Father (Jn. 20:17; Heb. 2:11, 12).

The principal theme of today's scripture is "praise to the LORD in the coming kingdom." The king will praise Him (v. 22). The descendants of Jacob will praise and glorify Him (v. 23). The psalmist will praise Him (v. 25). The lowly will praise Him (v. 26). All individuals and all nations shall worship Him (vs. 27-29).

"A seed shall serve Him" (v. 30). In order to understand the impact of this prophecy, read Isaiah 53:8-10.

In His crucifixion He was cut off without physical descendants. In His resurrection, the multitude of His progeny cannot be numbered (Jn. 12:24).

Application_____

Psalm 22:31 reminds us that we are like the second runner in a four-man relay race. We are responsible for the truths that were brought to us by the preceding generation. We must relay them to the next generation of believers in such a forceful manner that they will not fail to effectually pass them on to a generation not yet born. God has something to say on this subject in Psalm 78:3-6 and 2 Timothy 2:2.

Psalm 23

A Psalm of David.

1. THE LORD *is* my shepherd; I shall not want.
2. He maketh me to lie down in green pastures: he leadeth me beside the still waters.
3. He restoreth my soul: he leadeth me in the paths of righteousness for his name's sake.
4. Yea, though I walk through the valley of the shadow of death, I will fear no evil: for thou *art* with me; thy rod and thy staff they comfort me.
5. Thou preparest a table before me in the presence of mine enemies: thou anointest my head with oil; my cup runneth over.
6. Surely goodness and mercy shall follow me all the days of my life: and I will dwell in the house of the LORD for ever.

Commentary_____

"I have gone astray like a lost sheep---"(Ps. 119:176). (See also Isa. 53:6). Whereas Psalm 22 presents the Good Shepherd who gave His life for the sheep (Jn. 10:11), Psalm 23 is a song about the living Great Shepherd who currently oversees His sheep (Heb. 13:20, 21; 1 Pet. 2:25). Our earthly pastors might be desirous of giving their lives in shepherding their flocks. They might even be willing to die for their flocks if necessary. But only Jesus could provide for me my total need—a shepherd that could live for me after He died for me. None of this world's religions can provide such a shepherd! After providing the needed sacrifice for my sins (Ps. 22), He now provides my total needs (Ps. 23) for my walk.

My Shepherd attends to my needs day by day (v.1). I have the "peace of God" (Phil. 4:7) as He leads me because He has provided "peace with God" (Rom. 5:1) through His perfect sacrifice (v. 2). Since I am incapable of directing my own steps (Jer. 10:23), my Shepherd guides me along the correct pathway in my daily walk (v. 3). Since the day I was born, I have lived in the shadow of death. But my Shepherd is the conqueror of death in verse 4 (See also 1 Cor. 15:54-57). I banquet peacefully in the presence of the enemy of my soul. Why shouldn't my cup of joy overflow (v. 5)? My enemy cannot pursue me because I am pursued by my Shepherd's goodness and mercy every day all the way to my eternal abode!

Application_____

The only barrier to the enjoyment of the blessings of Psalm 23 is a lack of trust in the Shepherd. If a sheep were in a desert surrounded by predatory animals could it enjoy life without complete reliance upon its shepherd?

Pslam 24

A Psalm of David.

1. THE EARTH *is* the LORD'S, and the fulness thereof; the world, and they that dwell therein.
2. For he hath founded it upon the seas, and established it upon the floods.
3. Who shall ascend into the hill of the LORD? or who shall stand in his holy place?
4. He that hath clean hands, and a pure heart; who hath not lifted up his soul unto vanity, nor sworn deceitfully.
5. He shall receive the blessing from the LORD, and righteousness from the God of his salvation.
6. This *is* the generation of them that seek him, that seek thy face, O Jacob. Selah
7. Lift up your heads, O ye gates; and be ye lift up, ye everlasting doors; and the King of glory shall come in.
8. Who *is* this King of glory? The LORD strong and mighty, the LORD mighty in battle.
9. Lift up your heads, O ye gates; even lift *them* up, ye everlasting doors; and the King of glory shall come in.
10. Who is this King of glory? The LORD of hosts, he *is* the King of glory. Selah.

Commentary

Historians find the setting for this psalm in the bringing of the Ark of God into the City of David (2 Sam. 6:12-19). Tradition says the psalm was later arranged for antiphonal singing. It was sung as the worshipers ascended to the Holy Hill of Zion for the Feasts of Jehovah. The section from verses 7 to 10 was reserved for the triumphal entry through the gates. Church fathers entitled the psalm, "The ascension to the throne by the King of Glory." Many see it as the third psalm of a trilogy about the Good Shepherd (Ps. 22), the Great Shepherd (Ps. 23), and the Chief Shepherd (Ps. 24). The Good Shepherd died for us to pay the penalty for sin (Jn. 10:11; 1 Pet. 2:24). The Great Shepherd lives in us to protect from the power of sin (Heb. 13:20, 21; 1 Pet. 2:25). The Chief Shepherd comes for us to part us from the presence of sin (1 Pet. 5:4).

The Earth and all that pertains to it, including its inhabitants, belong to the LORD (v. 1) because He created all (v. 2). Therefore, He has the right to determine who controls the government and worship (v. 3). The prime requirements are righteousness for both the King and His subjects (vv. 4-6).

Open the gates of Zion! The LORD has appointed His King to sit upon the throne (v. 7). He has conquered every opponent (v. 8) and is ready to enter (v. 9). The King of Glory and the LORD of Hosts are one and the same (v. 10). Be still and meditate upon that!

Application

"Lift up your heads"! If you have received that which was done in the past for you by the Good Shepherd, and you are not now rejoicing in that which the Great Shepherd is doing in and through you, lift up your head! Look toward that which the Chief Shepherd will do in the future with you! (Heb. 12:1-3)

Psalm 25:1-11

A Psalm of David.

1. UNTO THEE, O LORD, do I lift up my soul.
2. O my God, I trust in thee: let me not be ashamed, let not mine enemies triumph over me.
3. Yea, let none that wait on thee be ashamed: let them be ashamed which transgress without cause.
4. Shew me thy ways, O LORD; teach me thy paths.
5. Lead me in thy truth, and teach me: for thou *art* the God of my salvation; on thee do I wait all the day.
6. Remember, O LORD, thy tender mercies and thy lovingkindnesses; for they *have been* ever of old.
7. Remember not the sins of my youth, nor my transgressions: according to thy mercy remember thou me for thy goodness' sake, O LORD.
8. Good and upright *is* the LORD: therefore will he teach sinners in the way.
9. The meek will he guide in judgment: and the meek will he teach his way.
10. All the paths of the LORD *are* mercy and truth unto such as keep his covenant and his testimonies.
11. For thy name's sake, O LORD, pardon mine iniquity; for it *is* great.

Commentary

There are nine alphabetical psalms. Originally, this one was structured so that each of the 22 verses began with the next succeeding letter of the Hebrew alphabet—*ALEPH* through *TAV.* Apparently, this psalm and some other psalms were somewhat rearranged in form for liturgical purposes. However, most of the acrostic structure has been preserved in Hebrew manuscripts.

"Let none that wait on thee be ashamed" (v. 3)—David is not speaking of feelings of guilt, disgrace, or embarrassment. "Ashamed" here means being let down or disappointed because of misplaced trust. He was never in danger of being "ashamed" because his trust was in the LORD! (v. 20)

In verses 4 and 5, David petitions for guidance and instruction in knowing and following God's ways. He bases his request upon that which he already knows about the LORD's character and past performance (vv. 6-8). His God is, and always has been, loving, kind, good, and upright. He forgives and teaches sinful ones who confess before Him.

Both Moses (Num. 12:3) and Jesus (Mt. 11:29) were declared to be meek. The word here means compliant and supple, not deficient in spirit or courage.

Application

When we bring our petitions before the Lord, we should verbalize to Him that which we know about Him from His Word and from our past experiences with Him. We also confess what we are in His presence. We present a basis for Him to grant our requests. If our petitions are according to His promise and character, He will surely grant them "for [His] name's sake" (v. 11). He is both merciful and true!

Psalm 25:12-22

12. What man *is* he that feareth the LORD? him shall he teach in the way *that* he shall choose.
13. His soul shall dwell at ease; and his seed shall inherit the earth.
14. The secret of the LORD *is* with them that fear him; and he will shew them his covenant.
15. Mine eyes *are* ever toward the LORD; for he shall pluck my feet out of the net.
16. Turn thee unto me, and have mercy upon me; for I *am* desolate and afflicted.
17. The troubles of my heart are enlarged: O bring thou me out of my distresses.
18. Look upon mine affliction and my pain; and forgive all my sins.
19. Consider mine enemies; for they are many; and they hate me with cruel hatred.
20. O keep my soul, and deliver me: let me not be ashamed; for I put my trust in thee.
21. Let integrity and uprightness preserve me; for I wait on thee.
22. Redeem Israel, O God, out of all his troubles.

Commentary

Psalm 25 consists of a collection of petitions by David. These are interspersed with instructions by David concerning his knowledge and experiences of how God deals with people (vv. 8-10 and 12-15).

No doubt the petition in verses 16-21 was prayed during a time in the past when David was in deep distress. David, under the inspiration of the Holy Spirit (2 Sam. 23:1, 2) may also have recorded it here for future distresses that would be experienced by the nation of Israel (v. 22). See Psalm 102:18.

Jeremiah's designation for the Great Tribulation (Mt. 24:21) is "the time of Jacob's troubles" (Jer. 30:7). Jeremiah adds "but he shall be saved out of it." Certainly, the words of verses 16-22 would be a proper prayer for Israel during that time.

There are three great prayers of national confession in the Old Testament. In Ezra 9, that great leader identifies with his nation in confession as though he were the chiefest among the sinners. In Nehemiah 9, while confessing on behalf of the nation, the petitioners say, "We have done wickedly" (Neh. 9:33). In Daniel's great prayer of national confession, he says, "confessing my sin and the sin of my people, Israel" (Dan. 9:20). Here, the psalmist may be identifying prophetically with the nation's future distress.

Application

Did you know that the LORD makes known his secrets only to those who qualify (v. 14)? The following individuals qualify—His friends (Gen. 18:17; Jn. 15:15), the righteous (Pr. 3:32), His prophets (Dan. 2:19; Amos 3:7), those who will to do His will (Jn. 7:17), and "he that is spiritual" (1 Cor. 2:10-16). Do you qualify? How much do you really desire to qualify?

Psalm 26

A Psalm of David.

1. JUDGE ME, O LORD; for I have walked in mine integrity: I have trusted also in the LORD; *therefore* I shall not slide.
2. Examine me, O LORD, and prove me; try my reins and my heart.
3. For thy lovingkindness *is* before mine eyes: and I have walked in thy truth.
4. I have not sat with vain persons, neither will I go in with dissemblers.
5. I have hated the congregation of evildoers; and will not sit with the wicked.
6. I will wash mine hands in innocency: so will I compass thine altar. O LORD:
7. That I may publish with the voice of thanksgiving, and tell of all thy wondrous works.
8. LORD, I have loved the habitation of thy house, and the place where thine honour dwelleth.
9. Gather not my soul with sinners, nor my life with bloody men:
10. In whose hands *is* mischief, and their right hand is full of bribes.
11. But as for me, I will walk in mine integrity: redeem me, and be merciful unto me.
12. My foot standeth in an even place: in the congregations will I bless the LORD.

Commentary

In petitioning the LORD to judge him, David is asking to be distinguished from the evildoers of verse 5. He is not claiming to be without sin; rather, he is asserting that his deep desire has been to walk (maintain a manner of life) pleasing to God. The basis for his claim of integrity is threefold: 1) his trust in the LORD; 2) his continuous desire to have his motives, intents, and purposes examined, proven, and tested by the LORD; 3) his walk in God's truth as he keeps his eyes upon the goodness of God.

David continues his petition (vv. 4, 5) by pointing out that he doesn't keep company with idolaters, pretenders, or people who plot evil deeds. He will remain clean in his actions (v. 6) by regularly attending the place of worship. David will not be a silent believer but will publicly thank the LORD and tell of His wondrous works (v. 7). David has congregated with those who worship and honor the LORD. He vows to continue to avoid violent people (v. 9) and those who seek ill-gotten gains (v. 10). In the future, David purposes to continue his walk of integrity (v. 11). He asks for redemption and mercy based on a walk that arises from a heart that seeks after God. David declares that he stands upon a firm foundation (v.12) and that is his assurance that he will not slip (v. 1). He ends his petition by emphasizing the importance of public worship.

Application

When the LORD selected a king for Israel, He "sought a man after His own heart" (1 Sam. 13:14). The LORD told Samuel, "man looketh upon the outward appearance, but the LORD looketh on the heart" (1 Sam. 16:7). In spite of our failures, the LORD will have a place of productive service for us if His examination proves our hearts to be toward Him and His purposes.

Psalm 27

A Psalm of David.

1. THE LORD *is* my light and my salvation; whom shall I fear? the LORD *is* the strength of my life; of whom shall I be afraid?
2. When the wicked, *even* mine enemies and my foes, came upon me to eat up my flesh, they stumbled and fell.
3. Though an host should encamp against me, my heart shall not fear: though war should rise against me, in this *will* I *be* confident.
4. One *thing* have I desired of the LORD, that will I seek after; that I may dwell in the house of the LORD all the days of my life, to behold the beauty of the LORD, and to inquire in his temple.
5. For in the time of trouble he shall hide me in his pavilion: in the secret of his tabernacle shall he hide me; he shall set me up upon a rock.
6. And now shall mine head be lifted up above mine enemies round about me: therefore will I offer in his tabernacle sacrifices of joy; I will sing, yea, I will sing praises unto the LORD.
7. Hear, O LORD, *when* I cry with my voice: have mercy also upon me, and answer me.
8. *When thou saidst*, Seek ye my face; my heart said unto thee, Thy face, LORD, will I seek.
9. Hide not thy face *far* from me; put not thy servant away in anger: thou hast been my help; leave me not, neither forsake me, O God of my salvation.
10. When my father and my mother forsake me, then the LORD will take me up.
11. Teach me thy way, O LORD, and lead me in a plain path, because of mine enemies.
12. Deliver me not over unto the will of mine enemies: for false witnesses are risen up against me, and such as breathe out cruelty.
13. *I had fainted,* unless I had believed to see the goodness of the LORD in the land of the living.
14. Wait on the LORD: be of good courage, and he shall strengthen thine heart: wait, I say, on the LORD.

Commentary_____

This psalm is in the form of a petition by David in which he is asking the LORD for deliverance from a powerful enemy. He asks the LORD to hear him (v.7), teach him (v. 11), and deliver him (v. 12). However, before he presents his plea, he expresses confident trust (v. 1) based upon previous experiences of faith in the LORD that brought victorious results (v. 2).

More than thirty Hebrew words in the Old Testament are translated as "strength" in the English language. The word in verse 1 is elsewhere translated as "refuge," "defense," "fortress," and "stronghold" as well as "strength." David is declaring in verses 1 and 3 that no enemy can overcome him because he is in the LORD's stronghold.

In verses 4-6, David envisions himself as a guest in the LORD's dwelling place delightfully beholding His glory and seeking to understand His ways. By faith he is appropriating victory and anticipating the rejoicing that will follow. Praise and thanksgiving are often described in the Bible as an acceptable sacrifice unto the LORD (Ps. 54:6, 69:30-31,107:22; Heb. 13:15).

In verse 13, David confesses that without reliance upon the LORD, he would fail. He ends the psalm by offering to the reader advice based upon his own experiences. A strengthened heart is only one of the many benefits promised in Scriptures to those who "wait on the LORD" (v. 14).

Application_____

Are you missing the blessedness of "waiting on the LORD" (Is. 30:18; Dan.12:12)? Perhaps it is because you don't understand in what way you are to occupy yourself while waiting. Why don't you try the advice given in Joshua 1:8 and Psalm 1:2?

Psalm 28

A Psalm of David.

1. UNTO THEE will I cry, O LORD my rock; be not silent to me: lest, *if* thou be silent to me, I become like them that go down into the pit.
2. Hear the voice of my supplications, when I cry unto thee, when I lift up my hands toward thy holy oracle.
3. Draw me not away with the wicked, and with the workers of iniquity, which speak peace to their neighbors, but mischief *is* in their hearts.
4. Give them according to their deeds, and according to the wickedness of their endeavors: give them after the work of their hands; render to them their desert.
5. Because they regard not the works of the LORD, nor the operation of his hands, he shall destroy them, and not build them up.
6. Blessed *be* the LORD, because he hath heard the voice of my supplications.
7. The LORD *is* my strength and my shield; my heart trusted in him, and I am helped: therefore my heart greatly rejoiceth; and with my song will I praise him.
8. The LORD *is* their strength, and he *is* the saving strength of his anointed.
9. Save thy people, and bless thine inheritance: feed them also, and lift them up for ever.

Commentary_____

David wrote this psalm at a time when his life was in peril at the
hands of his enemies—probably when he fled before Absalom and his
conspirators (2 Sam. 15:12-14). They were accusing him of being
dethroned by the LORD because of evilness (2 Sam. 16:8). The pit
(v.1) is the place God is preparing for the wicked (Ps. 94:13; Mt. 25:41).
David cried out to the Lord not to turn a deaf ear to the plea that he not
be classified with the wicked. Those who do deeds of iniquity with their
hands do so because there is deceit and mischief in their hearts
(vv. 3, 4). The wicked do not regard the Lord and therefore obstruct His
work (v. 5) by oppressing the LORD's people (Ps. 17:9).

In verse 6, David, by faith, blesses the LORD for hearing his plea.
He manifests that faith by discontinuing his petition and glorifying the
LORD with rejoicing and praise. His rock (v.1) has become his strength
for offense and his shield for defense (v. 7). He has won the victory by
faith while he is still fleeing and before the foe is faced!

By faith David freed himself from the distressing concern for his
own life to focus on the welfare of his people (vv. 8, 9). He declares the
LORD to be both their offensive strength and their defensive stronghold.
He confidently trusts the LORD to save His people, to bless them, to
feed (shepherd) them, and to carry them. He declares these people to
be the LORD's heritage forever.

Application_____

While earnestly petitioning your LORD, have you had the experience of receiving full assurance of an answer before your prayer is
ended? Such appropriation by faith brings forth rejoicing and songs of
praise. That's the way our God desires true faith to operate.

Psalm 29

A Psalm of David.

1. GIVE UNTO the LORD, O ye mighty, give unto the LORD glory and strength.
2. Give unto the LORD the glory due unto his name; worship the LORD in the beauty of holiness.
3. The voice of the LORD *is* upon the waters: the God of glory thundereth: the LORD *is* upon many waters.
4. The voice of the LORD *is* powerful; the voice of the LORD *is* full of majesty.
5. The voice of the LORD breaketh the cedars; yea, the LORD breaketh the cedars of Lebanon.
6. He maketh them also to skip like a calf; Lebanon and Sirion like a young unicorn.
7. The voice of the LORD divideth the flames of fire.
8. The voice of the LORD shaketh the wilderness; the LORD shaketh the wilderness of Kadesh.
9. The voice of the LORD maketh the hinds to calve, and discovereth the forests: and in his temple doth every one speak of *his* glory.
10. The LORD sitteth upon the flood; yea, the LORD sitteth King for ever.
11. The LORD will give strength unto his people; the LORD will bless his people with peace.

Commentary

The most prominent name for God in the Hebrew Old Testament is *Yahweh.* For centuries in English we have called this name *Jehovah.* Most scholars now agree that it was vocalized *Yahweh.* One respected scholar defines the name as "He causes to be." In most English translations the name is rendered *LORD* with all letters capitalized. This name of God is repeated eighteen times in Psalm 29.

In Psalm 19:1-3, David sees the created universe as declaring "the glory of God." In Psalm 29, he sees the "God of Glory" speaking by means of a violent storm venting its fury upon the land of Israel from north to south.

The psalmist begins by calling upon the angels of Heaven (v.1) and the inhabitants of the earth (v. 2) to glorify and worship *Jehovah.* The phrase "in the beauty of holiness" is also found in Psalm 96 and Psalm 110 as well as in 1 and 2 Chronicles. It probably means "because of His holy splendor."

Lebanon and Sirion (Mt. Hermon) are located in the northern extremity of David's realm. The Wilderness of Kadesh is in the southernmost part. The Hebrew word translated *flood* (v. 10) is found only here and in Genesis 6-11. The psalmist is pointing out that the LORD was in total control during Noah's flood, remains in control, and will continue to be in control forever! Verse 11 may very well look forward to the millennial reign of Jesus Christ on Earth (Isa. 32:16-18).

Application

Our politicians supply billions of dollars of public funds to scientists for building and operating devices directed towards the discovery of life beyond the limits of this planet. Yet a totally deaf ear is turned towards a God who knows the answer and speaks through creation, nature, and His Holy Word.

Psalm 30

A Psalm *and* Song *at* the dedication of the house of David.

I. I WILL extol thee, O LORD; for thou hast lifted me up, and hast not made my foes to rejoice over me.
2. O LORD my God, I cried unto thee, and thou hast healed me.
3. O LORD, thou hast brought up my soul from the grave: thou hast kept me alive, that I should not go down to the pit.
4. Sing unto the LORD, O ye saints of his, and give thanks at the remembrance of his holiness.
5. For his anger *endureth but* a moment; in his favour *is* life: weeping may endure for a night, but joy *cometh* in the morning.
6. And in my prosperity I said, I shall never be moved.
7. LORD, by thy favour thou hast made my mountain to stand strong: thou didst hide thy face, *and* I was troubled.
8. I cried to thee, O LORD; and unto the LORD I made supplication.
9. What profit *is there* in my blood, when I go down to the pit? Shall the dust praise thee? shall it declare thy truth?
10. Hear, O LORD, and have mercy upon me: LORD, be thou my helper.
11. Thou hast turned for me my mourning into dancing: thou hast put off my sackcloth, and girded me with gladness;
12. To the end that *my* glory may sing praise to thee, and not be silent. O LORD my God, I will give thanks unto thee for ever.

Commentary_____

David gives seven reasons in this psalm to extol his LORD:

(1)"Thou hast lifted me up" (v. 1). Scripture records a number of
occasions when David was in deep despair. However, his low
est point was reached when he realized the great reproach he
had brought upon the LORD through his sin with Bathsheba
(2 Sam. 12:14; Ps. 38:3-8).

(2)"Thou hast healed me" (v. 2). Healing in the Bible often refers to
the soul and spirit rather than the body
(2 Chr. 7:14; Ps. 6:2, 3; Hos. 14:4; Heb.12:13).

(3)"Thou hast brought my soul from the grave" (v. 3). David often
gives thanks for deliverance both from physical and eternal
death (Ps. 37:39; Ps. 62:1).

(4)"Thou hast kept me alive" (v. 3). Many times David faced death,
but God spared his life (1 Sam. 19:1, 10; 2 Sam. 15:14).

5)"Thou hast made my mountain to stand strong" (v. 7). By
"mountain," David is referring to his kingdom
(Isa. 2:2; Dan. 2:35, 44).

(6)"Thou hast turned for me my mourning into dancing" (v. 11). This
is a parallel thought to "weeping may endure for a night, but joy
cometh in the morning" (v. 5).

(7)"Thou hast put off my sackcloth, and girded me with gladness"
(v. 11). The wearing of sackcloth was the outward or observable
way of expressing grief, remorse or penitence. To be girded
with gladness is to show outward evidence of inner joy.

Application_____

One's spiritual temperature can be measured by that which causes
one to give thanks (v. 4) and by the frequency of the expression of
thanks (v. 12). The psalmist understands that adversity and affliction
are more profitable spiritually than prosperity is
(v. 6, Ps.10:6; Ps. 119:71).

Psalm 31:1-13

To the chief Musician, A Psalm of David.

1. IN THEE, O LORD, do I put my trust; let me never be ashamed: deliver me in thy righteousness.
2. Bow down thine ear to me; deliver me speedily: be thou my strong rock, for an house of defence to save me.
3. For thou *art* my rock and my fortress; therefore for thy name's sake lead me, and guide me.
4. Pull me out of the net that they have laid privily for me: for thou *art* my strength.
5. Into thine hand I commit my spirit: thou hast redeemed me, O LORD God of truth.
6. I have hated them that regard lying vanities: but I trust in the LORD.
7. I will be glad and rejoice in thy mercy: for thou hast considered my trouble; thou hast known my soul in adversities;
8. And hast not shut me up into the hand of the enemy: thou hast set my feet in a large room.
9. Have mercy upon me, O LORD, for I am in trouble: mine eye is consumed with grief, *yea*, my soul and my belly.
10. For my life is spent with grief, and my years with sighing: my strength faileth because of mine iniquity, and my bones are consumed.
11. I was a reproach among all mine enemies, but especially among my neighbors, and a fear to mine acquaintance: they that did see me without fled from me.
12. I am forgotten as a dead man out of mind: I am like a broken vessel.
13. For I have heard the slander of many: fear *was* on every side: while they took counsel together against me, they devised to take away my life.

Commentary_____

This psalm probably arises from David's experiences as he fled from Absalom (2 Sam. 15-17). Textual indications suggest that the psalm was compiled over a period of several days as events caused his faith to waiver and then grow firm as he considered his LORD's faithfulness in past deliverances.

He begins his supplication with a firm declaration of his trust in the LORD as his fortress at a time when he is fleeing the fortress he built for himself on Mt. Zion. Often, David saw himself as a bird for which his enemies had set a snare (v. 4).

Compare verse 5 with the words of our Lord on the cross (Lk. 23:46) and the words of Stephen as he was stoned (Acts 7:59). "Lying vanities" (v. 6) is a biblical term for idols (Jonah 2:8; Acts 14:15).

Verses 9-13 demonstrate for us what happens to faith when we take our eyes off the Lord and fix them upon self and circumstances. When Peter, by faith, stepped from the boat and onto the sea (Mt. 14:29), he had his eyes on the Lord. When he was distracted by the wind and waves, he sank. Thankfully, that wasn't the end of the story, and verse 13 isn't the end of this psalm.

In verse 13, David is no doubt referring to the conspiracy recorded in 2 Samuel 15:12. The chief conspirators, Absalom and Ahithophel, certainly proved the truth of Proverbs 11:19- "he that pursueth evil pursueth it to his own death" (2 Sam. 17:23, 18:15).

Application_____

The faith of the strongest Christian may waiver when adverse circumstances strike suddenly. That is the reason we need an armory of verses like Romans 8:35 well planted in our hearts for use in an emergency.

Psalm 31:14-24

14. But I trusted in thee, O LORD: I said, Thou *art* my God.
15. My times *are* in thy hand: deliver me from the hand of mine enemies, and from them that persecute me.
16. Make thy face to shine upon thy servant: save me for thy mercies' sake.
17. Let me not be ashamed, O LORD; for I have called upon thee: let the wicked be ashamed, *and* let them be silent in the grave.
18. Let the lying lips be put to silence; which speak grievous things proudly and contemptuously against the righteous.
19. *Oh* how great is thy goodness, which thou hast laid up for them that fear thee; *which* thou hast wrought for them that trust in thee before the sons of men!
20. Thou shalt hide them in the secret of thy presence from the pride of man: thou shalt keep them secretly in a pavilion from the strife of tongues.
21. Blessed *be* the LORD: for he hath shewed me his marvellous kindness in a strong city.
22. For I said in my haste, I am cut off from before thine eyes: nevertheless thou heardest the voice of my supplications when I cried unto thee.
23. O love the LORD, all ye his saints: *for* the LORD preserveth the faithful, and plentifully rewardeth the proud doer.
24. Be of good courage, and he shall strengthen your heart, all ye that hope in the LORD.

Commentary_____

What brought David from the despair of verses 9-12 to the victorious faith of verses 19-21? Notice in verse 10 that his eyes are upon his own weakness and inadequacy. In verses 11-13 his eyes are upon his enemies and their actions. In verse 14, he simply takes his eyes off himself and his circumstances and fixes his gaze upon his God. The end result is that he stops pitying himself (v. 9) and begins encouraging others (v. 24).

"My times are in thy hand" (v. 15). When we conclude that God is in complete control of our length of days upon Earth, we relax within our circumstances and rest in Him. That makes us usable to Him and gives Him good reason to deliver us from our circumstances in response to our prayer (vv. 14-18). The immediate result for us is that anxiety is converted to praise (v. 19). Praise strengthens trust. Now we regard ourselves as protected in God's bosom from anything the enemy can do against us (v. 20).

"Strong city" (v. 21)—David now sees himself in an impregnable fortress under siege which is impervious to the attacks of the besieger. In verse 22, David refers to the thoughts expressed in verse 12. In spite of his failing faith, God heard the supplication of verses 15-18.

The psalm concludes triumphantly with David not only looking to the LORD but also ardently turning the eyes of others upon the LORD.

Application_____

In order to profit from the psalms, we must firmly believe that the Spirit is speaking to us through the psalmist (2 Sam. 23:2). We should continually remind ourselves that the Divine Author had us in mind when He caused the words to be written
(Ps. 102:18; Rom. 15:4; 1 Cor. 10:11).

Psalm 32

A *Psalm* of David, Maschil.

1. BLESSED *IS he whose* transgression *is* forgiven, *whose* sin *is* covered.
2. Blessed *is* the man unto whom the LORD imputeth not iniquity, and in whose spirit *there is* no guile.
3. When I kept silence, my bones waxed old through my roaring all the day long.
4. For day and night thy hand was heavy upon me: my moisture is turned into the drought of summer. Selah.
5. I acknowledged my sin unto thee, and mine iniquity have I not hid. I said, I will confess my transgressions unto the LORD; and thou forgavest the iniquity of my sin. Selah.
6. For this shall every one that is godly pray unto thee in a time when thou mayest be found: surely in the floods of great waters they shall not come nigh unto him.
7. Thou *art* my hiding place; thou shalt preserve me from trouble; thou shalt compass me about with songs of deliverance. Selah.
8. I will instruct thee and teach thee in the way which thou shalt go: I will guide thee with mine eye.
9. Be ye not as the horse, *or* as the mule, *which* have no understanding: whose mouth must be held in with bit and bridle, lest they come near unto thee.
10. Many sorrows *shall be* to the wicked: but he that trusteth in the LORD, mercy shall compass him about.
11. Be glad in the LORD, and rejoice, ye righteous: and shout for joy, all *ye that are* upright in heart.

Commentary

Psalm 32 is a sequel to Psalm 51 in which David confesses his sin with Bathsheba. David confesses three aspects of his unrighteousness. Compare verses 1, 2, and 5 to Psalm 51: 1-3. See also Romans 4:6-8 where the Apostle Paul quotes from Psalm 32: 1, 2.

A "transgression" is an action against God's known law such as violating one of the Ten Commandments. "Sin" is falling short of God's righteous standard. "Iniquity" is that which is inherently wrong whether or not it violates a law. Examples are cruelty, disregard for the well-being of others, and guile (v. 2).

For those who enjoy alliteration, here is an outline for the psalm. Sins are forgiven (v. 1) when the spirit is right (v. 2) whereas silence (v. 3) brings summer drought (v. 4). Sins acknowledged (v. 5) bring sure safety (v. 6), songs of deliverance (v. 7) and Spirit guidance (v. 8). The choice is between stubbornness (v. 9) and sorrows (v. 10) or shouts of joy (v. 11).

"He that covereth his sins shall not prosper, but whoso confesseth and forsaketh them shall have mercy" (Pr. 28:13). If we uncover sins by confessing, God covers them in the depths of the sea (Mic. 7:19). David's personal experience as recorded in Psalm 32 is scriptural proof of the proverb. He kept his sins covered for about a year before Nathan forced him to face them (2 Sam. 12). "Godly sorrow" (2 Cor. 7:10) changed his "many sorrows" (v. 10) into rejoicing (v. 11).

Application

The New Testament provision for the sinning child of God is found in the first chapter of 1 John. We have fellowship in Christ (v. 3) and fullness of joy (v. 4) as we walk in the light (v. 7) through the cleansing of the blood of Christ (v. 7) when we confess our sins (v. 9). Then we can say with the psalmist, "Blessed is he whose transgression is forgiven, whose sin is covered."

Psalm 33:1-9

1. REJOICE IN the LORD, O ye righteous: *for* praise is comely for the upright.
2. Praise the LORD with harp: sing unto him with the psaltry *and* an instrument of ten strings.
3. Sing unto him a new song; play skilfully with a loud noise.
4. For the word of the LORD *is* right; and all his works *are done* in truth.
5. He loveth righteousness and judgment: the earth is full of the goodness of the LORD.
6. By the word of the LORD were the heavens made; and all the host of them by the breath of his mouth.
7. He gathereth the waters of the sea together as an heap: he layeth up the depth in storehouses.
8. Let all the earth fear the LORD: let all the inhabitants of the world stand in awe of him.
9. For he spake, and it was *done;* he commanded, and it stood fast.

Commentary

The probable reason Psalm 33 is anonymous is that, as a medley of four songs, it was composed at different times by different authors and compiled as one psalm for worship purposes. The first song (vs. 1-5) might well be titled "A Joyful Song of the Righteous." It calls for praise to the LORD for His word and His work (v. 4) and for His righteousness and His goodness (v. 5). Verse 2 lets us know that the proper use of musical instruments is for praise to the LORD (Ps. 92:3).

Four times in the Psalms (33:3, 96:1, 98:1, 149:1) and once in Isaiah the LORD's people are exhorted to sing a new song unto the LORD. Why a _new_ song? "He hath put a new song in my mouth" so that "many shall see it, and fear, and shall trust in the LORD" (Ps. 40:3). "His mercies are new every morning" (Lam. 3:23). He declares new things "before they spring forth" (Isa. 42: 9, 10).

I must "show forth His salvation from day to day" (Ps. 96:2). "He hath done marvelous things" (Ps. 98:1). "The LORD taketh pleasure in His people" (Ps. 149:4).

The second song of the medley (vv. 6-9) could be titled "A Song of Allegiance to the Creator." The "scientific world" spends countless dollars and many lifetimes attempting to discover how the universe came to be. Whatever they conclude will surely be proven false if they omit a Creator God. "The worlds were framed by the word of God" (Heb. 11:3). The schedule of events in the origin of the universe is precisely related in Genesis 1. Believe that and you will never need to change your position. Neither will you ever be proven wrong!

Application

"The word of the LORD is right and all His works are done in truth" (v. 4). If you are squarely settled on that word from the LORD, you have adequate reason to "rejoice in the LORD" (v. 1) and to "sing unto Him a new song" (v. 3) every day. The righteous praise Him because praise is befitting to the upright (v. 1).

Psalm 33:10-22

10. The LORD bringeth the counsel of the heathen to nought: he maketh the devices of the people of none effect.

11. The counsel of the LORD standeth for ever, the thoughts of his heart to all generations.

12. Blessed *is* the nation whose God *is* the LORD; *and* the people *whom* he hath chosen for his own inheritance.

13. The LORD looketh from heaven; he beholdeth all the sons of men.

14. From the place of his habitation he looketh upon all the inhabitants of the earth.

15. He fashioneth their hearts alike; he considereth all their works.

16. There is no king saved by the multitude of an host: a mighty man is not delivered by much strength.

17. An horse *is* a vain thing for safety: neither shall he deliver *any* by his great strength.

18. Behold, the eye of the LORD *is* upon them that fear him, upon them that hope in his mercy;

19. To deliver their soul from death, and to keep them alive in famine.

20. Our soul waiteth for the LORD: he *is* our help and our shield.

21. For our heart shall rejoice in him, because we have trusted in his holy name.

22. Let thy mercy, O LORD, be upon us, according as we hope in thee.

Commentary

We shall entitle the third song (vv. 10-17) of our Psalm 33 medley, "The Lord of Heaven and the People of His Earth" (v. 13). When the creating originator of this universe spoke it into existence, He already had fully developed plans for its future (Isa. 46:10). Throughout history, when the actions of men have attempted to counsel and devise against His program, He exercises His veto power (v. 10). His carefully thought out plans overrule in every generation (v. 11). He knows precisely what every person is thinking before action follows thought (Ps. 94:11). This is awesome beyond human comprehension (Ps. 139:4-6; Isa. 55:9).

The deliverance of Israel from Pharoah (Ex. 14:28-30) and the victory of David over Goliath (1 Sam. 17:47-50), along with other Bible accounts and historical events, prove the veracity of verse 16 and 17. Let the "Hitlers" of history and the Antichrist of the future be assured this truth continues through all generations.

For the title of song four (vv. 18-22) we suggest, "The LORD and Those Who Fear Him." Men rebel against God's program for this world because "there is no fear of God before their eyes" (Rom. 3:18). The ultimate deliverance (v. 19) for "those who hope in His mercy" is rescue from the certain fate of those who fear not the LORD.

We know we are among those who are truly trusting (v. 21) by the joy in our hearts. If we are rejoicing regardless of circumstances, we are trusting. Hope in the LORD is not wishful desire—it is the present appropriation of a future joyous certainty (Tit. 1:2; Heb. 6:19).

Application

Where is there literature on this Earth of any kind more profitable for contemplation and consolation in times of trial or distress than Psalm 33? Deliberate meditation on each verse will surely result in fulfillment of the promise of Psalm 1:3.

Psalm 34:1-10

A *Psalm* of David, when he changed his behaviour before Abimelech; who drove him away, and he departed.

1. I WILL bless the LORD at all times: his praise *shall* continually *be* in my mouth.
2. My soul shall make her boast in the LORD: the humble shall hear *thereof*, and be glad.
3. O magnify the LORD with me, and let us exalt his name together.
4. I sought the LORD, and he heard me, and delivered me from all my fears.
5. They looked unto him, and were lightened: and their faces were not ashamed.
6. This poor man cried, and the LORD heard *him*, and saved him out of all is troubles.
7. The angel of the LORD encampeth round about them that fear him, and delivereth them.
8. O taste and see that the LORD *is* good: blessed *is* the man *that* trusteth in him.
9. O fear the LORD, ye his saints: for *there is* no want to them that fear him.
10. The young lions do lack, and suffer hunger: but they that seek the LORD shall not want any good *thing*.

Commentary_____

Originally this psalm was composed as an acrostic with each of the 22 verses beginning with the next succeeding letter of the Hebrew alphabet. According to the superscription, David wrote the psalm following his experience that is related in 1 Samuel 21:10-15. Abimelech, meaning "royal father," is a title designating several Philistine kings from Abraham (Gen. 20:2) to David. The name of the king with whom David was involved was Achish (1 Sam. 21:10).

As I meditate on the first three verses of Psalm 34 they say to me, "I will continue to speak well of the LORD in every situation and will always give Him credit for the good things of life. This will cause the people around me, who are not arrogantly self-reliant, to have glad hearts. Please join me in praising the LORD so we can rejoice together in Him."

Verse 4 expresses the theme of the psalm: "The LORD heard; the LORD delivered." Read verse 5 as an imperative- "Look unto Him and your face will glow and you will never be confounded." Verse 6 rephrases the theme of verse 4.

"The Angel of the LORD" is a frequent Old Testament designation for God as He manifests Himself to individuals on Earth. (Gen. 16:9; Ex. 3:2-6; Jud. 13:3-22).

The apostle Peter applies verse 8 to the Lord Jesus Christ in 1 Peter 2:3. There our Lord is presented as the Chief Cornerstone of the spiritual abode of which every believer is a living part.

Application_____

A good spiritual exercise would be to rephrase verses 8-10 in your own words as you apply the truths of those verses to your own life. What does it mean to "taste" the LORD? How does one "seek" the LORD? What will be the result for you if you taste, trust, fear and seek the LORD?

Psalm 34:11-22

11. Come, ye children, hearken unto me: I will teach you the fear of the LORD.

12. What man *is he that* desireth life, *and* loveth *many* days, that he may see good?

13. Keep thy tongue from evil, and thy lips from speaking guile.

14. Depart from evil, and do good; seek peace, and pursue it.

15. The eyes of the LORD *are* upon the righteous, and his ears *are open* unto their cry.

16. The face of the LORD *is* against them that do evil, to cut off the remembrance of them from the earth.

17. *The righteous* cry, and the LORD heareth, and delivereth them out of all their troubles.

18. The LORD *is* nigh unto them that are of a broken heart; and saveth such as be of a contrite spirit.

19. Many *are* the afflictions of the righteous: but the LORD delivereth him out of them all.

20. He keepeth all his bones: not one of them is broken.

21. Evil shall slay the wicked: and they that hate the righteous shall be desolate.

22. The LORD redeemeth the soul of his servants: and none of them that trust in him shall be desolate.

Commentary_____

If you desire a long and satisfying life (v. 12), the psalmist exhorts you to actively proceed in four respects. First, learn what it means to fear the LORD (v. 11). Second, be very careful about what comes forth from your mouth (v. 13). Third, stay away from evil by actively involving yourself in doing good (v. 14). Fourth, diligently pursue peace (v. 14). As a result, the LORD will keep a protective eye upon you and will be attentive to your petitions (v. 15). The LORD also has His eye on evildoers (v. 16).

Verse 17 returns us to the principal theme of the psalm. Not only has the LORD heard and delivered in past circumstances (vv. 4, 6), but He will continue to hear and deliver those described in verse 18. The psalmist employs four different Hebrew words in speaking of the LORD's deliverance. They are variously translated "deliver" (vv. 4, 7, 17, 19), "save" (vv. 6, 18), and "redeem" (v. 22). All four Hebrew words share a common thought. In different ways, they all speak of rescuing one from a place or situation of danger to a safe haven.

Notice that verse 19 does not promise the righteous exemption from affliction. It promises that the LORD will make His presence known in the affliction and will ultimately deliver the righteous from the affliction (Dan. 3:25; 2 Cor. 12:9).

Verse 20 is quoted in John 19:36 and applied to Jesus Christ at His crucifixion. The passover lamb pointed to "the Lamb of God who taketh away the sin of the world" (Jn. 1:29). See Exodus 12:46 and Numbers 9:12.

Application_____

Psalm 34 ends by reminding us that judgment is according to works (Rom. 2:6; Rev. 20:13), but redemption is apart from works and according to trust, which is the psalmist's word for faith (Eph. 2: 8, 9). Make certain that your trust for eternal soul salvation rests solely upon the redemption wrought for you by Jesus Christ on Calvary.

Psalm 35:1-14

A Psalm of David.

1. PLEAD *MY cause*, O LORD, with them that strive with me: fight against them that fight against me.
2. Take hold of shield and buckler, and stand up for mine help.
3. Draw out also the spear, and stop *the way* against them that persecute me: say unto my soul, I *am* thy salvation.
4. Let them be confounded and put to shame that seek after my soul: let them be turned back and brought to confusion that devise my hurt.
5. Let them be as chaff before the wind: and let the angel of the LORD chase *them*.
6. Let their way be dark and slippery: and let the angel of the LORD persecute them.
7. For without cause have they hid for me their net *in* a pit, *which* without cause they have digged for my soul.
8. Let destruction come upon him at unawares; and let his net that he hath hid catch himself: into that very destruction let him fall.
9. And my soul shall be joyful in the LORD: it shall rejoice in his salvation.
10. And my bones shall say, LORD, who *is* like unto thee, which deliverest the poor from him that is too strong for him, yea, the poor and the needy from him that spoileth him?
11. False witnesses did rise up; they laid to my charge *things* that I knew not.
12. They rewarded me evil for good *to* the spoiling of my soul.
13. But as for me, when they were sick, my clothing *was* sackcloth: I humbled my soul with fasting; and my prayer returned into mine own bosom.
14. I behaved myself as though *he had been* my friend *or* brother: I bowed down heavily, as one that mourneth *for his* mother.

Commentary_____

We can better understand what may seem to be vindictiveness on the part of David in Psalm 35 if we consider the history recorded in 1 Samuel beginning in chapter 16. As a lad, David was anointed king by Samuel the prophet (1 Sam. 16: 1, 13). In chapters 17 and 18, David demonstrated his willingness to serve King Saul until it was God's time for him to ascend to the throne. Although Saul knew David was innocent of any ill will against him(1 Sam. 19:5; 20:1; 24:11, 17), Saul relentlessly pursued David for more than ten years. Twice David had the opportunity to slay Saul but refused to avenge himself. In Psalm 35 David is beseeching his LORD to vindicate him because vengeance belongs to Him (Deut. 32:35; Heb. 10:30). In verses 1-3, David recognizes that "the battle is the LORD's" (1 Sam. 17:47).
(See also Ex. 14:14, Josh. 5:14, 2 Chron. 20:15 and Zech. 14:3.)

In verse 8, David calls upon the LORD to use one of His favorite ways of dealing with evil men (Ps. 9:15; Pr. 28:10; Est. 7:10). In verses 9 and 10, he presents to the LORD a good reason for the LORD to hear his plea. A favorable answer will result in joyful praise to the LORD.

While David was a fugitive, he and his army came to the aid of a city besieged by the Philistines. The inhabitants of that city returned evil for good by betraying David into the hands of Saul (1 Sam. 23:1-12). When David wrote verses 12-14, he probably had that incident in mind as well as the episode involving Nabal (1 Sam. 25).

Application_____

When we have vengeful feelings toward someone who is mistreating us, we should follow David's example and express our frustrations to the Lord. He will turn our resentment into compassion (1 Sam. 26:21-25). He will also teach us that He is in control and that in His time the issue will be resolved correctly.

Psalm 35:15-28

15. But in mine adversity they rejoiced, and gathered themselves together: *yea*, the abjects gathered themselves together against me, and I knew *it* not; they did tear *me*, and ceased not:
16. With hypocritical mockers in feasts, they gnashed upon me with their teeth.
17. Lord, how long wilt thou look on? rescue my soul from their destructions, my darling from the lions.
18. I will give thee thanks in the great congregation: I will praise thee among much people.
19. Let not them that are mine enemies wrongfully rejoice over me: *neither* let them wink with the eye that hate me without a cause.
20. For they speak not peace: but they devise deceitful matters against *them that are* quiet in the land.
21. Yea, they opened their mouth wide against me, *and* said, Aha, aha, our eye hath seen *it*.
22. *This* thou hast seen, O LORD: keep not silence: O Lord, be not far from me.
23. Stir up thyself, and awake to my judgment, *even* unto my cause, my God and my Lord.
24. Judge me, O LORD my God, according to thy righteousness; and let them not rejoice over me.
25. Let them not say in their hearts, Ah, so would we have it: let them not say, We have swallowed him up.
26. Let them be ashamed and brought to confusion together that rejoice at mine hurt: let them be clothed with shame and dishonour that magnify *themselves* against me.
27. Let them shout for joy, and be glad, that favour my righteous cause: yea, let them say continually, Let the LORD be magnified, which hath pleasure in the prosperity of his servant.
28. And my tongue shall speak of thy righteousness *and* of thy praise all the day long.

Commentary_____

"In my adversity they rejoiced." Four times (vv. 15, 19, 24, 26) David cries out against those who rejoice because of his troubles. To rejoice in another's adversity is the very opposite of "love thy neighbor as thyself" (Lev. 19:18; Mt. 22:39; Rom. 13:9). In Psalm 35, David is reasoning thusly with the LORD: "they are rejoicing in evil while my desire is to lead many in rejoicing because of Your goodness (vv. 9, 18, 27, 28). Therefore act on my behalf!"

"How long O LORD?" This has been the cry of the LORD's servants through the ages—Job (Job 7:19), David (Ps. 6:3, 35:17), Asaph (Ps. 74:10, 79:5), Moses (Ps. 90:13), the psalmist (Ps. 94:3), Jeremiah (Jer. 12:4, 47:6), and Habakkuk (Hab. 1:2). It is even the cry of the Angel of the LORD on behalf of Jerusalem (Zech. 1:12) because when things are right in Jerusalem, they will be right everywhere forever! In times of travail, it seems that the LORD is so slow to rebuke evil and establish righteousness. Why doesn't He hurry up and do something?

In verses 22-24, twice in each verse, David invokes the three principal Old Testament names of God—LORD (*Jehovah* or *Yahweh*), Lord (*Adonai*) and God (*Elohim*). A study of the significance of each of these names would be of much value in understanding the intensity of David's plea. He is "pulling out all of the stops"!

Application_____

How often have we been made aware of the need to say "I'm sorry" when we have brought discomfort to someone by word or deed? It is sinful to play practical jokes upon, poke fun at, or embarrass others in order to enjoy their reactions. It is sinful to take pleasure at another's expense. If we confess such actions as sin, we would seldom need to use the pitifully inadequate words, "I'm sorry."

Psalm 36

To the chief Musician, *A Psalm* of David the servant of the LORD.

1. THE TRANSGRESSION of the wicked saith within my heart, *that there is* no fear of God before his eyes.
2. For he flattereth himself in his own eyes, until his iniquity be found to be hateful.
3. The words of his mouth *are* iniquity and deceit: he hath left off to be wise, *and* to do good.
4. He deviseth mischief upon his bed; he setteth himself in a way *that is* not good; he abhorreth not evil.
5. Thy mercy, O LORD, *is* in the heavens; *and* thy faithfulness *reacheth* unto the clouds.
6. Thy righteousness *is* like the great mountains; thy judgments *are* a great deep: O LORD, thou preservest man and beast.
7. How excellent *is* thy lovingkindness, O God! therefore the children of men put their trust under the shadow of thy wings.
8. They shall be abundantly satisfied with the fatness of thy house; and thou shalt make them drink of the river of thy pleasures.
9. For with thee *is* the fountain of life: in thy light shall we see light.
10. O continue thy lovingkindness unto them that know thee; and thy righteousness to the upright in heart.
11. Let not the foot of pride come against me, and let not the hand of the wicked remove me.
12. There are the workers of iniquity fallen: they are cast down, and shall not be able to rise.

Commentary_____

The last half of verse 1 is quoted in Romans as the finale of a long list of the characteristics that describe the condition of the unregenerate human heart (Rom. 3:10-18). The word "fear" in verse 1 is not the same as the word translated "fear" in Psalm 33:8, 18 and Psalm 34:7, 9, 11. In those psalms "fear" denotes the proper regard for an awesome Creator by His creatures. Here in Psalm 36 the usage denotes the proper regard of a sinner facing a righteous Divine Judge. For a fuller understanding of the word, see how it is used in Isaiah 2:10, 19, 21.

The word "mercy" in verse 5 is translated from the original word which is rendered "loving kindness" in verses 7 and 10. Verses 5 and 6 are stating in poetic language that the LORD's lovingkindness and faithfulness, as well as His righteous judgments, surpass human comprehension (Rom. 11:33).

"The fountain of life" (v. 9) is one of the LORD's favorite designations for Himself. From that fountain flows the river of God (Ps. 36:8, 46:4, 65:9, Isa. 66:12 Rev. 22:1, 17) which brings delights that will "abundantly satisfy " eternally the "upright in heart" (v. 10). On the other hand, "the workers of iniquity" will be "cast down, and shall not be able to rise" (v. 12).

Application_____

Psalm 36 emphasizes the truth that the choices made in this life have profound eternal consequences. Those who choose to disregard their Maker are described in verses 1-4, and their certain fate is pointed out in verse 12. Those who "put their trust under the shadow of His wings" (v. 7) will forever "be abundantly satisfied with the fatness of His house" and will drink eternally from "the river of His delights" (v. 8).

Psalm 37:1-13

A Psalm of David.

1. FRET NOT thyself because of evildoers, neither be thou envious against the workers of iniquity.
2. For they shall soon be cut down like the grass, and wither as the green herb.
3. Trust in the LORD, and do good; *so* shalt thou dwell in the land, and verily thou shall be fed.
4. Delight thyself also in the LORD; and he shall give thee the desires of thine heart.
5. Commit thy way unto the LORD; trust also in him; and he shall bring *it* to pass.
6. And he shall bring forth thy righteousness as the light, and thy judgment as the noonday.
7. Rest in the LORD, and wait patiently for him: fret not thyself because of him who prospereth in his way, because of the man who bringeth wicked devices to pass.
8. Cease from anger, and forsake wrath: fret not thyself in any wise to do evil.
9. For evildoers shall be cut off: but those that wait upon the LORD, they shall inherit the earth.
10. For yet for a little while, and the wicked *shall* not *be*: yea, thou shalt diligently consider his place, and it *shall* not *be*.
11. But the meek shall inherit the earth; and shall delight themselves in the abundance of peace.
12. The wicked plotteth against the just, and gnasheth upon him with his teeth.
13. The Lord shall laugh at him: for he seeth that his day is coming.

Commentary_____

In its original form Psalm 37 was an acrostic poem with 22 stanzas of varying size. Each stanza began with the next succeeding letter of the Hebrew alphabet. When the psalm was later divided into 40 verses, the original structure was not precisely followed. The purpose of the psalm is to encourage the righteous not to fret about the prosperity of the wicked but rather to trust the Lord to rectify all things in His time.

Between the "fret not" of verse 1 and the "fret not" of verse 7, we find seven words of exhortation teaching the righteous how to grow to spiritual maturity. One who is intent upon growing is not fretting, and one who is fretting is not growing. The seven words are *trust, do good, delight, commit, trust* (again), *rest*, and *wait*. They give us a yardstick by which to measure our spiritual progress.

First, we trust solely in Christ for eternal salvation. Good works follow salvation as proof of genuine conversion
(Eph. 2:8-10, Tit. 3:5-8, Jam. 2:18). A growing Christian delights in the Word and in prayer (1 Pet. 2:2). This brings one to a point of decision in which one commits himself completely to the LORD
(Rom. 6:13, 12:1). One then trusts the LORD not only for salvation but also for step-by-step guidance in one's daily walk (Pr. 3:5, 6). A full grown Christian rests completely in the LORD and waits patiently while He brings fruitfulness into his life and all things to consummation
(vv. 9-11).

Application_____

"There is a place of quiet rest near to the heart of God" wrote hymnist Cleland B. McAfee. Do you have a heart desire to enter into His place of rest? (Mt. 11:29, Heb. 4:1) Where are you now in regards to the measuring stick of Psalm 37:3-7?

Psalm 37:14-26

14. The wicked have drawn out the sword, and have bent their bow, to cast down the poor and needy, *and* to slay such as be of upright conversation.

15. Their sword shall enter into their own heart, and their bows shall be broken.

16. A little that a righteous man hath *is* better than the riches of many wicked.

17. For the arms of the wicked shall be broken: but the LORD upholdeth the righteous.

18. The LORD knoweth the days of the upright: and their inheritance shall be for ever.

19. They shall not be ashamed in the evil time: and in the days of famine they shall be satisfied.

20. But the wicked shall perish, and the enemies of the LORD *shall be* as fat of lambs: they shall consume; into smoke shall they consume away.

21. The wicked borroweth, and payeth not again: but the righteous sheweth mercy, and giveth.

22. For *such as be* blessed of him shall inherit the earth; and *they that be* cursed of him shall be cut off.

23. The steps of a *good* man are ordered by the LORD: and he delighteth in his way.

24. Though he fall, he shall not be utterly cast down: for the LORD upholdeth *him with* his hand.

25. I have been young, and *now* am old; yet have I not seen the righteous forsaken, nor his seed begging bread.

26. *He is* ever merciful, and lendeth; and his seed *is* blessed.

Commentary

Psalm 37 considers the character and the conduct of two different classes of people. Thirteen times one group is designated "the wicked." These people are also called "evildoers," "workers of iniquity," "enemies of the LORD," and "transgressors." The psalmist accuses the wicked of bringing wicked devices to pass (v. 7). They plot against the just (v. 12). They cast down the poor and needy with drawn sword and bent bow (v. 14). They seek to slay the righteous (v. 32).

The other class of people is designated "the righteous," "the upright," and "the just." These are characterized by showing mercy and giving to others (vv. 21, 26). They speak wisdom and justice (v. 30). The steps of the righteous are directed by the LORD, and therefore, the LORD takes great delight in their ways (v. 23).

Although Psalm 37 has much to say about the wicked and the righteous, the principal personage of the psalm is "the LORD" who is named fifteen times. He knows exactly what is happening every day in the lives of the upright (v. 18). At the same time, He keeps His eye on the wicked and foresees their judgment (v. 13). In the words of the psalmist, He "upholds" the righteous and will "cut off" the wicked. If the righteous will rest upon that assurance, they will be blessed by the LORD in many ways, and that blessing will be passed on to their descendents (vv. 25, 26).

Application

Today there are those who cause the problems of society and those who are part of the solution. We must instill into the hearts of the next generation a deep desire to be a part of the solution instead of the problem. This is possible only when their steps are ordered by the LORD (v. 23, Ps. 119:133; Jer. 10:23).

Psalm 37:27-40

27. Depart from evil, and do good; and dwell for evermore.
28. For the LORD loveth judgment, and forsaketh not his saints; they are preserved for ever: but the seed of the wicked shall be cut off.
29. The righteous shall inherit the land, and dwell therein for ever.
30. The mouth of the righteous speaketh wisdom, and his tongue talketh of judgment.
31. The law of his God *is* in his heart; none of his steps shall slide.
32. The wicked watcheth the righteous, and seeketh to slay him.
33. The LORD will not leave him in his hand, nor condemn him when he is judged.
34. Wait on the LORD, and keep his way, and he shall exalt thee to inherit the land: when the wicked are cut off, thou shall see *it*.
35. I have seen the wicked in great power, and spreading himself like a green bay tree.
36. Yet he passed away, and, lo, he *was* not: yea, I sought him, but he could not be found.
37. Mark the perfect *man*, and behold the upright: for the end of *that* man *is* peace.
38. But the transgressors shall be destroyed together: the end of the wicked shall be cut off.
39. But the salvation of the righteous *is* of the LORD: *he is* their strength in the time of trouble.
40. And the LORD shall help them, and deliver them: he shall deliver them from the wicked, and save them, because they trust in him.

Commentary

"Dwell forevermore," "preserved forever," "dwell therein forever"—
the psalmist wants us to gain an eternal perspective. That will cause us
to "depart from evil and do good." The time will surely come when the
wicked will no longer be on Earth or in Heaven
(vv. 2, 9, 10, 17, 20, 22, 28, 34, 38). Their apparent prosperity is temporary. The righteous are forever.

Psalm 37 enumerates many temporal benefits for living righteously
(vv. 3, 23, 24, 39, 40). The psalm also looks forward to the blessedness of the Messiah's kingdom when He reigns on Earth
(vv. 9, 11, 22, 34). However, the greatest rewards for the righteous are
eternal. The wicked fail to evaluate life from the eternal viewpoint.
They live entirely for the here and now. Their eternal destiny is dread-
ful, beyond human comprehension (Mt. 25:41; Rev. 20:11-15)!

How does one learn to live day to day with eternity's values in
view? The answer is in the last three words of the psalm—"trust in
Him." The salvation that is of the LORD (v. 39) not only furnished
strength in the time of trouble but also transports the souls safely from
time into eternity. The deliverance is not only from the wicked (v. 40)
but also from the "wicked one" (Jn 17:15). We will know that we are living daily with an eternal perspective when we are resting in the "Lord"
and not fretting because of those who are prospering while they are
bringing wicked devices to pass (v. 7).

Application

Living one's life with an eternal perspective will solve every problem
offered by the circumstances which befall us. Such a life is acquired by
immersing oneself in the promises contained in the Scriptures. The
Word of God produces for us the necessary faith to believe and rely
upon that which the Word of God declares (Rom. 10:17).

Psalm 38:1-11

A Psalm of David, to bring to remembrance.

1. O LORD, rebuke me not in thy wrath: neither chasten me in thy hot displeasure.
2. For thine arrows stick fast in me, and thy hand presseth me sore.
3. *There is* no soundness in my flesh because of thine anger; neither *is there any* rest in my bones because of my sin.
4. For mine iniquities are gone over mine head: as an heavy burden they are too heavy for me.
5. My wounds stink *and* are corrupt because of my foolishness.
6. I am troubled; I am bowed down greatly; I go mourning all the day long.
7. For my loins are filled with a loathsome *disease:* and *there is* no soundness in my flesh.
8. I am feeble and sore broken: I have roared by reason of the disquietness of my heart.
9. Lord, all my desire *is* before thee; and my groaning is not hid from thee.
10. My heart panteth, my strength faileth me: as for the light of mine eyes, it also is gone from me.
11. My lovers and my friends stand aloof from my sore; and my kinsmen stand afar off.

Commentary_____

This is one of four psalms believed to have been penned by David after he was confronted by the prophet Nathan concerning his sin with Bathsheba (2 Sam. 12:7-9). Textual content indicates they were written over a period of months in the following sequence—Psalm 38, 6, 51 and 32. Studied in that order, the four psalms describe David's progress from overwhelming misery (38:1-11) to the overflowing joy of one basking in the assurance of forgiveness and restoration (32:11).

God's attitude towards gross sin is wrath, hot displeasure and anger. "Hot displeasure" (v. 1) is translated from a word usually rendered "fury." "Anger" (v.3) comes from a word usually translated "indignation."

Although David has confessed and has received forgiveness (2 Sam. 12:13), he still must face the dire consequences of his sin. He was so overcome by guilt, remorse, and the consequences of his sin that it took many months for him to appropriate the blessedness of forgiveness.

Sin brings displeasure to the LORD (v. 1). To the sinner it brings conviction (v. 2), restlessness (v. 3), burdensomeness (v. 4), corruption (v. 5), trouble, shame, mourning (v. 6), sickness (v. 7) feebleness, disquietness (v. 8), groaning (v. 9), weakness (v. 10), loneliness and loathsomeness (v. 11). Such is the terrible price for a moment's lustful gratification. How grateful we should be that a merciful God has preserved this record for our benefit (Rom. 15:4; 1 Cor. 10:11-13)!

Application_____

Within the scope of our acquaintances, there are fellow believers weighed down with conviction who need to read these psalms. Let us pray to our Lord that he would lead us to such ones that we might bring God's message of forgiveness and restoration.

Psalm 38:12-22

12. They also that seek after my life lay snares *for me:* and they that seek my hurt speak mischievous things, and imagine deceits all the day long.

13. But I, as a deaf *man*, heard not; and *I was* as a dumb man *that* openeth not his mouth.

14. Thus I was as a man that heareth not, and in whose mouth *are* no reproofs.

15. For in thee, O LORD, do I hope: thou wilt hear, O Lord my God.

16. For I said, *Hear me*, lest *otherwise* they should rejoice over me: when my foot slippeth, they magnify *themselves* against me.

17. For I *am* ready to halt, and my sorrow *is* continually before me.

18. For I will declare mine iniquity; I will be sorry for my sin.

19. But mine enemies *are* lively, *and* they are strong: and they that hate me wrongfully are multiplied.

20. They also that render evil for good are mine adversaries; because I follow *the thing that* good *is.*

21. Forsake me not, O LORD: O my God, be not far from me.

22. Make haste to help me, O Lord my salvation.

Commentary_____

There were conspirators within David's kingdom who saw his sad plight as an opportunity to depose him. There were also subjugated kingdoms surrounding him who were threatening. He was aware of their maneuvers and threats but had no strength or courage to thwart them (v. 10). As far as any response from him was concerned, he was both deaf and dumb.

In verse 15, David proclaims that his expectation and reliance are upon his God. He invokes the three principal names of God. God (*Elohim*) is He who possesses full capabilities to help him. The LORD (*Jehovah* or *Yahweh*) is that same omnipotent One who thinks it fitting to act in the direction of the dependent worshippers. The Lord (*Adonai*) is the Master David serves and to whom he is reaching upwards.

In verse 16, David confesses his inability to cope with the enemy. In verse 17, he confesses his current condition, and in verse 18 he repeats his confession of guilt and his repentance. In verses 19 and 20, David expresses the reasons a just God should come to his aid: first, his enemies are strong and confident of their ability to carry out their threats; second, they are against David because his purposes are good and theirs are evil; finally, they hate him without cause. (See John 15:25 for a parallel passage.)

David ends the psalm with a very pointed plea for help, again invoking the three names of God.

Application_____

When we were unsaved, our plight was similar to David's. We had no strength to resist the power of Satan. God had the ability to save us. He looked down and saw our need. When we confessed our state and our need, He heard our plea.

Psalm 39

To the chief Musician, *even to* Jeduthun, A Psalm of David.

1. I SAID, I will take heed to my ways, that I sin not with my tongue: I will keep my mouth with a bridle, while the wicked is before me.
2. I was dumb with silence, I held my peace, *even* from good; and my sorrow was stirred.
3. My heart is hot within me, while I was musing the fire burned: *then* spake I with my tongue.
4. LORD, make me to know mine end, and the measure of my days, what it *is; that* I may know how frail I *am*.
5. Behold, thou hast made my days *as* an handbreadth; and mine age *is* as nothing before thee: verily every man at his best state *is* altogether vanity. Selah.
6. Surely every man walketh in a vain shew: surely they are disquieted in vain: he heapeth up *riches*, and knoweth not who shall gather them.
7. And now, Lord, what wait I for? my hope *is* in thee.
8. Deliver me from all my transgressions: make me not the reproach of the foolish.
9. I was dumb, I opened not my mouth; because thou didst *it.*
10. Remove thy stroke away from me: I am consumed by the blow of thine hand.
11. When thou with rebukes dost correct man for iniquity, thou makest his beauty to consume away like a moth: surely every man *is* vanity. Selah.
12. Hear my prayer, O LORD, and give ear unto my cry; hold not thy peace at my tears: for I *am* a stranger with thee, *and* a sojourner, as all my fathers *were*.
13. O spare me, that I may recover strength, before I go hence, and be no more.

Commentary

During the ten years or so that David was a fugitive, his faith sometimes wavered and at times he despaired of his life (1 Sam. 27:1). Near the end of King Saul's reign, David sought refuge from the Philistine King Achish for sixteen months (1 Sam. 27:7). It was discomforting to him to be allied with the principal adversary of his nation, Israel, and he felt estranged from and forsaken by his God. As his resentment for his plight built up within (v. 3), he resisted airing his complaint to wicked men (vv. 1, 2) and vocalized his emotion to the LORD (v. 4).

David acknowledges that it was futile for anyone to attempt to program his own future (v. 6) because God was in control of the length of one's life. He asked the LORD to let him know what the future held for him (vv. 4, 7). While he was voicing his request, he suddenly was struck dumb (v.9) by the thought that God Himself was permitting all of his adversity! God was buffeting him because of the iniquity in his life (v. 10). Actually, the LORD was molding him into "a vessel unto honor, sanctified and meet [fit] for the Master's use, prepared unto every good work" (2 Tim. 2:21).

In verse 13, David pleads that his life be spared so that he will not die having lived in vain. The words *vanity* (vv. 5, 11) and *vain* (v. 6) mean fruitless, empty, and devoid of purpose.

Application

God has chosen to do His work in this world through human beings. Since we don't think like He does (Isa. 55:9), we must be molded like a clay vessel before we are usable for His purposes. Affliction is one tool He uses for His purpose and our eternal benefit (Ps. 119:71, 75, 92; 2 Cor. 12:9, 10).

Psalm 40

To the chief Musician, A Psalm of David.

1. I WAITED patiently for the LORD; and he inclined unto me, and heard my cry.
2. He brought me up also out of an horrible pit, out of the miry clay, and set my feet upon a rock, *and* established my goings.
3. And he hath put a new song in my mouth, *even* praise unto our God: many shall see *it*, and fear, and shall trust in the LORD.
4. Blessed *is* that man that maketh the LORD his trust, and respecteth not the proud, nor such as turn aside to lies.
5. Many, O LORD my God, *are* thy wonderful works *which* thou hast done, and thy thoughts *which are* to us-ward: they cannot be reckoned up in order unto thee: *if* I would declare and speak *of them*, they are more than can be numbered.
6. Sacrifice and offering thou didst not desire; mine ears hast thou opened: burnt offering and sin offering hast thou not required.
7. Then said I, Lo, I come: in the volume of the book *it is* written of me.
8. I delight to do thy will, O my God: yea, thy law *is* within my heart.
9. I have preached righteousness in the great congregation: lo, I have not refrained my lips, O LORD, thou knowest.
10. I have not hid thy righteousness within my heart; I have declared thy faithfulness and thy salvation: I have not concealed thy lovingkindness and thy truth from the great congregation.
11. Withhold not thou thy tender mercies from me, O LORD: let thy lovingkindness and thy truth continually preserve me.
12. For innumerable evils have compassed me about: mine iniquities have taken hold upon me, so that I am not able to look up; they are more than the hairs of mine head: therefore my heart faileth me.
13. Be pleased, O LORD, to deliver me: O LORD, make haste to help me.
14. Let them be ashamed and confounded together that seek after my soul to destroy it; let them be driven backward and put to shame that wish me evil.
15. Let them be desolate for a reward of their shame that say unto me, Aha, aha.
16. Let all those that seek thee rejoice and be glad in thee: let such as love thy salvation say continually, The LORD be magnified.
17. But I *am* poor and needy; *yet* the Lord thinketh upon me: thou *art* my help and my deliverer; make no tarrying, O my God.

Commentary

Hebrews 10:5-9 quotes Psalm 40:6-8 and then explains that the psalmist is prophesying concerning the complete surrender of Christ to the Father's will in giving His body as a sacrifice. Psalm 40 is one of sixteen psalms designated as "Messianic Psalms." New Testament references to each of these psalms illustrate that all of them are referring, in whole or in part, to Jesus Christ's appearance on Earth.

As in several other messianic psalms, some portions speak of Christ, some of the psalmist (v. 12) and some of both (vv. 2-4). David's horrible pit experience came when he was consumed by remorse after his sin with Bathsheba (see Ps. 38:3-8). His new song came when he appropriated the blessedness of forgiveness (Ps. 32:1, 11). Jesus' pit occurred on Calvary when, laden with our sins, His soul suffered anguish beyond comprehension (Ps. 22:1), and His body was subjected to agony beyond measure (Ps. 22:15). His new song came in resurrection (Ps. 22:22, Heb. 2:12).

What does the LORD our God think about (v. 5)? His thoughts are deep (Ps. 92:5), they are high (Isa. 55:9), they are good (Jer. 29:11), and they are many (Ps. 139:18). His thoughts are precious (Ps. 139:17) because they are toward us (Ps. 40:5, 17)

When the Lord puts a new song in our mouths (v. 3), we must tell others (vv. 9, 10). This we will do if we saturate our hearts with His Word and delight in doing His will (v. 8). The answer to the prayer in verse 11 is bestowed upon those who offer their bodies to Him as a living sacrifice (v. 6 and Rom. 12:1).

Note: Verses 13-17 are repeated as Psalm 70 and will be discussed later.

Application

Before I was saved, I was in a horrible pit (Eph. 2:1-4) on course to utter damnation (Jn. 3:18, Rev. 20:15). Jesus Christ lifted me out of the miry clay and set my feet upon a rock. Now He desires to establish my goings (v. 2).

Psalm 41

To the chief Musician, A Psalm of David.

1. BLESSED *IS* he who considereth the poor: the LORD will deliver him in time of trouble.
2. The LORD will preserve him, and keep him alive; *and* he shall be blessed upon the earth: and thou wilt not deliver him unto the will of his enemies.
3. The LORD will strengthen him upon the bed of languishing: thou wilt make all his bed in his sickness.
4. I said, LORD, be merciful unto me: heal my soul; for I have sinned against thee.
5. Mine enemies speak evil of me, When shall he die, and his name perish?
6. And if he come to see *me,* he speaketh vanity: his heart gathereth iniquity to itself; *when* he goeth abroad, he telleth *it.*
7. All that hate me whisper together against me: against me do they devise my hurt.
8. An evil disease, *say they*, cleaveth fast unto him: and *now* that he lieth he shall rise up no more.
9. Yea, mine own familiar friend, in whom I trusted, which did eat of my bread, hath lifted up *his* heel against me.
10. But thou, O LORD, be merciful unto me, and raise me up, that I may requite them.
11. By this I know that thou favourest me, because mine enemy doth not triumph over me.
12. And as for me, thou upholdest me in mine integrity, and settest me before thy face for ever.
13. Blessed *be* the LORD God of Israel from everlasting, and to everlasting. Amen, and Amen.

Commentary_____

In considering Psalm 41 as one of the sixteen "Messianic Psalms," we focus on the context in which our Lord used verse 9 of the psalm on the night of His betrayal by Judas (Jn. 13:18-19). He wanted the disciples (and us) to know that the events which would soon engulf them were all foreknown by Him because He is the great "I Am" of Exodus 3:14. He was and is the God who sees our affliction, hears our groaning and came down to deliver (Acts 7:34). See also John 8:58 and 18:6.

Prophetically, the "familiar friend" in David's life was Ahithophel (2 Sam. 15:12; 16:23). This man, who was Bathsheba's grandfather (2 Sam. 11:3; 23:34), points to Judas in several respects. He was a close friend, bargained with the enemy, asked for a band of men, and ended his life by hanging himself (2 Sam. 17:23).

As mentioned previously, a number of psalms are based upon historical experiences in the lives of the psalmists, but they also convey prophetic implications. The same psalms contain poignant applications for our spiritual growth. The Apostle Peter, in Acts 1:16-20, cites this and three other psalms as predictive of Judas (Ps. 55:12, 13; 69:25; 109:8).

Verse 13 is not actually a part of the psalm; it is a benediction or doxology such as closes each of the five books of Psalms. (See 72:18, 19; 89:52; 106:48 and 150:6).

Application_____

The word *poor* in verse 1 refers to anyone who needs help because of unfortunate circumstances. If you are considerate of such people, what will the Lord do on your behalf according to verses 1-3?

Psalm 42

To the chief Musician, Maschil, for the sons of Korah.

1. AS THE hart panteth after the water brooks, so panteth my soul after thee, O God.
2. My soul thirsteth for God, for the living God: when shall I come and appear before God?
3. My tears have been my meat day and night, while they continually say unto me, Where *is* thy God?
4. When I remember these *things*, I pour out my soul in me: for I had gone with the multitude, I went with them to the house of God, with the voice of joy and praise, with the multitude that kept holyday.
5. Why art thou cast down, O my soul? and *why* art thou disquieted in me? hope thou in God: for I shall yet praise him *for* the help of his countenance.
6. O my God, my soul is cast down within me: therefore will I remember thee from the land of Jordan, and of the Hermonites, from the hill Mizar.
7. Deep calleth unto deep at the noise of thy waterspouts: all thy waves and thy billows are gone over me.
8. *Yet* the LORD will command his lovingkindness in the daytime, and in the night his song *shall be* with me, *and* my prayer into the God of my life.
9. I will say unto God my rock, Why hast thou forgotten me? why go I mourning because of the oppression of the enemy?
10. *As* with a sword in my bones, mine enemies reproach me; while they say daily unto me, Where *is* thy God?
11. Why art thou cast down, O my soul? and why art thou disquieted within me? hope thou in God: for I shall yet praise him, *who is* the health of my countenance, and my God.

Commentary_____

In passing from Book I to Book II of Psalms, one immediately notices that the principal name for God changes from LORD (*Yahweh*) to God (*Elohim*). The name *LORD* is found five times in Psalm 41; God is the designation thirteen times in Psalm 42. The doxology of Book I (Ps. 41:13) smooths the transition by employing both names. Notice also that Psalm 14 of Book I is almost identical to Psalm 53 of Book II except for the name difference in four places.

Structure and content indicate that Psalm 42 and Psalm 43 were originally composed as one psalm with three equal stanzas ending with the same refrain.

Every devout Israelite journeyed to Jerusalem for worship three times a year (Ex. 34:23; Dt. 16:16). This psalmist dwelt in the part of the land most distant from the proper place of assembly (v. 6). He was being restrained and taunted by an oppressive enemy (vv. 9-10). He felt as though God had forgotten him as his thirst for spiritual communion intensified. As he recalls the joys of past experiences (v. 4), he realizes that God is omnipresent and resolves to praise Him where he is (vv.5-6).

In spite of the reproaches of his enemies (v. 10), the psalmist will appropriate the loving-kindness of the LORD throughout the day. At night he will listen to the LORD's song and will pray unto his God (v. 8).

Application_____

Have you ever entertained the thought that God has forgotten you? If you will start praising Him for past mercies, He will honor your faith by making His presence known. When your mourning turns to joy and praise, you will know He is with you wherever you are.

Psalm 43

1. JUDGE ME, O God, and plead my cause against an ungodly nation: O deliver me from the deceitful and unjust man.
2. For thou *art* the God of my strength: why dost thou cast me off? why go I mourning because of the oppression of the enemy?
3. O send out thy light and thy truth: let them lead me; let them bring me unto thy holy hill, and to thy tabernacles.
4. Then will I go unto the altar of God, unto God my exceeding joy: yea, upon the harp will I praise thee, O God my God.
5. Why art thou cast down, O my soul? and why art thou disquieted within me? hope in God: for I shall yet praise him, *who is* the health of my countenance, and my God.

Commentary

"Why hast Thou forgotten me?"(42:9) "Judge me, O God" (43:1). "Why dost Thou cast me off?"(43:2) The psalmist is perplexed! According to God's Word, he is to go to the place of the altar (Jerusalem) to worship. He earnestly desires to go. He wants the light of God's truth to lead him. He knows that God has the strength to deliver him from the oppression of the enemy. So why doesn't God do something? He reasons that God has either abandoned him or is punishing him for some unknown sin.

Instead of delivering him out of his circumstance, God chooses to make His presence known within the circumstance. God does this by measuring to him sufficient faith to calm his disquieted soul and bring a smile to his countenance. His mourning (v. 2) is turned to praise (v. 5). His despair is conquered by hope!

Without affliction, it is impossible to experience the sufficiency of God's grace (2 Cor. 12:9). Without opposition, it is impossible to exercise faith. God is well pleased with praise and good works (Heb. 13:15-16), but "without faith it impossible to please Him" (Heb. 11:6).

Both the Old and New Testaments make it clear that God's people are to come together for worship through prayer and praise. However, acceptable worship is not restricted by distance or circumstance.

Application

As a Christian, have you ever been in circumstances which caused you to think that God had abandoned you? God put this psalm (along with many others) in the Bible to let you know that He will manifest His presence in response to the faith that comes from knowing His Word (Rom. 10:17; 12:3).

Psalm 44:1-14

To the chief Musician for the sons of Korah, Maschil.

1. WE HAVE heard with our ears, O God, our fathers have told us, *what* work thou didst in their days, in the times of old.
2. *How* thou didst drive out the heathen with thy hand, and plantedst them; *how* thou didst afflict the people, and cast them out.
3. For they got not the land in possession by their own sword, neither did their own arm save them: but thy right hand, and thine arm, and the light of thy countenance, because thou hadst a favour unto them.
4. Thou art my king, O God: command deliverances for Jacob.
5. Through thee will we push down our enemies: through thy name will we tread them under that rise up against us.
6. For I will not trust in my bow, neither shall my sword save me.
7. But thou hast saved us from our enemies, and hast put them to shame that hated us.
8. In God we boast all the day long, and praise thy name for ever. Selah.
9. But thou hast cast off, and put us to shame; and goest not forth with our armies.
10. Thou makest us to turn back from the enemy: and they which hate us spoil for themselves.
11. Thou hast given us like sheep *appointed* for meat; and hast scattered us among the heathen.
12. Thou sellest thy people for nought, and dost not increase *thy wealth* by their price.
13. Thou makest us a reproach to our neighbours, a scorn and a derision to them that are round about us.
14. Thou makest us a byword among the heathen, a shaking of the head among the people.

Commentary_____

This psalm is in the form of a lengthy complaint followed by a passionate plea. The psalmist speaks to God on behalf of his nation. He begins by acknowledging the obligation of each generation to pass God's message to succeeding generations (Deut.11:18-19; Ps. 78:3-6).

In verse 2, he points out that God had cast out the heathen nations in order to "plant" the nation of Israel in this special land (Ex.15:17). You will understand this concept of "planting" more fully by studying Psalm 80:8-15 and Isaiah 5:1-7.

In verse 3, the psalmist recognizes that the possession of the land is through the favor and strength of God and not by Israel's own merit or power.

The psalmist then tells God that, based on prior deliverances and the allegiance of the nation of God, he fully expects God to undertake again (vv. 4-8).

The complaint begins in verse 9. God has cast them off and brought them shame by not leading their army. Therefore, the enemy has defeated and plundered them. Some have been taken captive. They are objects of reproach and scorn.

God had forewarned Israel that these maladies would befall them. Compare verse 10 with Leviticus 26:17 and verse 11 with Deuteronomy 28:64-66. There is also a striking parallel between the condition described by the psalmist and Israel's plight since its rejection of Jesus Christ as Messiah.

Application_____

The New Testament emphasizes that our obligation to pass God's message to the next generation is not confined to our physical descendents. If you put yourself in Timothy's place in 2 Timothy 2:2, to how many generations do you have an obligation?

Psalm 44:15-26

15. My confusion *is* continually before me, and the shame of my face hath covered me.
16. For the voice of him that reproacheth and blasphemeth; by reason of the enemy and avenger.
17. All this is come upon us; yet have we not forgotten thee, neither have we dealt falsely in thy covenant.
18. Our heart is not turned back, neither have our steps declined from thy way.
19. Though thou hast sore broken us in the place of dragons, and covered us with the shadow of death.
20. If we have forgotten the name of our God, or stretched out our hands to a strange god;
21. Shall not God search this out? for he knoweth the secrets of the heart.
22. Yea, for thy sake are we killed all the day long; we are counted as sheep for the slaughter.
23. Awake, why sleepest thou, O Lord? arise, cast *us* not off for ever.
24. Wherefore hidest thou thy face, *and* forgettest our affliction and our oppression?
25. For our soul is bowed down to the dust: our belly cleaveth unto the earth.
26. Arise for our help, and redeem us for thy mercies' sake.

Commentary_____

Predominantly, in Psalm 44, the psalmist employs the first person plural, indicating that he is speaking on behalf of the nation. However, in verse 4, he addresses God as his own personal King. In verse 15, he uses first person singular to express how he is personally affected by the enemy's oppression. In his confusion and shame (vv. 9-14), he accuses God in a manner not found anywhere else in the Psalms.

In verse 17, he returns to the use of *us* and *we*. He vigorously defends his nation as undeserving of God's apparent abandonment. In verse 19, he again blames God for the nation's plight. He challenges God to consider the people's allegiance to Him by searching the secrets of their hearts. He pleads that it is their faithfulness to Him that is causing their slaughter.

Other psalmists have implied that God needed to be aroused from sleep in order to come to the aid of His people (Ps. 7:6; 78:65). However, nowhere else does one so blatantly accuse God of causing affliction and oppression by sleeping when He should be acting on behalf of His people. "Behold, He who keepeth Israel shall neither slumber nor sleep" (Ps. 121:4).

By the end of the psalm, the psalmist has finished venting his frustration and humbly bows and pleads for mercy.

Application_____

The apostle Paul quotes Psalm 44:22 in Romans 8:36 and applies it to the distress and persecution suffered by faithful Christians. Do you see a difference between his reaction to oppression and that of the psalmist? What would be your reaction in similar situations?

Psalm 45

To the chief Musician upon Shoshannim, for the sons of Korah, Maschil, A Song of loves.

1. MY HEART is inditing a good matter: I speak of the things which I have made touching the king: my tongue *is* the pen of a ready writer.
2. Thou art fairer than the children of men: grace is poured into thy lips: therefore God hath blessed thee for ever.
3. Gird thy sword upon *thy* thigh, O *most* mighty, with thy glory and thy majesty.
4. And in thy majesty ride prosperously because of truth and meekness *and* righteousness; and thy right hand shall teach thee terrible things.
5. Thine arrows *are* sharp in the heart of the king's enemies; *whereby* the people fall under thee.
6. Thy throne, O God, *is* for ever and ever: the sceptre of thy kingdom *is* a right sceptre.
7. Thou lovest righteousness, and hatest wickedness: therefore God, thy God, hath anointed thee with the oil of gladness above thy fellows.
8. All thy garments *smell* of myrrh, and aloes, *and* cassia, out of the ivory palaces, whereby they have made thee glad.
9. Kings' daughters *were* among thy honourable women: upon thy right hand did stand the queen in gold of Ophir.
10. Hearken, O daughter, and consider, and incline thine ear; forget also thine own people, and thy father's house;
11. So shall the king greatly desire thy beauty: for he *is* thy Lord; and worship thou him.
12. And the daughter of Tyre *shall be there* with a gift; *even* the rich among the people shall entreat thy favour.
13. The king's daughter *is* all glorious within: her clothing *is* of wrought gold.
14. She shall be brought unto the king in raiment of needlework: the virgins her companions that follow her shall be brought unto thee.
15. With gladness and rejoicing shall they be brought: they shall enter into the king's palace.
16. Instead of thy fathers shall be thy children, whom thou mayest make princes in all the earth.
17. I will make thy name to be remembered in all generations: therefore shall the people praise thee for ever and ever.

Commentary_____

The quotation of verse 6 and 7 of Psalm 45 in Hebrews 1:8-9 gives us the key to the prophetic impact of this Messianic Psalm. It points to the establishment of the future reign of Christ on Earth as prophesied in Daniel 2:44.

One early English translator renders the first line, "my heart bubbleth over with goodly word." The writer feels a compelling urge to share the revelation he received. There are seven divisions to the psalm:

--the King's majestic beauty and graciousness (vv. 1-2)
--the King's arrival in might, glory and majesty (vv. 3-5)
--the deity of the King and His authority (vv. 6-7)
--the marriage of the King (vv. 8-9)
--the bride's submission to the King (vv.10-11)
--the bride's entourage and the wedding guests (vv. 12-15)
--the worldwide and eternal homage to the King (vv.16-17)

This same King offered His glorious and gracious rule 2000 years ago (Jn. 1:14), but it was rejected (Jn. 1:11; 5:43).

For an expanded account of the events described in verses 3-5, see Revelation 19:11-21.

It is not only the psalmist who is calling the King "God" in verse 6. The context of the Hebrews 1:8-9 quotation emphasizes that the Father Himself calls His Son "God"!

The scepter is the symbol of the authority and obligation of the King. The crown speaks of His prerogative and privilege.

Application_____

Do you understand in what way your future fits into Psalm 45? If there are aspects that you can't grasp, be patient. If you are part of the Bride of Christ, you will be there to behold the glory of it all (2 Cor. 11:2; Eph. 5:32).

Psalm 46

To the chief Musician for the sons of Korah, A Song upon Alamoth.

1. GOD *IS* our refuge and strength, a very present help in trouble.
2. Therefore will not we fear, though the earth be removed, and though the mountains be carried into the midst of the sea;
3. *Though* the waters thereof roar *and* be troubled, *though* the mountains shake with swelling thereof. Selah.
4. *There is* a river, the streams whereof shall make glad the city of God, the holy *place* of the tabernacles of the most High.
5. God *is* in the midst of her; she shall not be moved: God shall help her, *and that* right early.
6. The heathen raged, the kingdoms were moved: he uttered his voice, the earth melted.
7. The LORD of hosts *is* with us; the God of Jacob *is* our refuge. Selah.
8. Come, behold the works of the LORD, what desolations he hath made in the earth.
9. He maketh wars to cease unto the end of the earth; he breaketh the bow, and cutteth the spear in sunder; he burneth the chariot in the fire.
10. Be still, and know that I *am* God: I will be exalted among the heathen, I will be exalted in the earth.
11. The LORD of hosts *is* with us; the God of Jacob *is* our refuge. Selah.

Commentary_____

Psalms 45-48 possess a commonality in that all four look forward to the millennial reign of Christ on Earth. No doubt each has its own historical basis, but we will focus on the prophetic aspect. In that regard we could entitle this group of psalms as follows:

Psalm 45—The Establishment of the Kingdom on Earth
Psalm 46—The King Dwelling among His Citizenry
Psalm 47—The Joyous Subjects Praise Their King
Psalm 48—The City of the Great King

Psalm 46 is comprised of three stanzas appended by the word *Selah*. There is a summarizing refrain at the end of Stanza Two which is repeated after Stanza Three.

Stanza One sings of "His Provided Protection." There will be no fear in the kingdom because no possible occurrence is beyond the strength of the King. He will forestall any catastrophe.

Stanza Two tells of "His Personal Presence." One of the compound names of God is *Yahweh Shammah* which means "The LORD is there" (Ezk. 48:35). There will never be a time again when the LORD will not dwell in the midst of His people (Rev. 21:3).

The theme of Stanza Three is "His Promised Peace" (Is. 2:4). "The work of righteousness shall be peace: and the effect of righteousness, quietness and assurance forever" (Isa. 32:17).

Application_____

Because the Prince of Peace has come to live within us, we now have peace with God through justification by faith (Rom. 5:1). The peace of God rules in our lives within this world's turmoil as we appropriate His peace moment by moment (Phil. 4:7).

Psalm 47

To the chief Musician, A Psalm for the sons of Korah.

1. O CLAP your hands, all ye people; shout unto God with the voice of triumph.
2. For the LORD most high *is* terrible; *he is* a great King over all the earth.
3. He shall subdue the people under us, and the nations under our feet.
4. He shall choose our inheritance for us, the excellency of Jacob whom he loved. Selah.
5. God is gone up with a shout, the LORD with the sound of a trumpet.
6. Sing praises to God, sing praises: sing praises unto our King, sing praises.
7. For God *is* the King of all the earth: sing ye praises with understanding.
8. God reigneth over the heathen: God sitteth upon the throne of his holiness.
9. The princes of the people are gathered together, *even* the people of the God of Abraham: for the shields of the earth *belong* unto God: he is greatly exalted.

Commentary_____

"Thy kingdom come. Thy will be done in Earth, as it is in Heaven" (Mt. 6:10). That prayer has been uttered countless times (often improperly) by human lips since it came from the lips of our Lord. Psalm 47 opens the curtain between us and the future that we may glory in the reaction of God's people who experience the answer to the prayer.

In verses 1-4, we join in the glad shout at the arrival of the triumphant King! In verses 5-7, we hear the trumpet announce the King's enthronement and join into the songs of praise. Verses 8-9 speak of the King's reign following His enthronement.

"All ye peoples" (v. 1) ; "over all the Earth" (v. 2) ; "King of all the Earth(v. 7) —although the psalmist would tend to think in terms of the physical descendents of Jacob (v. 4) and Abraham (v. 9), God extends the celebration to all who inhabit the Earth at the King's enthronement. In God's viewpoint, all who are born of the Spirit are Abraham's seed and therefore enter into God's covenant to him (Gen. 12:2-3; 17:6-8). The Apostle Paul explains the concept in Galatians 3:6-9, 16, 29).

The millennial conditions bringing about all of the singing and praise during the reign of the great King can be found in such Scripture portions as Isaiah 11:1-10 and 35:1-10. Some of the song content is in Isaiah 12:1-6.

Application_____

Because of the curse that sin brought upon Earth, we live in conditions far different from those that will prevail when Christ is seated on His earthly throne. However, through a good understanding of Bible prophecy we are able to be transported into the joy of that day (2 Pet. 1:19).

Psalm 48

A Song *and* Psalm for the sons of Korah.

1. GREAT *IS* the Lord, and greatly to be praised in the city of our God, *in* the mountain of his holiness.
2. Beautiful for situation, the joy of the whole earth, *is* mount Zion, *on* the sides of the north, the city of the great King.
3. God is known in her palaces for a refuge.
4. For, lo, the kings were assembled, they passed by together.
5. They saw *it, and* so they marveled; they were troubled, *and* hasted away.
6. Fear took hold upon them there, *and* pain, as of a woman in travail.
7. Thou breakest the ships of Tarshish with an east wind.
8. As we have heard, so have we seen in the city of the LORD of hosts, in the city of our God: God will establish it for ever. Selah.
9. We have thought of thy lovingkindness, O God, in the midst of thy temple.
10. According to thy name, O God, so *is* thy praise unto the ends of the earth: thy right hand is full of righteousness.
11. Let mount Zion rejoice, let the daughters of Judah be glad, because of thy judgments.
12. Walk about Zion, and go round about her: tell the towers thereof.
13. Mark ye well her bulwarks, consider her palaces; that ye may tell *it* to the generation following.
14. For this God *is* our God for ever and ever: he will be our guide *even* unto death.

Commentary_____

"Glorious things are spoken of thee, O city of God. Selah!" (Ps. 87:3). Twice in Psalm 48 Jerusalem is called "the city of our God." Once it is designated "the city of the LORD of Host" and once "the city of the Great King," which is the name Jesus applied to it in the Sermon on the Mount (Mt. 5:35). In Psalm 48 it is also described as "the mountain of His holiness," "the joy of the whole Earth," and "Mount Zion." This is the earthly Jerusalem from which Jesus the Messiah will reign during the coming Kingdom Age. It is the same as the "city of God" in Psalm 46:4 and Isaiah 60:14. However, it is to be distinguished from the heavenly Jerusalem of Hebrews 12:22 and Revelation 3:12, which is described more fully in Revelation 21.

"Sides of the North" (v. 2) is the place the ancients looked upon as God's heavenly dwelling place (Isa. 14:13, Ezk. 1:4). See also Psalm 75:6,7 and Job 37:22, where "fair weather" (KJV) could be better translated "golden splendor." The idea in Psalm 48 is that God has brought His dwelling place down to Earth.

Verses 4-7 refer to the conquest of the nations by Messiah in setting up His kingdom on Earth (Dan. 2:44).

Verses 8 and 14 project the earthly Jerusalem beyond the millennium into eternity. Some translations render the final word "forever" rather than "unto death."

Application_____

Although not all translators and/or godly expositors agree precisely on the order of end-time events, you can know from God's Word precisely how to live a life pleasing to God by meeting the condition set forth by Christ in John 7:17. See also I John 2:27.

Psalm 49:1-11

To the chief Musician, A Psalm for the sons of Korah.

1. HEAR THIS, all *ye* people; give ear, all *ye* inhabitants of the world:
2. Both low and high, rich and poor, together.
3. My mouth shall speak of wisdom; and the meditation of my heart *shall be* of understanding.
4. I will incline mine ear to a parable: I will open my dark saying upon the harp.
5. Wherefore should I fear in the days of evil, *when* the iniquity of my heels shall compass me about?
6. They that trust in their wealth, and boast themselves in the multitude of their riches;
7. None *of them* can by any means redeem his brother, nor give to God a ransom for him:
8. (For the redemption of their soul *is* precious, and it ceaseth for ever:)
9. That he should still live for ever, *and* not see corruption.
10. For he seeth *that* wise men die, likewise the fool and the brutish person perish, and leave their wealth to others.
11. Their inward thought *is, that* their houses *shall continue* for ever, *and* their dwelling places to all generations; they call *their* lands after their own names.

Commentary_____

In verses 1 and 2 the psalmist makes it clear that he has an urgent message for all people of all times. The word translated "world" connotes not only geographical extent but also time. The message is no less important today than it was in the psalmist's day or in the day when Jesus spoke the parable recorded in Luke 12:15-21. "Life consisteth not in the abundance of things one possesses" (Lk. 12:15).

This world's educational system teaches that one needs more knowledge because knowledge brings more opportunity for material prosperity. The Bible emphasizes wisdom and understanding (Ps. 49:3; Pr. 4:5-7). In order to speak wisdom, one must gain understanding through meditating on the right kind of knowledge. Knowledge without godly wisdom can be detrimental (1 Cor. 8:1).

The main message of this psalm is that material wealth is, and always has been, highly overrated. It cannot procure that which is most important—one's own eternal well-being and that of his brother (Mt. 16:26).

From the earliest days, men have attempted to perpetuate themselves by naming cities after themselves or their sons (Gen. 4:17). Look at any map to see the many cities, rivers, mountains and even nations that are named for men. Museums, universities and charitable foundations are also named for men of honor and wealth in exchange for their monetary contributions. However, not one iota of eternal value is obtained for the donor or his progeny.

Application_____

It has been wisely said that possessions will possess you. It is possible to own so many things that you no longer "own" anything. Instead, you are "owned" by the very items you have accumulated. The individual who has too many possessions is not to be envied; he is to be pitied. He is so occupied with protecting his possessions that he receives no joy from them. Then he dies and takes nothing with him!

Psalm 49:12-20

12. Nevertheless man *being* in honour abideth not: he is like the beasts *that* perish.

13. This their way *is* their folly: yet their posterity approve their sayings. Selah.

14. Like sheep they are laid in the grave; death shall feed on them; and the upright shall have dominion over them in the morning; and their beauty shall consume in the grave from their dwelling.

15. But God will redeem my soul from the power of the grave: for he shall receive me. Selah

16. Be not thou afraid when one is made rich, when the glory of his house is increased.

17. For when he dieth he shall carry nothing away: his glory shall not descend after him.

18. Though while he lived he blessed his soul: and *men* will praise thee, when thou doest well to thyself.

19. He shall go to the generation of his fathers; they shall never see light.

20. Man *that is* in honour, and understandeth not, is like the beasts *that* perish.

Commentary

Although verses 12 and 20 are translated the same in some versions, they are different in ancient texts. The verses in between develop both thoughts. Though a man has much honor and lives with great pomp, he will not endure (v.12) without understanding (v. 20). His fame may continue after death, but how does he differ from great race horses like Man O'War and Whirlaway who died more than a half century ago? As far as being a part of this present world is concerned, both famous horses and famous men are like sheep at death—"they are laid in the grave; death shall feed on them" (v. 14). Tragically, the next generation follows in the same folly (v. 13).

Verses 14 and 15 turn our attention to those who do have understanding— those who meet the requirements of a righteous God by receiving His own righteousness (1 Cor. 1:30). Such will have dominion in the morning of resurrection because God has redeemed them and received them.

"Be not thou afraid"—do not be awestruck by the glory of the mansions of the rich. Though they shine brightly in this life, beyond the grave "they shall never see light" (v. 19). For them "the mist of darkness is reserved forever" (2 Pet. 2:17).

An important theme in this psalm conveys the need to set our esteem on eternal values instead of on present gratifications. This keeps our perspective right.

Application

Whether we have little or much of this world's goods, wealth can be a blessing if we understand that all wealth belongs to God, and we are stewards of differing amounts. God uses the wealth of dedicated stewards to do His work on Earth.

Psalm 50:1-13

A Psalm of Asaph.

1. The mighty God, *even* the LORD, hath spoken, and called the earth from the rising of the sun unto the going down thereof.
2. Out of Zion, the perfection of beauty, God hath shined.
3. Our God shall come, and shall not keep silence: a fire shall devour before him, and it shall be very tempestuous round about him.
4. He shall call to the heavens from above, and to the earth, that he may judge his people.
5. Gather my saints together unto me; those that have made a covenant with me by sacrifice.
6. And the heavens shall declare his righteousness: for God *is* judge himself. Selah.
7. Hear, O my people, and I will speak; O Israel, and I will testify against thee: I *am* God, *even* thy God.
8. I will not reprove thee for thy sacrifices or thy burnt offerings, *to have been* continually before me.
9. I will take no bullock out of thy house, *nor* he goats out of thy folds.
10. For every beast of the forest *is* mine, *and* the cattle upon a thousand hills.
11. I know all the fowls of the mountains: and the wild beasts of the field *are* mine.
12. If I were hungry, I would not tell thee: for the world *is* mine, and the fullness thereof.
13. Will I eat the flesh of bulls, or drink the blood of goats?

Commentary_____

Human beings in general live their lives as though they will never face an all-seeing and all-knowing Creator acting as their judge. In Psalm 50, the mighty God as Judge of all is presented.

Zion originally was the headland on which King David built his fortress palace. After the temple was built, it became a designation for all of Jerusalem. When used figuratively, as in verse 2, it designates that place from which God's true governmental authority emanates. He will come in that respect to subject all people to judgment.

"Saints" in verse 5 refers to those who are set aside for God's holy purposes on Earth. The psalmist is thinking in terms of the nation of Israel which was given the covenant of sacrificial offerings under the Mosaic Law.

Beginning in verse 7, God reproves Israel for wrong motives in offering their animal sacrifices. He is not objecting to the procedures being used but to their reasoning. They think they are doing God a favor as if they were bringing food to Him. Their thinking is like that of the surrounding heathen worshipers--God is dependent upon them for His sustenance! They miss the whole point of a merciful God devising a means by which, as a holy God, He is able to have intimate communion with a sinful people. Their sacrifices should be offered in recognition of their sinfulness as it stands in contrast to God's holiness. Perverted worship is the ultimate sin committed against God by His own people.

Application_____

"God is a Spirit; and they that worship Him must worship Him in spirit and in truth" (Jn. 4:24). How much of our worship is a product of form and tradition rather than a genuine response from the heart?

Psalm 50:14-23

14. Offer unto God thanksgiving; and pay thy vows unto the most High:
15. And call upon me in the day of trouble: I will deliver thee, and thou shalt glorify me.
16. But unto the wicked God saith, What hast thou to do to declare my statutes, or *that* thou shouldest take my covenant in thy mouth?
17. Seeing thou hatest instruction, and castest my words behind thee.
18. When thou sawest a thief, then thou consentedst with him, and hast been partaker with adulterers.
19. Thou givest thy mouth to evil, and thy tongue frameth deceit.
20. Thou sittest and speakest against thy brother; thou slanderest thine own mother's son.
21. These *things* hast thou done, and I kept silence; thou thoughtest that I was altogether *such an one* as thyself: *but* I will reprove thee, and set *them* in order before thine eyes.
22. Now consider this, ye that forget God, lest I tear *you* in pieces, and *there be* none to deliver.
23. Whoso offereth praise glorifieth me: and to him that ordereth *his* conversation *aright* will I shew the salvation of God.

Commentary_____

For all those among His people who want to please their God, He presents the instructions of verses 14 and 15. First, offer thanksgiving to Him(Ps. 107:22; Hos. 14:2). Thanksgiving is a preventative for the sins of covetousness, envy, and greed. Next, be very careful to pay any vow made unto the LORD (Eccl. 5:4-7). Finally, call upon the LORD. This is a remedy for egotistic pride and self-reliance. God's continual complaint against His people was their failure to call upon Him (Isa. 43:21-22; Hos. 7:7). Notice how the psalmist delighted in observing these three requests by God in Psalm 116:16-18.

After giving words of instruction to those who will hear and heed, God points out the sin of the wicked in verses 16-20. In contemporary language, He is saying, "You proclaim my laws and speak of the covenant but toss aside my instructions. You overtly violate numbers seven, eight and nine of the Ten Commandments."

The supreme folly of these willful sinners is that they interpret God's silence as disinterest on His part. He makes it clear that the time will come when they will give answer to their Maker face-to-face (v. 21).

In Scripture, "the wicked" include all who live their lives as though they don't need God.

The warning of verse 22 is no idle threat nor is the offer of verse 23 an empty promise. The choice is given to every person of every age. Therefore, "now consider" (v. 22).

Application_____

Although a thankful heart is bestowed upon us at conversion, it must be cultivated by regularly voicing our thanksgiving to God. Increasing the thanksgiving portion of our prayers automatically decreases the length of the petition portion. Thanksgiving tends to put requests into proper perspective.

Psalm 51

To the chief Musician, A Psalm of David, when Nathan the prophet came unto him, after he had gone in to Bath-sheba.

1. HAVE MERCY upon me, O God, according to thy lovingkindness: according unto the multitude of thy tender mercies blot out my transgressions.
2. Wash me thoroughly from mine iniquity, and cleanse me from my sin.
3. For I acknowledge my transgressions: and my sin *is* ever before me.
4. Against thee, thee only, have I sinned, and done *this* evil in thy sight: that thou mightest be justified when thou speakest, *and* be clear when thou judgest.
5. Behold, I was shapen in iniquity; and in sin did my mother conceive me.
6. Behold, thou desirest truth in the inward parts: and in the hidden *part* thou shalt make me to know wisdom.
7. Purge me with hyssop, and I shall be clean: wash me, and I shall be whiter than snow.
8. Make me to hear joy and gladness; *that* the bones *which* thou hast broken may rejoice.
9. Hide thy face from my sins, and blot out all mine iniquities.
10. Create in me a clean heart, O God; and renew a right spirit within me.
11. Cast me not away from thy presence; and take not thy holy spirit from me.
12. Restore unto me the joy of thy salvation; and uphold me *with thy* free spirit.
13. *Then* will I teach transgressors thy ways; and sinners shall be converted unto thee.
14. Deliver me from bloodguiltness, O God, thou God of my salvation: *and* my tongue shall sing aloud of thy righteousness.
15. O Lord, open thou my lips: and my mouth shall shew forth thy praise.
16. For thou desirest not sacrifice; else would I give *it*: thou delightest not in burnt offering.
17. The sacrifices of God *are* a broken spirit: a broken and a contrite heart, O God, thou wilt not despise.
18. Do good in thy good pleasure unto Zion: build thou the walls of Jerusalem.
19. Then shalt thou be pleased with the sacrifices of righteousness, with burnt offering and whole burnt offering: then shall they offer bullocks upon thine altar.

Commentary

King David is believed to have written four penitential psalms following the confrontation by the prophet Nathan concerning David's sin with Bathsheba(2 Sam. 12:7-9). Textual content indicates he penned them over a period of months in this sequence—38, 6, 51 and 32. If read in that order, the four psalms describe his progress from overwhelming remorse (38:1-11) to overflowing joy in the assurance of forgiveness and restoration (Ps. 32).

By definition, *transgression* is overstepping the established boundaries of rules and conduct—such as breaking one or more of the Ten Commandments. *Iniquity* is that which emanates from an evil heart (Mk. 7:21-23). Sin is coming short of God's required righteousness (Rom. 3:23). In confessing these three aspects of wrongdoing, David makes a threefold plea: "blot out" (v. 1), "wash" and "cleanse" (v. 2).

David had been taught by the Spirit that all sin is against God (2 Sam. 12:13). God has all of eternity to compensate Uriah and Bathsheba for the temporary injury David brought upon them. In glory, there will be no barrier to perfect fellowship between Uriah and David. In the eternal perspective, Uriah was not harmed. But who will compensate for the injury our sins do to the tender heart of our gracious, loving, eternal Heavenly Father?

The steps back to full communion and service are confession (vv. 1-6), cleansing by the blood (vv. 7-10), joy and empowering by the Spirit (vv. 11-12), service (v. 13) and worship (vv. 14-17).

Application

There are many guilt-laden Christians who need full assurance of forgiveness and restoration. Sin has robbed them of the joy of their salvation. Use this psalm to return them to a productive role in the Lord's army.

Psalm 52

To the chief Musician, Maschil, *A Psalm* of David, when Doeg the Edomite came and told Saul, and said unto him, David is come to the house of Ahimelech.

1. WHY BOASTEST thou thyself in mischief, O mighty man? the goodness of God *endureth* continually.
2. Thy tongue deviseth mischiefs; like a sharp razor, working deceitfully.
3. Thou lovest evil more than good; *and* lying rather than to speak righteousness. Selah.
4. Thou lovest all devouring words, O *thou* deceitful tongue.
5. God shall likewise destroy thee for ever, he shall take thee away, and pluck thee out of *thy* dwelling place, and root thee out of the land of the living. Selah.
6. The righteous also shall see, and fear, and shall laugh at him:
7. Lo, *this is* the man *that* made not God his strength; but trusted in the abundance of his riches, *and* strengthened himself in his wickedness.
8. But I *am* like a green olive tree in the house of God: I trust in the mercy of God for ever and ever.
9. I will praise thee for ever, because thou hast done *it:* and I will wait on thy name; for *it is* good before thy saints.

Commentary

The superscription above Psalm 52 gives its historical setting as recorded in 1 Samuel 22:9-23. At the command of a vengeful King Saul, Doeg, the Edomite slew eighty-five priests and their families. The high priest, Ahimelech, had supplied bread and a sword to David and his men as they fled from Saul's army. David had deceived Ahimelech by saying he was on an errand for the king (1 Sam. 21:2).

In verses 1-4, David lashes out at the treacherous Doeg as though he were accusing him in a face-to-face confrontation. In verse 5, he makes a fourfold pronouncement of Doeg's doom at the hand of God.

Verse 6 assures the reader that the righteous will have "the last laugh" even though the wicked seem to prevail. A person's ultimate well-being depends upon what or upon whom his trust rests (v. 7).

According to Jeremiah 11:16, a green olive tree is both lovely and fruitful. Figuratively, a green tree represents abundant life (Ps. 1:3; Lk. 23:31; Rev. 22:2). An olive tree produces oil which symbolizes the empowering of the Spirit. When one is a green olive tree in God's household, trusting in His mercy, he will utter praise to his God regardless of the adversities that befall him. Thereby, he will cause other saints in the household of God to wait patiently upon the Lord to accomplish His purposes. That is good for the Lord's saints!

Application

David told an "innocent" lie trying to "help God" protect him. The outcome was disastrous. The Holy Spirit led him to write this psalm (see 2 Sam. 23:2) for our benefit (Rom. 15:4) and unto the praise of His mercy.

Psalm 53

To the chief Musician upon Mahalath, Maschil.
A Psalm **of David.**

1. THE FOOL hath said in his heart, *There is* no God. Corrupt are they, and have done abominable iniquity: *there is* none that doeth good.
2. God looked down from heaven upon the children of men, to see if there were *any* that did understand, that did seek God.
3. Every one of them is gone back: they are altogether become filthy; *there is* none that doeth good, no, not one.
4. Have the workers of iniquity no knowledge? who eat up my people *as* they eat bread: they have not called upon God.
5. There were they in great fear, *where* no fear was: for God hath scattered the bones of him that encampeth *against* thee: thou hast put *them* to shame, because God hath despised them.
6. Oh that the salvation of Israel *were come* out of Zion! When God bringeth back the captivity of his people, Jacob shall rejoice, *and* Israel shall be glad.

Commentary_____

Verses 1-4 of Psalm 53 are substantially the same as the first four verses of Psalm 14, except that Psalm 53 retains *Elohim* as the designation for God throughout the psalm, whereas Psalm 14 also utilizes *Yahweh* (Jehovah). Verse 5 replaces verses 5 and 6 of Psalm 14. The psalmist probably made the change in order to give God the credit for a major victory over a strong enemy in a battle fought after Psalm 14 was written. The two psalms end with the same prayer, a prayer that will be answered when Messiah sets up His kingdom on Earth (Dan. 2: 44). The victory of verse 5 is a precursor to Armageddon (Rev. 16:16).

The word *fool* in verse 1 does not indicate mental deficiency; rather, it denotes a disregard for God and therefore a mindset devoid of wisdom. Romans 3:10-12 quotes from verses 1-3 to begin a series of quotes that describe the depravity of the human heart.

The fool of verse 1 has the same "heart problem" as did Pharaoh (Ex. 9:34-35) who disregarded God (Ex. 5:1-2). Ananias (Acts 5:4) and Simon the Sorcerer (Acts 8:21) were afflicted with the same disease.

God changed Jacob's name to Israel in Genesis 32:28. Here, in verse 6, *Jacob* designates the people descended from Jacob. *Israel*, meaning "Prince of God" or "God's ruler," is the nation derived from those people. In a sense, they are the same group of people.

Application_____

Be aware that the Lord's people can "act the fool" by attempting to live without proper regard for God. The children of Israel wandered in the wilderness forty years because they "erred in their hearts" (Heb. 3:7-12). To prevent this problem we should carefully heed Proverbs 3:5-6 everyday.

Psalm 54

To the chief Musician on Neginoth, Maschil, *A Psalm* of David, when the Ziphims came and said to Saul, Doth not David hide himself with us?

1. SAVE ME, O God, by thy name, and judge me by thy strength.
2. Hear my prayer, O God; give ear to the words of my mouth.
3. For strangers have risen up against me, and oppressors seek after my soul: they have not set God before them. Selah.
4. Behold, God *is* mine helper: the Lord *is* with them that uphold my soul.
5. He shall reward evil unto mine enemies: cut them off in thy truth.
6. I will freely sacrifice unto thee: I will praise thy name, O LORD; for *it is* good.
7. For he hath delivered me out of all trouble: and mine eye hath seen his desire upon mine enemies.

Commentary_____

Many psalms have inscriptions above the text. Some of these contain untranslated Hebrew words because early translators weren't confident of the meanings. Examples are *maschil* in Psalm 52-55 and *michtam* in Psalm 56-60. Recent scholars have compiled lists with a considerable degree of confidence that they have arrived at the correct meanings. See J. Sidlow Baxter's *Explore the Book* (vol. 3, p. 97). He also declares that in Psalm 54, as well as in other psalms, the part of the superscription preceding the title *(A Psalm of David)* was originally a subscription at the end of the preceding psalm.

The historical event which occasioned the writing of Psalm 54 is recorded in 1 Samuel 23:19-29. Verses 1-3 express an urgent plea for protection against the armies of King Saul. David bases his petition upon the premise that his pursuers have no regard for God. In contrast, he declares his reliance upon the LORD's deliverance and vindication.

In verse 6, David is not speaking of animal sacrifice but of the acceptable sacrifice of praise unto God (Ps. 50:13-15; 69:30-31). See Hebrews 13:15 for New Testament comment on praise as a sacrifice.

In verse 7, David bases his faith upon deliverance by the LORD that he has witnessed in the past. If you want to know how God answered this prayer, read 1 Samuel 23:27-29.

Application_____

Do you ever find yourself in dire circumstances with faith wavering? Learn a lesson from David. Just recall the times in the past when you have experienced deliverance from the Lord. He cares for you now as much as He did when He gave His Son that you might have deliverance from the penalty of sin. He is today your faithful deliverer.

Psalm 55:1-14

To the chief Musician on Neginoth, Maschil, *A Psalm* **of David.**

1. GIVE EAR to my prayer, O God; and hide not thyself from my supplication.
2. Attend unto me, and hear me: I mourn in my complaint, and make a noise;
3. Because of the voice of the enemy, because of the oppression of the wicked: for they cast iniquity upon me, and in wrath they hate me.
4. My heart is sore pained within me: and the terrors of death are fallen upon me.
5. Fearfulness and trembling are come upon me, and horror hath overwhelmed me.
6. And I said, Oh that I had wings like a dove! *for then* would I fly away, and be at rest.
7. Lo, *then* would I wander far off, *and* remain in the wilderness. Selah.
8. I would hasten my escape from the windy storm *and* tempest.
9. Destroy, O Lord, *and* divide their tongues: for I have seen violence and strife in the city.
10. Day and night they go about it upon the walls thereof: mischief also and sorrow *are* in the midst of it.
11. Wickedness *is* in the midst thereof: deceit and guile depart not from her streets.
12. For *it was* not an enemy *that* reproached me; then I could have borne *it:* neither *was it* he that hated me *that* did magnify *himself* against me; then I would have hid myself from him:
13. But *it was* thou, a man mine equal, my guide, and mine acquaintance.
14. We took sweet counsel together, *and* walked unto the house of God in company.

Commentary

As predicted by the prophet Nathan in 2 Samuel 12, lawlessness and conspiracy existed in David's kingdom from the time of David's sin with Bathsheba until Absalom's rebellion. Psalm 55 portrays the anguish of soul suffered by David when he learned that close friends had betrayed him. The prayer of verses 1-5 was probably uttered during his flight from Absalom. In verses 6-8, he is reflecting upon his decision to flee to the wilderness. In verses 9-11, he envisions the conditions in the city from which he is fleeing.

David soon received word that his trusted counselor Ahithophel was among the conspirators (2 Sam. 15:31; 16:23). We deduce that he is the person in view in verses 12-14 of this psalm. By considering these verses, along with Psalm 41:9, John 13:18 and Acts 1:16, we see that Ahithophel pre-figures Judas. Both ended their lives by hanging themselves (2 Sam. 17:23; Mt. 27:5).

How is it that David called Ahithophel his equal (v. 13)? In rank, no one was David's equal. Neither is any human being equal in rank to our Lord Jesus. However, He chooses to look upon His disciples as equals (Jn. 15:15, 20:17; Heb. 2:11,12).

The untranslated Hebrew word *selah* is found seventy-one times in Psalms (also three times in Habakkuk). Some scholars believe it is a call to stop and meditate on what has been said. Others think it is a musical directive added after the psalm was written.

Application

Jesus Christ is our Lord, and we are His servants. All of the writing apostles recognized this at the beginning of their epistles (Rom.1:1, Jas. 1:1, 2 Pet. 1:1, Jude 1:1, Rev. 1:1). Let us follow their example while we rejoice that He deigns to speak of us as friends and brethren.

Psalm 55:15-23

15. Let death seize upon them, *and* let them go down quick into hell: for wickedness *is* in their dwellings, *and* among them.
16. As for me, I will call upon God; and the LORD shall save me.
17. Evening, and morning, and at noon, will I pray, and cry aloud: and he shall hear my voice.
18. He hath delivered my soul in peace from the battle *that was* against me: for there were many with me.
19. God shall hear, and afflict them, even he that abideth of old. Selah. Because they have no changes, therefore they fear not God.
20. He hath put forth his hands against such as be at peace with him: he hath broken his covenant.
21. *The words* of his mouth were smoother than butter, but war *was* in his heart: his words were softer than oil, yet *were* they drawn swords.
22. Cast thy burden upon the LORD, and he shall sustain thee: he shall never suffer the righteous to be moved.
23. But thou, O God, shalt bring them down into the pit of destruction: bloody and deceitful men shall not live out half their days; but I will trust in thee.

Commentary_____

The history of David's life given in Scripture proves that he well knew that vengeance belongs to God (Dt. 32:35). Therefore, read verse 15 as a pronouncement from God rather than a vindictive plea by David. The scriptural authority for that conclusion is 2 Samuel 23:1-3. The reason God will "bring them down into the pit of destruction" (v. 23) is "they fear not God" (v. 19).

If you want to know what David prayed in the morning when he was fleeing from Absalom, read Psalm 3. That prayer transported him from troubled (vv. 1-2) to trusting (vv. 3-4) to tranquil (vv. 5-6) to triumphant (vv. 7-8). His evening prayer was Psalm 4, and his prayer for guidance throughout the day was Psalm 5. For David, the result of all that praying was "peace from the battle that was against me" (v. 18).

Whereas verses 12-14 describe a trusted friend who joined the enemy, verses 20-21 tell of one who deceitfully feigned friendship because he had ulterior motives. In which category was his counselor Ahithophel? David may have been pondering that very question as he penned this psalm.

At any rate, David demonstrated the correct route to victory over evil antagonists. He called upon the LORD morning, noon and evening. He cast his burdens upon the LORD and trusted Him for deliverance and vindication. This will work for anyone of any age at all times.

Application_____

David not only learned the way to fight the Lord's battles on Earth, but he also shared his knowledge with us in Psalms (Rom. 15:4). Our problem is that we insist upon learning from experience rather than from instruction. Experience is a hard teacher and learning that way takes a lifetime.

Psalm 56

To the chief Musician upon Jonath-elem-rechokim, Michtam of David, when the Philistines took him in Gath.

1. BE MERCIFUL unto me, O God: for man would swallow me up; he fighting daily oppresseth me.
2. Mine enemies would daily swallow *me* up: for *they be* many that fight against me, O thou most High.
3. What time I am afraid, I will trust in thee.
4. In God I will praise his word, in God I have put my trust; I will not fear what flesh can do unto me.
5. Every day they wrest my words: all their thoughts *are* against me for evil.
6. They gather themselves together, they hide themselves, they mark my steps, when they wait for my soul.
7. Shall they escape by iniquity? in *thine* anger cast down the people, O God.
8. Thou tellest my wanderings: put thou my tears into thy bottle: *are they* not in thy book?
9. When I cry *unto thee*, then shall mine enemies turn back: this I know; for God *is* for me.
10. In God will I praise *his* word: in the LORD will I praise *his* word.
11. In God have I put my trust: I will not be afraid what man can do unto me.
12. Thy vows *are* upon me, O God: I will render praises unto thee.
13. For thou hast delivered my soul from death: *wilt* not *thou deliver* my feet from falling, that I may walk before God in the light of the living?

Commentary_____

By combining the information given in the superscriptions of Psalms 34 and 56, together with the narrative found in 1 Samuel 21, we may understand David's dire distress as he wrote this psalm. Fleeing for his life from King Saul, he sought refuge in Gath, a principal city of the Philistines, who were Saul's main enemies. Achish, the king of Gath, evidently received David, but Achish's servants recognized David as the slayer of thousands of Philistines. David escaped captivity by successfully feigning insanity before King Achish who drove him away.

Failing to save himself by his own devices, David placed his complete trust in the Most High God who is able to overrule any harm men could have done to him. David made his faith concrete by praising God for His Word (vv. 4, 10). God, through Samuel the prophet, had promised David the kingship of Israel. David believed that word.

Although pursued by some and forsaken by others, David perceived that God's eye of protection was upon him (vv.8-9). His faith was sustained by repeatedly announcing his trust and by praising his God via tongue and pen.

The psalm concludes with David recalling those instances in the past when God had preserved him from death. This gives him the confidence to believe that he would "walk before God in the light of the living" until God's purposes for him on Earth were finished (v. 13).

Application_____

Regardless of dire circumstances, we may walk day by day in victory by following David's example. First, renounce any confidence in yourself or your fellow humans to deliver you. Second, trust completely in the promises given in God's Word. Third, believe that He has a purpose for your life. Fourth, keep praising Him for His Word and keep rejoicing in His provision.

Psalm 57

To the chief Musician, Altaschith, Michtam of David, when he fled from Saul in the cave.

1. BE MERCIFUL unto me, O God, be merciful unto me: for my soul trusteth in thee: yea, in the shadow of thy wings will I make my refuge, until *these* calamities be overpast.
2. I will cry unto God most high; unto God that performeth *all things* for me.
3. He shall send from heaven, and save me *from* the reproach of him that would swallow me up. Selah. God shall send forth his mercy and his truth.
4. My soul *is* among lions: *and* I lie *even among* them that are set on fire, *even* the sons of men, whose teeth *are* spears and arrows, and their tongue a sharp sword.
5. Be thou exalted, O God, above the heavens; *let* thy glory *be* above all the earth.
6. They have prepared a net for my steps; my soul is bowed down: they have digged a pit before me, into the midst whereof they are fallen *themselves*. Selah.
7. My heart is fixed, O God, my heart is fixed: I will sing and give praise.
8. Awake up, my glory; awake, psaltery and harp: I *myself* will awake early.
9. I will praise thee, O Lord, among the people: I will sing unto thee among the nations.
10. For thy mercy *is* great unto the heavens, and thy truth unto the clouds.
11. Be thou exalted, O God, above the heavens: *let* thy glory *be* above all the earth.

Commentary_____

David twice took refuge in a cave while fleeing from Saul. (See the superscription above this psalm). The first time immediately followed his escape from Gath (1 Sam. 22:1). Psalm 57 is one of several psalms probably written on that occasion. It has the same structure as Psalm 56, consisting of two stanzas, each followed by a refrain. (Compare 56:4 and 11 with 57:5 and 11). Psalm 56 adds a vow to render praise unto God. Psalm 57 could be considered a sequel fulfillment of that vow. Both psalms begin with the same plea. However, the tone in Psalm 57 is more victorious because David is more focused on his God than on his enemies.

"Under the shadow of Thy wings" is a favorite metaphorical refuge for David (Ps. 17:8, 61:4, 63:7). He pictures himself as a helpless little chick nestling under its mother's wing at any sign of danger. There he finds a place of complete repose, unafraid of any predator that would "swallow me up" (Ps. 56:1-2; 57:3).

Many who live wickedly receive little retribution for their evil ways on this side of the grave. But some, particularly those who oppress others, "fall into the pit" they have dug for their prey (Ps. 7:15; Pr. 26:27, 28:10). Like Haman, who died on the gallows he had prepared for Mordecai (Est. 7:10), these oppressors are "taken in the devices that they have imagined" (Ps. 10:2). God does it so that men might fear Him.

Application_____

The psalmist is "among lions," men "whose teeth are spears and arrows" (v. 4). But he declares that his heart is fixed upon God. Therefore he will sing, give praise and exalt God—publicly! His one goal is that the glory of the God of Heaven be known on Earth.

Psalm 58

To the chief Musician, Altaschith, Michtam of David.

1. DO YE indeed speak righteousness, O congregation? do ye judge uprightly, O ye sons of men?
2. Yea, in heart ye work wickedness; ye weigh the violence of your hands in the earth.
3. The wicked are estranged from the womb: they go astray as soon as they be born, speaking lies.
4. Their poison *is* like the poison of a serpent: *they are* like the deaf adder *that* stoppeth her ear;
5. Which will not hearken to the voice of charmers, charming never so wisely.
6. Break their teeth, O God, in their mouth: break out the great teeth of the young lions, O LORD.
7. Let them melt away as waters *which* run continually: *when* he bendeth *his bow* to *shoot* his arrows, let them be as cut in pieces.
8. As a snail *which* melteth, let *every one of them* pass away: *like* the untimely birth of a woman, *that* they may not see the sun.
9. Before your pots can feel the thorns, he shall take them away as with a whirlwind, both living, and in *his* wrath.
10. The righteous shall rejoice when he seeth the vengeance: he shall wash his feet in the blood of the wicked.
11. So that a man shall say, Verily *there* is a reward for the righteous: verily he is a God that judgeth in the earth.

Commentary_____

This psalm begins with an indictment against those placed in governmental authority (vv. 1-2). On Earth they sit in the place of God (Rom. 13:1), and are therefore obligated to rule in righteousness. However, because they are wicked, they rule in wickedness. They refuse to listen to God on whose behalf they are appointed (Dan. 4:17). The psalmist likens them to a poisonous serpent that is deaf to his charmer and therefore destroys him with his fangs.

In verses 6-8, the psalmist uses colorful figurative language in beseeching God to destroy the ability of wicked rulers to continue their evil ways.

It takes time for burning thorns to heat a pot to the boiling point. Then suddenly, the contents are seething with action. So it is with God's wrath against wickedness. God waited with longsuffering in the days of Noah—then came the flood!

The psalm closes with a reminder that God is the final judge of all that transpires on Earth. One day the righteous will rejoice, and the wicked will meet their doom. The Almighty has already chosen His righteous ruler (Ps. 2:6). "With righteousness shall He judge the poor, and reprove with equity for the meek of the earth; and He shall smite the earth with the rod of His mouth and with the breath of His lips shall He slay the wicked" (Isa. 11:4).

Application_____

As we read and hear the daily news that is filled with wickedness and violence, we long for His coming. But He "is longsuffering toward us, not willing that any should perish, but that all should come to repentance" (2 Pet. 3:9). Therefore, "what manner of persons ought we to be" (2 Pet. 3:11)?

Psalm 59

To the chief Musician, Altaschith, Michtam of David; when Saul sent, and they watched the house to kill him.

1. DELIVER ME from mine enemies, O my God: defend me from them that rise up against me.
2. Deliver me from the workers of iniquity, and save me from bloody men.
3. For, lo, they lie in wait for my soul: the mighty are gathered against me; not *for* my transgression, not *for* my sin, O LORD.
4. They run and prepare themselves without *my* fault: awake to help me, and behold.
5. Thou therefore, O LORD God of hosts, the God of Israel, awake to visit all the heathen: be not merciful to any wicked transgressors. Selah.
6. They return at evening: they make a noise like a dog, and go round about the city.
7. Behold, they belch out with their mouth: swords *are* in their lips: for who, *say they*, doth hear?
8. But thou, O LORD, shalt laugh at them; thou shalt have all the heathen in derision.
9. *Because of* his strength will I wait upon thee: for God *is* my defence.
10. The God of my mercy shall prevent me: God shall let me see *my desire* upon mine enemies.
11. Slay them not, lest my people forget: scatter them by thy power; and bring them down, O Lord our shield.
12. *For* the sin of their mouth *and* the words of their lips let them even be taken in their pride: and for cursing and lying *which* they speak.
13. Consume *them* in wrath, consume *them*, that they *may* not *be:* and let them know that God ruleth in Jacob unto the ends of the earth. Selah.
14. And at evening let them return; *and* let them make a noise like a dog, and go round about the city.
15. Let them wander up and down for meat, and grudge if they be not satisfied.
16. But I will sing of thy power; yea, I will sing aloud of thy mercy in the morning: for thou hast been my defence and refuge in the day of my trouble.
17. Unto thee, O my strength, will I sing: for God *is* my defence, *and* the God of my mercy.

Commentary_____

King Saul was determined to kill David because God, through Samuel, made it clear that David would replace Saul as king. Saul's plan was to require David to slay 100 Philistines in exchange for receiving Saul's daughter Michal for a bride. Saul was confident that David would be killed in his attempt (1 Sam. 18:25). David slew 200, received his bride, and gained the admiration of the people.

Furious, Saul tried to thrust David through with a javelin. David escaped to his house, and Saul sent soldiers to surround his house and kill him in the morning (1 Sam. 19:9-11). According to the superscription, that is the scenario for Psalm 59.

In verses 1-5, David recognizes his predicament and calls upon his God to deliver, defend, and save. He declares his innocence and reminds God that His future plans call for using David to reach the nations. Verses 6 and 7 are David's poetic description of Saul's soldiers.

In verses 8-10, David declares his confidence that God can and will defend him and bring retribution to his adversaries.

Next, David suggests that God need not kill his enemies but can use them as reminders for others to see. Examples are Cain (Gen.4:12) and the generation of Israelites who wandered in the wilderness forty years.

The psalm closes with David singing aloud of God's power and mercy.

Application_____

To see how God used David's bride for his deliverance instead of his death, read 1 Samuel 19:12-18. Saul failed to consider that her love for David superseded her devotion to her father. Can you think of other instances recorded in the Bible in which the devices of Satan were turned into God's method for bringing about His purposes?

Psalm 60

To the chief Musician upon Shushan-eduth, Michtam of David, to teach; when he strove with Aram-naharaim and with Aram-zobah, when Joab returned, and smote of Edom in the valley of salt twelve thousand.

1. O GOD, thou hast cast us off, thou hast scattered us, thou hast been displeased; O turn thyself to us again.
2. Thou hast made the earth to tremble; thou hast broken it: heal the breaches thereof; for it shaketh.
3. Thou hast shewed thy people hard things: thou hast made us to drink the wine of astonishment.
4. Thou hast given a banner to them that fear thee, that it may be displayed because of the truth. Selah.
5. That thy beloved may be delivered; save *with* thy right hand, and hear me.
6. God hath spoken in his holiness; I will rejoice, I will divide Shechem, and mete out the valley of Succoth.
7. Gilead *is* mine, and Manasseh *is* mine; Ephriam also *is* the strength of mine head; Judah *is* my lawgiver;
8. Moab *is* my washpot; over Edom will I cast out my shoe: Philistia, triumph thou because of me.
9. Who will bring me *into* the strong city? who will lead me into Edom?
10. *Wilt* not thou, O God, *which* hadst cast us off? and *thou*, O God, *which* didst not go out with our armies?
11. Give us help from trouble: for vain *is* the help of man.
12. Through God we shall do valiantly: for he *it is that* shall tread down our enemies.

Commentary

God assigned King David the task of preserving a nation on Earth that regarded the true God and from which the Savior would come. David had two serious character flaws that interfered with his ability to fulfill his assignment—he didn't control his fleshly passions, and he failed to discipline his sons. Satan desired to use David's flaws and the surrounding heathen nations to thwart God's purposes.

On occasion, God permitted enemy nations to defeat Israel in battle in order to bring His people to complete reliance upon Him rather than their own devices. Psalm 60:1-3 tells of David's reaction to one of those defeats. The banner represents both God and His purposes (v. 4; Ps. 20:5).

Verses 5-12 are repeated as Psalm 108:6-13 except for the last line of 60:8. Context indicates that the original text is preserved in 108:9. This is recognized in some more recent versions of the Bible.

God answers the prayer of verse 5 in verses 6-8. He names six areas of the Land of Promise to emphasize that it is His land, and He is in control. Then He announces the subjugation of three surrounding enemy nations. The complete triumph over those nations is recorded in 2 Samuel 8 and 1 Chronicles 18.

In verses 9-12 David proclaims his dependence upon God and God alone and thereby appropriates His might for the battle.

Application

Satan uses the same tactics today in our lives to thwart God's purposes—the power of the world around us and our fleshly desires. The only way to victory is complete reliance upon the Lord who saved us.

Psalm 61

To the chief Musician upon Neginah, *A Psalm* **of David.**

1. HEAR MY cry, O God; attend unto my prayer.
2. From the end of the earth will I cry unto thee, when my heart is over-whelmed: lead me to the rock *that* is higher than I.
3. For thou hast been a shelter for me, *and* a strong tower from the enemy.
4. I will abide in thy tabernacle for ever: I will trust in the covert of thy wings. Selah.
5. For thou, O God, hast heard my vows: thou hast given *me* the her-itage of those that fear thy name.
6. Thou wilt prolong the king's life: *and* his years as many generations.
7. He shall abide before God for ever: O prepare mercy and truth, *which* may preserve him.
8. So will I sing praise unto thy name for ever, that I may daily perform my vows.

Commentary

2 Samuel 17:24-29 most likely gives us the historical setting for Psalm 61. David perceived the protecting hand of God in his flight from the army of Absalom. The battle was imminent. "[E]nd of the earth" (v. 2) could also be translated "far reaches of the land." David was in Mahanaim, far to the northeast of Jerusalem.

"[T]he Rock that is higher than I" (v. 2) is David's designation for the "Captain of the LORD's host," who led Joshua to victory against superior forces (Josh. 5:13-15). As recognized by several discerning songwriters of our time, that Rock was the pre-incarnate Son of God! The LORD his Rock had already manifested Himself as shelter and fortress and would forever be his abiding place and covert (protected hiding place). The need of the hour was someone with a capability higher than David's or that of David's pursuers.

Verses 5-8 look forward to God's future purposes for David and his progeny. There are four ways in which God would "prolong the king's life." First, he would live the full threescore and ten years allotted to man (Ps. 90:10). David died at age seventy (2 Sam. 5:4). Any years beyond that is a bonus. Second, his lineal descendants would reign over Israel for several centuries. Third, he would be the ancestor of the Messiah, and fourth, he would "abide before God forever" (v. 7). Because God is merciful and truthful, David can be confident that God will fulfill all that He promised David in the Davidic Covenant (2 Sam. 7:8-16). Therefore, David will carry out his vow to "sing praise unto thy name forever" (v. 8).

Application

In His Word, the Lord has "given unto us exceeding great and precious promises" (2 Pet. 1:4). Therefore, as did David of old, let us purpose in our hearts to sing praise unto His name daily and forever. This will empower us to live in this sinful world on a plane above its allurements.

Psalm 62

To the chief Musician, to Jeduthun, A Psalm of David.

1. TRULY MY soul waiteth upon God: from him *cometh* my salvation.
2. He only *is* my rock and my salvation: *he is* my defence; I shall not be greatly moved.
3. How long will ye imagine mischief against a man? ye shall be slain all of you: as a bowing wall *shall ye be, and as* a tottering fence.
4. They only consult to cast *him* down from his excellency: they delight in lies: they bless with their mouth, but they curse inwardly. Selah.
5. My soul, wait thou only upon God; for my expectation *is* from him.
6. He only *is* my rock and my salvation: *he is* my defence; I shall not be moved.
7. In God *is* my salvation and my glory: the rock of my strength, *and* my refuge, *is* in God.
8. Trust in him at all times: ye people, pour out your heart before him: God *is* a refuge for us. Selah.
9. Surely men of low degree *are* vanity, *and* men of high degree *are* a lie: to be laid in the balance, they *are* altogether *lighter* than vanity.
10. Trust not in oppression, and become not vain in robbery: if riches increase, set not your heart *upon them.*
11. God hath spoken once; twice have I heard this; that power *belongeth* unto God.
12. Also unto thee, O Lord, *belongeth* mercy: for thou renderest to every man according to his work.

Commentary_____

Psalm 62 consists of three stanzas of four verses each. In the original text, verses 1, 2, 4, 5, 6, and 9 begin with the Hebrew word *akh* which is usually translated "only" if the thought is restrictive; otherwise, it is translated "surely" (see Ps. 23:6) if the thought is positive. In the Gospels, when the word begins a sentence, it is basically the equivalent of "verily." It announces that the sentence is true regardless of any other conclusion one might reach!

The noun rock is introduced as a metaphor for God (*Elohim*) manifesting Himself to man as the LORD (*Jehovah*) in the Song of Moses (Dt. 32:4, 15, 18 and 31). In Hannah's prayer of praise, she also uses this symbol (1 Sam. 2:2). David further develops the metaphor in 2 Samuel 22:2 and 3, and in Psalm 18:2. The LORD, his Rock, is his fortress, his deliverer, his shield, the horn of his salvation, his high tower, his refuge, and his Savior.

Because of what his Rock is, David "shall not be greatly moved" (v. 2); whereas his enemies shall fall like a crumbling wall or "a tottering fence" (v. 3).

Verses 5-7 repeat David's declaration of confidence in his Rock and add to that pronouncement. He concludes stanza two by exhorting others to trust in God.

In stanza three he gives the reasons man is not trustworthy and warns against trusting in force or in riches. The final line of the psalm is quoted and expounded upon by the Apostle Paul in Romans 2:6-11.

Application_____

How many songs of the faith can you name that speak of the Lord Jesus Christ as our Rock? For what reasons is a rock such an apt metaphor for Christ? How many other metaphors in scriptures and/or songs are used to describe Christ?

Psalm 63

A Psalm of David, when he was in the wilderness of Judah.

1. O GOD, thou *art* my God; early will I seek thee: my soul thirsteth for thee, my flesh longeth for thee in a dry and thirsty land, where no water is;

2. To see thy power and thy glory, so *as* I have seen thee in the sanctuary.

3. Because thy lovingkindness *is* better than life, my lips shall praise thee.

4. Thus will I bless thee while I live: I will lift up my hands in thy name.

5. My soul shall be satisfied as *with* marrow and fatness: my mouth shall praise *thee* with joyful lips:

6. When I remember thee upon my bed, *and* meditate on thee in the *night* watches.

7. Because thou hast been my help, therefore in the shadow of thy wings will I rejoice.

8. My soul followeth hard after thee: thy right hand upholdeth me.

9. But those *that* seek my soul, to destroy *it*, shall go into the lower parts of the earth.

10. They shall fall by the sword: they shall be a portion for foxes.

11. But the king shall rejoice in God; every one that sweareth by him shall glory: but the mouth of them that speak lies shall be stopped.

Commentary_____

See 1 Samuel 23:14 for the probable historical setting of this psalm. When David was being relentlessly pursued by King Saul, he had a sufficient resource. By faith he saw the power and glory of God in His sanctuary (Ps. 102:19; Isa. 6:5).

In verses 1-7, David shows us the pathway to joy in the midst of the direst of circumstances (Heb. 12:2). He begins by acknowledging that _The_ God is _his_ God. He tells his God that he seeks, thirsts, and longs for Him. He praises and blesses his God with lips and uplifted hands. When he awakes during the night, he presently appropriates the total future satisfaction that will be his in God's presence. His faith becomes future satisfaction that will be his in God's presence. His faith becomes sufficient as he meditates on how God has sheltered him in the past.

David was upheld because of his dedication to follow God's leading and by trusting God for future vindication.

Let us meditate again upon the psalm as we observe David acknowledging, seeking, thirsting, longing, seeing, praising, blessing, meditating and rejoicing. The psalm shows us the right perspective concerning the past, present and future. As we live in the present, we constantly keep in mind how God has dealt with us in the past. All the while, we rejoice in that which He has promised for our future. We are upheld in the present "in hope of eternal life, which God, who cannot lie, promised before the world began" (Ti. 1:2).

Application_____

David had the perfect cure for insomnia. He didn't need sleeping pills(v. 6).He trusted God to turn meditation into restful sleep when He foresaw that sleep was needed for tomorrow's tasks (Ps. 3:5, 4:4). The psalmist in Psalm 119:148 looked forward to waking up at night so that he might meditate on God's Word!

Psalm 64

To the chief Musician, A Psalm of David.

1. HEAR MY voice, O God, in my prayer: preserve my life from fear of the enemy.
2. Hide me from the secret counsel of the wicked; from the insurrection of the workers of iniquity:
3. Who whet their tongue like a sword, *and* bend *their bows to shoot* their arrows, *even* bitter words:
4. That they may shoot in secret at the perfect: suddenly do they shoot at him, and fear not.
5. They encourage themselves *in* an evil matter: they commune of laying snares privily; they say, Who shall see them?
6. They search out iniquities; they accomplish a diligent search: both the inward *thought* of every one *of them,* and the heart, *is* deep.
7. But God shall shout at them *with* an arrow; suddenly shall they be wounded.
8. So they shall make their own tongue to fall upon themselves: all that see them shall flee away.
9. And all men shall fear, and shall declare the work of God; for they shall wisely consider of his doing.
10. The righteous shall be glad in the LORD, and shall trust in him; and all the upright in heart shall glory.

Commentary_____

The theme of Psalm 64 is "the wicked versus the righteous." The psalmist begins with a threefold plea to God—hear my voice; preserve my life; hide me from the wicked. "Wicked" denotes what his enemies are; "iniquity" is that which they think and do because of what they are. "Iniquity" designates that which is inherently wrong even if there is no law against it. Examples of iniquity are spite, cruelty, oppression and bullying.

Verses 3-6 describe ones who are wicked. They speak words designed to hurt compared to weapons shot from ambush. "Perfect" means blameless (Job 1:1). The victim did nothing wrong to cause the attack of the wicked. The wicked think and act as though no one is watching their evil deeds. Society fails in its efforts to reform such people because the problem is deep within the heart (Mk. 7:21-23). Regeneration, not reformation, is the only solution short of eternal condemnation. Only the power of the Gospel can change the heart (Rom. 1:16).

"But God"—the wicked disregard the God who defends the righteous. His arrows are sharper than theirs and never miss the mark. He knows the intent of the hearts of the wicked before they act. Therefore His timing is perfect. He remembers every evil word spoken and those words will be arrows piercing their hearts for all eternity. This should cause men to fear and the righteous to be glad as they trust (take refuge) in the LORD.

Application_____

The Lord Jesus Christ loves all men regardless of their wickedness. At the cost of dying on a cross, He provided a way to avoid the punishment that justice requires. Some will heed if they are told the saving message of the gospel by one who has the type of love He manifested.

Psalm 65

To the chief Musician, A Psalm *and* Song of David.

1. PRAISE WAITETH for thee, O God, in Sion: and unto thee shall the vow be performed.
2. O thou that hearest prayer, unto thee shall all flesh come.
3. Iniquities prevail against me: *as for* our transgressions, thou shalt purge them away.
4. Blessed *is the man whom* thou choosest, and causest to approach *unto thee, that* he may dwell in thy courts: we shall be satisfied with the goodness of thy house, *even* of thy holy temple.
5. *By* terrible things in righteousness wilt thou answer us, O God of our salvation; *who art* the confidence of all the ends of the earth, and of them that are afar off *upon* the sea:
6. Which by his strength setteth fast the mountains; *being* girded with power:
7. Which stilleth the noise of the seas, the noise of their waves, and the tumult of the people.
8. They also that dwell in the uttermost parts are afraid at thy tokens: thou makest the outgoings of the morning and evening to rejoice.
9. Thou visitest the earth, and waterest it: thou greatly enrichest it with the river of God, *which* is full of water: thou preparest them corn, when thou hast so provided for it.
10. Thou waterest the ridges thereof abundantly: thou settlest the furrows thereof: thou makest it soft with showers: thou blessest the springing therof.
11. Thou crownest the year with thy goodness; and thy paths drop fatness.
12. They drop *upon* the pastures of the wilderness: and the little hills rejoice on every side.
13. The pastures are clothed with flocks; the valleys also are covered over with corn; they shout for joy, they also sing.

Commentary

Psalm 65 is probably a compilation of several psalms prepared for the beginning of worship at one or more of the "Feasts of the LORD" (Lev. 23). Verses 1-4 express the joyous anticipation of the festive proceedings. Verses 5-8 present to God the honor due Him as the awesome Creator and Sustainer. Verses 9-13 sing a celebration to God for His benevolent and gracious provision.

Delving deeper we detect prophetic implications in the psalm. Verses 1 and 2 look forward to a time still future (Isa. 66:23; Zech. 14:16). Verse 3 surely sees beyond the upcoming animal sacrifices to the work of Christ on the cross (Heb. 9:13, 14). Verse 4 foresees the complete satisfaction that will be ours when we are "present with the Lord" (Ps. 17:15; 2 Cor. 5:8).

"The noise of the seas . . . the tumult of the peoples"—this simile in verse 7 introduces a series of passages that tell us the figurative meaning of the word *sea* in the Bible. Notice how the figure is developed in Isaiah 17:12-13, Luke 21:25 and Revelation 17:15. When used figuratively, the "sea" stands for the great mass of unregenerate humanity. This knowledge is the key that unlocks a number of passages like Daniel 7: 2-3 and Revelation 13:1.

The "river of God" is His benevolent provision of water on Earth (v. 9). Figuratively, it is that satisfying stream that flows from the fountain of life eternally.

Application

The psalms don't tell us much about what heaven will be like. However, several psalms emphasize the fact that we will be satisfied. That we will be present with the Lord Jesus Christ in heaven is all we really need to know!

Psalm 66

To the chief Musician, A Song *or* Psalm.

1. MAKE A joyful noise unto God, all ye lands:
2. Sing forth the honour of his name: make his praise glorious.
3. Say unto God, How terrible *art thou in* thy works! through the greatness of thy power shall thine enemies submit themselves unto thee.
4. All the earth shall worship thee, and shall sing unto thee; they shall sing *to* thy name. Selah.
5. Come and see the works of God: *he is* terrible *in his* doing toward the children of men.
6. He turned the sea into dry *land:* they went through the flood on foot: there did we rejoice in him.
7. He ruleth by his power for ever; his eyes behold the nations: let not the rebellious exalt themselves. Selah.
8. O bless our God, ye people, and make the voice of his praise to be heard:
9. Which holdeth our soul in life, and suffereth not our feet to be moved.
10. For thou, O God, has proved us: thou hast tried us, as silver is tried.
11. Thou broughtest us into the net; thou laidst affliction upon our loins.
12. Thou hast caused men to ride over our heads; we went through fire and through water: but thou broughtest us out into a wealthy *place.*
13. I will go into thy house with burnt offerings: I will pay thee my vows,
14. Which my lips have uttered, and my mouth hath spoken, when I was in trouble.
15. I will offer unto thee burnt sacrifices of fatlings, with the incense of rams; I will offer bullocks with goats. Selah.
16. Come *and* hear, all ye that fear God, and I will declare what he hath done for my soul.
17. I cried unto him with my mouth, and he was extolled with my tongue.
18. If I regard iniquity in my heart, the Lord will not hear *me*:
19. *But* verily God hath heard *me;* he hath attended to the voice of my prayer.
20. Blessed *be* God, which hath not turned away my prayer, nor his mercy from me.

Commentary

This psalm of praise is comprised of five stanzas. The end of stanzas one, two and four is marked by the word *selah*. Stanza three ends at verse 12 and at that point, there is a transition from the first person plural (we) to the first person singular (I).

In the first stanza, the psalmist calls upon all people everywhere to give God the honor and praise due His name. However, the fulfillment of the prophetic words of verses 3 and 4 will not occur until the appearance and reign of Messiah.

In stanza two, all people are exhorted to consider how God has intervened in the affairs of men in the past. The psalmist warns them to recognize that God, in His sovereignty, overrules in the governmental affairs of nations (Dan. 2:21; 4:17).

Stanza three is a special call to God's people to praise Him for upholding them. Verse 10 recognizes that there is divine purpose in trials, testings and affliction. (Compare verse 11 with 119:71, 75). The prophet Isaiah must have had verse 12 in mind when he wrote Isaiah 43:2).

In stanza four, the psalmist expresses that which he personally purposes to do in fulfilling his worship obligations to God.

In stanza five, he invites all "that fear God" to listen to his testimonial. When he cried out to God and praised God, he was heard because his heart was right before the Lord. He ends the psalm by gratefully blessing God for mercifully hearing his prayer.

Application

"He that covers his sins shall not prosper, but whoever confesses and forsakes them shall have mercy" (Pr. 28:13). Repeatedly, the Bible warns us that it is futile to petition God while harboring sin in our lives. "Whatever we ask, we receive of Him, because we keep His commandments, and do those things that are pleasing in His sight" (1 Jn. 3:22).

Psalm 67

To the chief Musician on Neginoth, A Psalm *or* Song.

1. GOD BE merciful unto us, and bless us; *and* cause his face to shine upon us; Selah.
2. That thy way may be known upon earth, thy saving health among all nations.
3. Let the people praise thee, O God; let all the people praise thee.
4. O let the nations be glad and sing for joy: for thou shalt judge the people righteously, and govern the nations upon earth. Selah.
5. Let the people praise thee, O God; let all the people praise thee.
6. *Then* shall the earth yield her increase; *and* God, *even* our own God, shall bless us.
7. God shall bless us; and all the ends of the earth shall fear him.

Commentary_____

The psalm before us is one of several that demonstrate the nation of Israel understood that God had commissioned it to take His saving message to "the ends of the earth." Historically, they did little to fulfill that commission. However, the promise given to Abraham (Gen. 12:3) and confirmed to Isaac and Jacob (Gen. 28:13-14) will not fail. As progenitors of our Lord Jesus Christ (Mt. 1:1-2), these patriarchs will see the fulfillment of the promises (Gal. 3:16).

Verse 1 quotes from the Aaronic benediction (Num. 6:22-27). Several other psalms, including Psalm 80, which quotes Numbers 6:25 three times, draw from that passage.

The invitation of verses 3 and 4 will not come to fruition until the Messiah is seated on His throne in Jerusalem for His reign of righteousness and peace. Therefore, "pray for peace of Jerusalem" (Ps. 122:6). The world wants peace with its standard of righteousness that disregards God and His righteousness; therefore the world's standard is actually wickedness. "There is no peace, saith my God, to the wicked" (Isa. 57:21).

Verse 6 begins with a quotation from Leviticus 26:4. However, the preceding verse in Leviticus 26 makes it clear that for Israel that promise is conditional. The promise to Abraham, Isaac and Jacob is unconditional because it depends upon the faithfulness of God rather than the faithfulness of a nation. So does the expectation of verse 7.

Application_____

In Matthew 28:19-20 and Acts 1:8, the Lord gave the church the commission to take the saving gospel message "unto the uttermost part of the earth." Considering that we have both the written record of the completed work of our Lord and the availability of the empowerment of the indwelling Holy Spirit, how much better is our record than that of the nation of Israel?

Psalm 68:1-10

To the chief Musician, A Psalm *or* Song of David.

1. LET GOD arise, let his enemies be scattered: let them also that hate him flee before him.
2. As smoke is driven away, *so* drive *them* away: as wax melteth before the fire, *so* let the wicked perish at the presence of God.
3. But let the righteous be glad; let them rejoice before God: yea, let them exceedingly rejoice.
4. Sing unto God, sing praises to his name: extol him that rideth upon the heavens by his name JAH, and rejoice before him.
5. A father of the fatherless, and a judge of the widows, *is* God in his holy habitation.
6. God setteth the solitary in families: he bringeth out those which are bound with chains: but the rebellious dwell in a dry *land.*
7. O God, when thou wentest forth before thy people, when thou didst march through the wilderness; Selah:
8. The earth shook, the heavens also dropped at the presence of God: *even* Sinai itself *was moved* at the presence of God, the God of Israel.
9. Thou O God, didst send a plentiful rain, whereby thou didst confirm thine inheritance, when it was weary.
10. Thy congregation hath dwelt therein: thou, O God, hast prepared of thy goodness for the poor.

Commentary_____

The purpose of Psalm 68 is to extol the God of Israel as victor over all of God's enemies and the oppressors of God's people past, present and future. In so doing, the psalmist utilizes seven Hebrew names for God—*Elohim* (v. 1), *Jah* (v. 4), *El Shaddai* (v. 14), *Yahweh* (v. 16), *Yah Elohim* (v. 18), *Adonai* (v. 19) and *Yahweh Adonai* (v. 20).

In order to accomplish his purpose, the psalmist draws upon the Scriptures that were available at his time. Verse 1 is the recorded call by Moses to Israel each time the pillar of cloud led them to resume the journey from Mt. Sinai to the Promised Land (Num. 10:35).

The wicked of verse 2 are those who disregard the true God. The righteous of verse 3 are God's chosen ones. The exhortation to the righteous is to be glad, rejoice, sing, praise and extol exceedingly.

Verses 5 and 6 emphasize a God who manifests a very personal interest in each individual. He is not only a powerful victor over enemies but also a tenderhearted Father.

Verses 7 and 8 come from the Song of Deborah (Jud. 5:4-5). She was singing of how God manifested Himself both at the giving of the law at Mt. Sinai and also at the events that followed.

"Plentiful rain" (v. 9) is emblematic of God's total provision for His people. It includes the water, manna and meat supplied in the wilderness as well as the "milk and honey" of the Promised Land.

Application_____

This psalm illustrates that the best way to stir God's people is to present what He has written. Much sermonizing today uses too much of the speaker's thoughts and too little exposition of God's Word (Neh. 8:8). This evidences a lack of reliance upon the power of God's own words (Heb. 4:12).

Psalm 68:11-23

11. The Lord gave the word: great *was* the company of those that published *it*.

12. Kings of armies did flee apace: and she that tarried at home divided the spoil.

13. Though ye have lien among the pots, *yet shall ye be as* the wings of a dove covered with silver, and her feathers with yellow gold.

14. When the Almighty scattered kings in it, it was *white* as snow in Salmon.

15. The hill of God *is as* the hill of Bashan; an high hill *as* the hill of Bashan.

16. Why leap ye, ye high hills? *this is* the hill *which* God desireth to dwell in; yea, the LORD will dwell *in it* for ever.

17. The chariots of God *are* twenty thousand, *even* thousands of angels: the Lord *is* among them, *as in* Sinai, in the holy *place*.

18. Thou hast ascended on high, thou hast led captivity captive: thou hast received gifts for men; yea, *for* the rebellious also, that the LORD God might dwell *among them*.

19. Blessed *be* the Lord, *who* daily loadeth us *with benefits, even* the God of our salvation. Selah.

20. *He that is* our God *is* the God of salvation; and unto GOD the Lord *belong* the issues from death.

21. But God shall wound the head of his enemies, *and* the hairy scalp of such an one as goeth on still in his trespasses.

22. The Lord said, I will bring again from Bashan, I will bring *my people* again from the depths of the sea:

23. That thy foot may be dipped in the blood of *thine* enemies, *and* the tongue of thy dogs in the same.

Commentary_____

Psalm 68 celebrates some great victory wrought by God on behalf of Israel during the psalmist's lifetime. The occasion may have been the result of the campaigns described in 2 Samuel 8.

Verses 11-13 focus on those who kept the home front while the army faced the enemy. The women celebrated in the manner instituted by Miriam (Ex. 15:20) and continued by Deborah (Jud. 5:1). See also 1 Samuel 18:6. They were enriched by their share of the spoils of war.

Verses 14-16 speak of the LORD's selection of the seemingly insignificant hill of Zion as His earthly dwelling, rather than the mountains of Bashan which culminate into the majestic snow-capped Mt. Hermon.

Verse 17 looks back to the host that brought the law to Moses at Sinai (Dt. 33:2; Acts 7:53; Gal. 3:19). It may also look forward to the host that will accompany the Lord when He establishes His throne (Dan. 7:10; Rev. 19:14).

According to Ephesians 4:8, verse 18 prophesied the ascension of Christ (Acts 1:9-11) which climaxed the victory over Satan and death wrought on the cross (Jn. 12:31-33; Heb. 2:14).

God should be glorified because He provides day by day and also because He has the only answer to death (vv. 19, 20).

Verses 21-23 prophesy both the ultimate defeat of God's enemies and the re-gathering of Israel at the end of the age.

Application_____

"And the God of peace shall bruise Satan under your feet shortly" (Rom. 16:20). Do you see any way that this New Testament verse relates to Psalm 68:21? Who is the instigator of all trespasses and the chief among the enemies of God? In what way does God use His servants to bring an end to all of the evil devices of that one?

Psalm 68:24-35

24. They have seen thy goings, O God; *even* the goings of my God, my King, in the sanctuary.
25. The singers went before, the players on instruments *followed* after; among *them were* the damsels playing with timbrels.
26. Bless ye God in the congregations, *even* the Lord, from the fountain of Israel.
27. There *is* little Benjamin *with* their ruler, the princes of Judah *and* their council, the princes of Zebulun, *and* the princes of Naphtali.
28. Thy God hath commanded thy strength: strengthen, O God, that which thou hast wrought for us.
29. Because of thy temple at Jerusalem shall kings bring presents unto thee.
30. Rebuke the company of spearmen, the multitude of the bulls, with the calves of the people, *till every one* submit himself with pieces of silver: scatter thou the people *that* delight in war.
31. Princes shall come out of Egypt; Ethiopia shall soon stretch out her hands unto God.
32. Sing unto God, ye kingdoms of the earth; O sing praises unto the Lord; Selah:
33. To him that rideth upon the heavens of heavens, *which were* of old; lo, he doth send out his voice, *and that* a mighty voice.
34. Ascribe ye strength unto God: his excellency *is* over Israel, and his strength *is* in the clouds.
35. O God, *thou art* terrible out of thy holy places: the God of Israel *is* he that giveth strength and power unto *his* people. Blessed *be* God.

Commentary

Verses 24-28 tell of a victorious procession to the sanctuary David had prepared for worship before Solomon's temple was built. The singers were a specially appointed group of Levites. They lived with their families at the place of worship. They were full-time keepers of the sanctuary provided for by special decree (1 Chr. 9:33, 15:16; Neh. 11:22-23, 12:47). In Jehoshaphat's day, the singers were placed in front of the army as it marched into the midst of the enemy! This so confused the enemy that they slaughtered one another, and not one Israelite was slain (2 Chr. 20:21-22).

Naming Benjamin and Judah from the far south and Zebulun and Naphtali from the far north is another way of saying that the entire nation was represented in the procession.

The use of the future tense is a signal that verses 29-32 project us into the future millennial reign of Messiah. All the rulers on Earth will pay homage by bringing gifts to the King at Jerusalem (Isa. 60:6).

The author of the Christmas hymn "We Three Kings of Orient Are" discerned that the potentates who brought gifts to Jesus (Mt. 2:11) foreshadowed the kings who would bring gifts to the King in the future. Stanzas two, three, and four of that hymn explain the spiritual significance of gold, frankincense and myrrh.

In verse 33-35, the psalmist closes with a tribute to the greatness of the God of Israel. All hearers are admonished to recognize that Israel's God is the God of the universe and all that is therein.

Application

There are sixteen messianic psalms including Psalm 68. These psalms contain prophecies concerning either the first or the second coming of Christ, and each is clearly documented in the New Testament as referring to Christ. We should, however, look for Christ in all of the psalms (Lk. 24:44).

Psalm 69:1-12

To the chief Musician upon Shoshannim, *A Psalm* of David.

1. SAVE ME, O God; for the waters are come in unto *my* soul.
2. I sink in deep mire, where *there is* no standing: I am come into deep waters, where the floods overflow me.
3. I am weary of my crying: my throat is dried: mine eyes fail while I wait for my God.
4. They that hate me without a cause are more than the hairs of mine head: they that would destroy me, *being* mine enemies wrongfully, are mighty: then I restored *that* which I took not away.
5. O God, thou knowest my foolishness; and my sins are not hid from thee.
6. Let not them that wait on thee, O Lord GOD of hosts, be ashamed for my sake: let not those that seek thee be confounded for my sake, O God of Israel.
7. Because for thy sake I have borne reproach; shame hath covered my face.
8. I am become a stranger unto my brethren, and an alien unto my mother's children.
9. For the zeal of thine house hath eaten me up; and the reproaches of them that reproached thee are fallen upon me.
10. When I wept, *and chastened* my soul with fasting, that was to my reproach.
11. I make sackcloth also my garment; and I became a proverb to them.
12. They that sit in the gate speak against me; and I *was* the song of the drunkards.

Commentary_____

The New Testament quotes from Psalm 69 four times and makes reference to it several other times. The psalm well illustrates the characteristics of messianic psalms. Some verses apply only to the psalmist; some only to Christ. Other verses apply to both the psalmist and Christ.

When verses 1-4 are applied to David, they reflect his desperation during his flight from King Saul as recorded in 1 Samuel 21. When applied to Jesus, the words could speak of the anguish of His soul at Gethsemane. The words "mire," "waters" and "floods" (v. 2) are used figuratively. Our Lord applied the first part of verse 4 to Himself in John 15:25.

Verses 5 and 6 apply only to David. In his flight from Saul, his actions at Nob brought disaster to the LORD's servants (1 Sam. 22:18-22). His behavior at Gath brought reproach to his followers (1 Sam. 21:13-15).

Verses 7-9 could apply to both David and Christ. Compare verse 8 with John 7:2-9. John 2:17 and Romans 15:3 quote from verse 9 and apply it to Christ.

Wearing sackcloth depicted an individual's mourning or his dedication to a burdensome task. Verses 10 and 11 likely apply to David, and the sackcloth is probably figurative.

"They that sit in the gate" (v.12) represent the most highly regarded citizens of a city. "Drunkards" represent those who are the least esteemed. Used together, these appellations signify that both David and Christ were disdained by all, from the "highest" to the "lowest."

Application_____

Psalm 69 should teach us that we must be diligent students of the entire Bible if we are to discern the deep things of God. Spirit-led teachers and commentators are helpful, but dependence upon the teaching ministry of the indwelling Holy Spirit is essential if He is to "teach you all things" (Jn. 14:26) and "guide you into all truth" (Jn. 16:13).

Psalm 69:13-21

13. But as for me, my prayer *is* unto thee, O LORD, *in* an acceptable time: O God, in the multitude of thy mercy hear me, in the truth of thy salvation.
14. Deliver me out of the mire, and let me not sink: let me be delivered from them that hate me, and out of the deep waters.
15. Let not the waterflood overflow me, neither let the deep swallow me up, and let not the pit shut her mouth upon me.
16. Hear me, O LORD; for thy lovingkindness *is* good: turn unto me according to the multitude of thy tender mercies.
17. And hide not they face from thy servant; for I am in trouble: hear me speedily.
18. Draw nigh unto my soul, *and* redeem it: deliver me because of mine enemies.
19. Thou hast known my reproach, and my shame, and my dishonour: mine adversaries *are* all before thee.
20. Reproach hath broken my heart; and I am full of heaviness: and I looked *for some* to take pity, but *there was* none; and for comforters, but I found none.
21. They gave me also gall for my meat; and in my thirst they gave me vinegar to drink.

Commentary_____

Verses 13-19 report David's solution to the distressful situation described in verses 2-4. He is still in anguish of soul, but his eyes have turned from his plight to his God. He addresses God first as LORD (*Yahweh*) and then as *Elohim*. *Elohim* is the One Who Is Omnipotent and therefore is able. *Yahweh* is that same omnipotent One when He acts on behalf of his own. David is beseeching the One who can solve his problem, and the One who will deliver at the time He chooses. David is confident that God will both hear and act because He is merciful to those who call upon Him and because He keeps His promises.

"Deliver me"; "turn unto me"; "hide not thy face from thy servant"; "draw nigh unto my soul"—to emphasize the urgency of his plea, David employs all the words at his command without using vain repetition. He addresses his God as a servant would because that presents to God a reason to deliver him speedily. He reasons, "How can I perform my duties as your servant unless You bring deliverance?"

Although verse 20 may well describe David's distress of soul, consider also that the Holy Spirit may have inspired him to write prophetically of the agony of Jesus in the Garden of Gethsemane when "his sweat was as it were great drops of blood falling down to the ground" (Lk. 22:44). The verse could also describe His heart suffering (Ps. 22:1-13) as distinguished from his physical suffering (Ps. 22:14-18) on the Cross.

Certainly, verse 21 looks at the cross. It is this scripture which is spoken of in John 19:28. See also Matthew 27:34.

Application_____

When David found himself sinking into the mire of despondency, he was extricated from his plight mentally and spiritually before he experienced physical deliverance. Such release comes only by the prayer of faith--faith in the merciful One who is able and willing to deliver those who call upon Him.

Psalm 69:22-36

22. Let their table become a snare before them: and *that which should have been* for *their* welfare, *let it become* a trap.
23. Let their eyes be darkened, that they see not; and make their loins continually to shake.
24. Pour out thine indignation upon them, and let thy wrathful anger take hold of them.
25. Let their habitation be desolate; *and* let none dwell in their tents.
26. For they persecute *him* whom thou hast smitten; and they talk to the grief of those whom thou hast wounded.
27. Add iniquity unto their iniquity: and let them not come into thy righteousness.
28. Let them be blotted out of the book of the living, and not be written with the righteous.
29. But I *am* poor and sorrowful: let thy salvation, O God, set me up on high.
30. I will praise the name of God with a song, and will magnify him with thanksgiving.
31. *This* also shall please the LORD better than an ox *or* bullock that hath horns and hoofs.
32. The humble shall see *this, and* be glad: and your heart shall live that seek God.
33. For the LORD heareth the poor, and despiseth not his prisoners.
34. Let the heaven and earth praise him, the seas, and every thing that moveth therein.
35. For God will save Zion, and will build the cities of Judah: that they may dwell there, and have it in possession.
36. The seed also of his servants shall inherit it: and they that love his name shall dwell therein.

Commentary_____

    Verses 22-28 prophesy the status of the nation of Israel during the time of "great indignation" (Deut. 29:28). It speaks particularly of the time between the rejection of Jesus as Israel's Messiah and the time still future when "the indignation is past" (Isa. 26:20, Dan. 8:19). The apostle Paul quotes verses 22-23 in Romans 11:9-10 and gives their application.

    In Acts 1:20, the apostle Peter quotes from verse 25 and applies it to Judas Iscariot by changing "their" to "his." Judas, like the religious leaders of Israel, rejected Jesus as Messiah and thereby brought disaster upon himself.

    Verse 26 speaks of the Jewish treatment of the One "despised and rejected of men, a man of sorrows, and acquainted with grief and. . .smitten of God" (Isa. 53:3,4).

    "Iniquity unto their iniquity"—we all, like David, are "shaped in iniquity" (Ps. 51:5). By refusing to acknowledge our iniquity and receive God's provision for our sin, we add the ultimate iniquity to that with which we were born. Israel set "about to establish their own righteousness, and have not submitted themselves unto the righteousness of God" (Rom. 10:3), thereby excluding themselves from "the book of the living" (v. 28).

    Verses 29-36 look forward to that day when Israel as a nation will see itself as "poor and sorrowful." The indignation will be past, and the people of Israel will receive their Messiah, praising God with song and thanksgiving.

Application_____

    Let us keep in mind that thousands of individual Jewish people are saved every year by receiving Jesus Christ as Savior. The Gospel "is the power of God unto salvation to everyone that believes: to the Jew first. . ." (Rom. 1:16).

Psalm 70

To the chief Musician, *A Psalm* of David, to bring to remembrance.

1. MAKE HASTE, O God, to deliver me; make haste to help me, O LORD.
2. Let them be ashamed and confounded that seek after my soul: let them be turned backward, and put to confusion, that desire my hurt.
3. Let them be turned back for a reward of their shame that say, Aha, aha.
4. Let all those that seek thee rejoice and be glad in thee: and let such as love thy salvation say continually, Let God be magnified.
5. But I *am* poor and needy: make haste unto me, O God: thou *art* my help and my deliverer; O LORD, make no tarrying.

Commentary_____

This psalm is almost identical to the final five verses of Psalm 40, with some interesting variations. The psalm is an urgent petition for deliverance from pursuers and is the type of prayer David might have prayed on a number of occasions. For instance, it fits well for the experience recorded in 2 Samuel 16:5-14. While David was fleeing from Absalom, a group of Benjamites threw stones at him, mocking and taunting him, probably because David had replaced Saul, a Benjamite, as king of Israel.

David invokes the name of God five times in the psalm—as *Elohim* three times and as *Yahweh* twice. In Psalm 40:13-17, he called upon *Yahweh* three times, *Elohim* once, and *Adonai* once. He used the words of verse 2 in several other psalms—twice in Psalm 35 (vv. 4, 26). So Psalm 70 and Psalm 40:13-17 are probably two similar prayers for two separate occasions.

David urges God to hurry! That is the way he both begins and ends his plea. He makes four requests in regards to his pursuers. First, "let them be ashamed" (v. 2). Second, let them be "confounded," meaning humiliated (v. 2). Third, "let them be turned back" (vv. 2, 3). Finally, let them be "put to confusion," meaning dishonored (v. 2).

Then he makes a request on behalf of those who seek God and love His salvation: "Let all those who seek thee rejoice and be glad" and magnify God continually (v. 4).

David closes by expressing his complete lack of resources to help himself and his entire dependency on a God who is able (*Elohim*) and a God who acts on behalf of His own (*Yahweh*).

Application_____

The Holy Spirit had this psalm written for our comfort and hope (Rom. 15:4) so that we might be "thoroughly furnished unto all good works" (2 Tim. 3:17). Let us meditate upon it so that our "profiting may appear to all" (1 Tim. 4:15).

Psalm 71:1-13

1. IN THEE, O LORD, do I put my trust: let me never be put to confusion.

2. Deliver me in thy righteousness, and cause me to escape: incline thine ear unto me, and save me.

3. Be thou my strong habitation, whereunto I may continually resort: thou hast given commandment to save me; for thou *art* my rock and my fortress.

4. Deliver me, O my God, out of the hand of the wicked, out of the hand of the unrighteous and cruel man.

5. For thou *art* my hope, O Lord GOD: *thou art* my trust from my youth.

6. By thee have I been holden up from the womb: thou art he that took me out of my mother's bowels: my praise *shall be* continually of thee.

7. I am as a wonder unto many; but thou *art* my strong refuge.

8. Let my mouth be filled *with* thy praise *and with* thy honour all the day.

9. Cast me not off in the time of old age; forsake me not when my strength faileth.

10. For mine enemies speak against me; and they that lay wait for my soul take counsel together,

11. Saying, God hath forsaken him: persecute and take him; for *there is* none to deliver *him.*

12. O God, be not far from me: O my God, make haste for my help.

13. Let them be confounded *and* consumed that are adversaries to my soul; let them be covered *with* reproach and dishonour that seek my hurt.

Commentary_____

Verses 1-13 of Psalm 71 comprise a petition. The remainder of the psalm is primarily praise. Though we are not told who authored the psalm, it was likely David in his old age (vv. 9, 18). The word *trust* in verse 1 means "to take refuge," and the psalmist was literally escaping (v. 2). Thus we assume the historical setting was David's flight from Absalom (2 Sam. 15:14). The first three verses are very nearly identical to the first three verses of Psalm 31, which almost certainly was penned during this episode.

In the past, God had always performed for David according to the request of verse 4. Therefore, he has a firm basis for hope and trust, which causes him to praise his God instead of cowering in fear as he flees.

"A wonder unto many" (v. 7)—certainly David was a wonderment to the man who cursed him and threw stones in 2 Samuel 16:5-8. The giant-slayer and conqueror of nations was fleeing in disgrace from his own son! This Benjamite thought God was punishing David and was ready to help God finish the job (v. 11). Some onlookers at the crucifixion of Jesus had similar thoughts (Lk. 23:35-37, 48). A few days after Jesus had been hailed in the city as King, He was condemned as a malefactor.

Verse 10 could well describe both the conspiracy against David (2 Sam. 15:12) and the conspiracy against Jesus (Mt. 26:3, 4; Acts 4:26, 27).

The historical account in 2 Samuel gives a graphic answer to the petition of verse 13. The two principle conspirators died very soon and very ignominiously (2 Sam. 17:23; 18:9, 14).

Application_____

The apostle Paul actually thought he was serving God as he persecuted believers. Many today are doing Satan's work in the name of God—even among believers! They err because they are "unskillful in the word of righteousness" and need to "have their senses exercised to discern both good and evil" (Heb. 5:13-14).

Psalm 71:14-24

14. But I will hope continually, and will yet praise thee more and more.
15. My mouth shall shew forth thy righteousness *and* thy salvation all the day; for I know not the numbers *thereof.*
16. I will go in the strength of the Lord GOD: I will make mention of thy righteousness, *even* of thine only.
17. O God, thou hast taught me from my youth: and hitherto have I declared thy wondrous works.
18. Now also when I am old and grayheaded, O God, forsake me not; until I have shewed thy strength unto *this* generation, *and* thy power to every one *that* is to come.
19. Thy righteousness also, O God, *is* very high, who hast done great things: O God, who *is* like unto thee!
20. *Thou,* which hast shewed me great and sore troubles, shall quicken me again, and shalt bring me up again from the depths of the earth.
21. Thou shalt increase my greatness, and comfort me on every side.
22. I will also praise thee with the psaltery, *even* thy truth, O my God: unto thee will I sing with the harp, O thou Holy One of Israel.
23. My lips shall greatly rejoice when I sing unto thee; and my soul, which thou hast redeemed.
24. My tongue also shall talk of thy righteousness all the day long: for they are confounded, for they are brought unto shame, that seek my hurt.

Commentary

In verses 1-13, the psalmist declared his trust and hope in the Lord God (vv. 1, 5). He also expressed a desire to praise God (vv. 6, 8). However, that portion of the psalm is mostly an urgent petition for deliverance from his enemies.

At verse 14 he stops praying about his enemies and turns his eyes upon the righteousness (vv. 15, 16, 19, 24), strength (vv. 16, 17) and wondrous works (vv. 17, 19) of his God. That causes him to appropriate the hope that he expressed in verse 5. Firmly trusting in God's salvation (deliverance), he begins to praise God more and more with his mouth, his lips and his tongue in accordance with the petition of verse 8. Since he is praising "all the day," there is no time for worry about circumstances or enemies!

In verse 17, the psalmist reminds God that from his youth he has declared the wondrous works of God. Now in his old age, he asks for the privilege of telling present and future generations of God's delivering power.

In verse 20, is the psalmist speaking of his bodily resurrection from the grave, or is he using figurative language to express deliverance from his present dire circumstances? Old Testament saints certainly expected to be resurrected bodily (Job 19:25-26; Ps. 17:15; Isa. 26:19).

The psalmist will sing joyously and accompany his singing with musical instruments. With every means available, he will praise God continually and that will confound his enemies!

Application

Keep in mind that although hope is about future expectations, it is meant for present utilization. Biblical hope is the present appropriation of a future joyous certainty (Ti. 1:2; Heb. 6:19). There is no hope in Hell, and hope is not needed in Heaven. It must be appropriated in this life.

Psalm 72:1-11

A Psalm of Solomon.

1. GIVE THE king thy judgments, O God, and thy righteousness unto the king's son.
2. He shall judge thy people with righteousness, and thy poor with judgment.
3. The mountains shall bring peace to the people, and the little hills, by righteousness.
4. He shall judge the poor of the people, he shall save the children of the needy, and shall break in pieces the oppressor.
5. They shall fear thee as long as the sun and moon endure, throughout all generations.
6. He shall come down like rain upon the mown grass: as showers *that* water the earth.
7. In his days shall the righteous flourish; and abundance of peace so long as the moon endureth.
8. He shall have dominion also from sea to sea, and from the river unto the ends of the earth.
9. They that dwell in the wilderness shall bow before him; and his enemies shall lick the dust.
10. The kings of Tarshish and of the isles shall bring presents: the kings of Sheba and Seba shall offer gifts.
11. Yea, all kings shall fall down before him: all nations shall serve him.

Commentary_____

Psalm 72 is a song deriving from the Davidic Covenant (2 Sam. 7:10-16). There God gives David promises which were partially fulfilled in Solomon's forty year reign of peace and rest (1 Chr. 22:9). However, complete fulfillment of the covenant awaits the earthly establishment of the future glorious kingdom of Jesus Christ, the Messiah (Dan. 2:44).

The superscription above the psalm appears to ascribe authorship to Solomon. Some commentators, however, suggest that the meaning is "concerning" Solomon rather than "by" Solomon and that the author is really David. (See verse 20.)

Verses 1-7 present the character of the kingdom, which is righteousness and peace. Righteousness must precede peace because "the work of righteousness shall be peace; and the effect of righteousness, quietness and assurance forever" (Isa. 32:17).

Together verses 3 and 6 form a poetic portrait of serenity and well-being for the citizenry of the kingdom. A chief concern of the King as sovereign will be the protection of "the children of the needy" (v. 4). There will be no oppressors.

Verses 8-11 present the breadth of the kingdom which is "to the ends of the earth" (v. 8) and to "all nations" (v. 11). God's original allotment to Israel extended from the Dead Sea to the Great Sea (Mediterranean Sea). However, He promised to "enlarge their borders" (Ex. 34:24a). David stretched the borders to the Euphrates River, and Messiah will expand them to the ends of the earth (Ex. 23:30-31).

Application_____

If we diligently pray the prayer of Jabez (1 Chr. 4:10), little by little the Holy Spirit will drive out the things in our lives that impede spiritual progress. The Lord will then enlarge the borders of our opportunities for productive service.

Psalm 72:12-20

12. For he shall deliver the needy when he crieth; the poor also, and *him* that hath no helper.

13. He shall spare the poor and needy, and shall save the souls of the needy.

14. He shall redeem their souls from deceit and violence: and precious shall their blood be in his sight.

15. And he shall live, and to him shall be given of the gold of Sheba: prayer also shall be made for him continually; *and* daily shall he be praised.

16. There shall be an handful of corn in the earth upon the top of the mountains; the fruit thereof shall shake like Lebanon: and *they* of the city shall flourish like grass of the earth.

17. His name shall endure for ever: his name shall be continued as long as the sun: and *men* shall be blessed in him: all nations shall call him blessed.

18. Blessed *be* the LORD God, the God of Israel, who only doeth wondrous things.

19. And blessed *be* his glorious name for ever: and let the whole earth be filled *with* his glory; Amen, and Amen.

20. The prayers of David the son of Jesse are ended.

Commentary_____

As it portrays Messiah's glorious future kingdom, Psalm 72 could be outlined as follows:
  I.   The Character of the Kingdom – righteousness and peace
       (vv. 1-7)
  II. The Extent of the Kingdom – to the ends of the earth (vv. 8-11)
  III. The Prosperity of the Kingdom – abundance for all (vv. 12-16)
  IV. The Duration of the Kingdom – never ending (vv. 17-19)

The King will give special attention to the poor and needy who have been so neglected in this age. Every individual is precious to Him (vv. 12-14).

The abundant life is expressed by "showers"(v. 7), "grain" and "fruit" (v.16). The King will be honored by gifts (vv. 10, 15), by homage (vv. 9, 11) and by praise (vv. 15,17).

The Thousand Year Kingdom Age (Millennium) will end with the destruction of Satan and death, followed by the the Great White Throne judgment (Rev. 20). However, there will be a new heaven and a new earth (Rev. 21:1), in which the throne of God and the Lamb will continue forever (Rev. 22:1-5). The promises to David (2 Sam. 7:13, 16) and the prophecy of Daniel (Dan. 2:44) emphatically declare the eternality of the throne and the Kingdom.

Although verses 18 and 19 make a fitting close for Psalm 72, the consensus of scholars ends the psalm at verse 17. The rest of the psalm is considered to be a doxology concluding Book 2. Books 1, 3 and 4 all end with somewhat shorter doxologies. In the Bible, the double *Amen* is found only at the end of each of the first three books of Psalms.

Application_____

Ten psalms, including Psalm 72, prophesy the coming Kingdom that Christ will establish on Earth. These have been designated "Royal Psalms." They motivate us to search out other Scriptures that give details of this glorious time on Earth which is still future. A good study Bible (with cross-referencing and a concordance) will help you in this endeavor.

Psalm 73:1-14

A Psalm of Asaph.

1. TRULY GOD *is* good to Israel, *even* to such as are of a clean heart.
2. But as for me, my feet were almost gone; my steps had well nigh slipped.
3. For I was envious at the foolish, *when* I saw the prosperity of the wicked.
4. For *there are* no bands in their death: but their strength *is* firm.
5. They *are* not in trouble *as other* men; but neither are they plagued like *other* men.
6. Therefore pride compasseth them about as a chain; violence covereth them *as* a garment.
7. Their eyes stand out with fatness: they have more than heart could wish.
8. They are corrupt, and speak wickedly *concerning* oppression: they speak loftily.
9. They set their mouth against the heavens, and their tongue walketh through the earth.
10. Therefore his people return hither: and waters of a full *cup* are wrung out to them.
11. And they say, How doth God know? and is there knowledge in the most High?
12. Behold, these *are* the ungodly, who prosper in the world; they increase *in* riches.
13. Verily I have cleansed my heart *in* vain, and washed my hands in innocency.
14. For all the day long have I been plagued, and chastened every morning.

Commentary

Book Three of Psalms consists of eleven consecutive psalms ascribed to Asaph, followed by six others authored by the Sons of Korah (4), David (1) and Ethan (1). Asaph, who also wrote Psalm 50, was King David's chief singer (1 Chron. 15:19; 16:5).

In Psalm 73, Asaph recounts how the age old question—why do the wicked prosper?—caused him to stumble and almost fall. This question also perplexed Job, Jeremiah and Habakkuk.

"The foolish" of verse 3 denotes those who arrogantly live their lives without regard to their Creator. Such appear to continue till death, living full lives with no evidence of recompense for their evil deeds. Their actions are controlled by pride of person and position as they indulge themselves in every desire. They are given over to corruption, oppression, and boasting. They vaunt themselves wherever they go, defying both God and man with no apparent penalty.

Asaph observes the people of the Most High God following after the ways of the wicked, having concluded that God isn't aware of what's happening on Earth. The ungodly increase in wealth and prosperity, so that must be the way to live!

Asaph, himself, almost decided that it was useless to live a clean life. Every morning and all day long he was filled with consternation because he was doing that which God says not to do in Psalm 37:1, 7.

Application

If Psalm 73 ended with verse 14, it would be a sad lament indeed. However, we shall see that Asaph did not fall. Just like Job and Habakkuk, he had a God of justice who gave him understanding. His experience has been a recourse for God's people throughout the centuries.

Psalm 73:15-28

15. If I say, I will speak thus; behold, I should offend *against* the generation of thy children.
16. When I thought to know this, it *was* too painful for me;
17. Until I went into the sanctuary of God; *then* understood I their end.
18. Surely thou didst set them in slippery places: thou castedst them down into destruction.
19. How are they *brought* into desolation, as in a moment! they are utterly consumed with terrors.
20. As a dream when *one* awaketh; *so,* O Lord, when thou awakest, thou shalt despise their image.
21. Thus my heart was grieved, and I was pricked in my reins.
22. So foolish *was* I, and ignorant: I was *as* a beast before thee.
23. Nevertheless I *am* continually with thee: thou hast holden *me* by my right hand.
24. Thou shalt guide me with thy counsel, and afterward receive me *to* glory.
25. Whom have I in heaven *but thee?* and *there is* none upon earth *that* I desire beside thee.
26. My flesh and my heart faileth: *but* God *is* the strength of my heart, and my portion for ever.
27. For, lo, they that are far from thee shall perish: thou hast destroyed all them that go a-whoring from thee.
28. But *it is* good for me to draw near to God: I have put my trust in the Lord GOD, that I may declare all thy works.

Commentary_____

Asaph knew there was something wrong with his thinking in verse 13. What about his obligation to the generations to come? Someone must stay true to God for their sake. How else will they know God's way? In Psalm 78:1-7, Asaph demonstrates that he took his obligation to future generations seriously.

The "sanctuary" is the place one draws near to God in order to communicate with Him (Ps. 20:2, 77:13, 96:6). It is the place God showed Asaph the foolishness of his thoughts. It is the place Asaph found the answer to the problem that caused his pain (v. 16). It is the place God brought conviction to his heart and the place Asaph freely confessed his sin (Job 42:5-6). In the sanctuary Aspah realized that his God was with him, holding his hand all the while. There Asaph gained the assurance that God would counsel and guide him during his life on Earth and safely bring him into God's very presence in Heaven. His God was his total desire here and his portion forever (vv. 25, 26).

As for those who are far from God because they shun His sanctuary—He will take care of that in His time. Those who follow after the ways of the wicked will perish with the ones who led them astray. At the end of the psalm, the same man is in the same circumstances, but he has a new perspective on the role he is to play on life's stage.

Application_____

According to verse 28, what two things must take place in my life before I will be involved in declaring all the works of God? Considering the ministry of the indwelling Holy Spirit, where is *my* sanctuary? See John 14:16 and 16:13,14.

Psalm 74:1-12

Maschil of Asaph.

1. O GOD, why hast thou cast *us* off for ever? *why* doth thine anger smoke against the sheep of thy pasture?
2. Remember thy congregation, *which* thou hast purchased of old; the rod of thine inheritance, *which* thou hast redeemed; this mount Zion, wherein thou hast dwelt.
3. Lift up thy feet unto the perpetual desolations; *even* all *that* the enemy hath done wickedly in the sanctuary.
4. Thine enemies roar in the midst of thy congregations; they set up their ensigns *for* signs.
5. A *man* was famous according as he had lifted up axes upon the thick trees.
6. But now they break down the carved work thereof at once with axes and hammers.
7. They have cast fire into thy sanctuary, they have defiled *by casting down* the dwelling place of thy name to the ground.
8. They said in their hearts, Let us destroy them together: they have burned up all the synagogues of God in the land.
9. We see not our signs: *there is* no more any prophet: neither *is there* among us any that knoweth how long.
10. O God, how long shall the adversary reproach? shall the enemy blaspheme thy name for ever?
11. Why withdrawest thou thy hand, even thy right hand? pluck *it* out of thy bosom.
12. For God *is* my King of old, working salvation in the midst of the earth.

Commentary_____

Because of the textual content, scholars have concluded that some of the twelve psalms attributed to Asaph were compiled by his descendants known as "the Sons of Asaph." These were leaders of worship for many generations after Asaph's time (2 Chr. 20:14; Ezra 3:10; Neh. 11:22). The sad plight of the nation described in Psalm 74:3-9 resulted from the destruction of Jerusalem by the Chaldeans (Babylonians) in 586 BC (2 Ki. 25:8-12).

In Romans 11, the apostle Paul answers the questions posed in verses 1 and 10. Full restoration for Israel as a nation will not come before three "untils" of the New Testament are fulfilled:

--"*Until* the time come when ye shall say, Blessed is He that cometh in the name of the Lord" (Lk. 13:35). Israel must receive Jesus as Messiah.

--"*Until* the times of the Gentiles be fulfilled" (Lk. 21:24). Jerusalem shall be trodden down by the Gentiles from 586 BC until Messiah crushes the world powers at the battle of Armageddon.

--"*Until* the fullness of the Gentiles be come in" (Rom. 11:25). The calling out of a people from the nations for His name must be completed (Acts 15:14).

Although it appeared to the psalmist that God had His hand idle in His bosom, actually He is "working salvation in the midst of the earth" (v. 12).

Application_____

In the power of the risen Christ and through the Spirit-controlled believers, God has an active program on Earth today. The question is, to what extent do I desire to be controlled by the Spirit that I might be an effective part of that program? What will be the evidence in my life that I am Spirit-controlled?

Psalm 74:13-23

13. Thou didst divide the sea by thy strength; thou brakest the heads of the dragons in the waters.
14. Thou brakest the heads of leviathan in pieces; *and* gavest him *to be* meat to the people inhabiting the wilderness.
15. Thou didst cleave the fountain and the flood: thou driest up mighty rivers.
16. The day *is* thine, the night also *is* thine: thou hast prepared the light and the sun.
17. Thou hast set all the borders of the earth: thou hast made summer and winter.
18. Remember this, *that* the enemy hath reproached, O LORD, and *that* the foolish people have blasphemed thy name.
19. O deliver not the soul of thy turtledove unto the multitude *of the wicked:* forget not the congregation of thy poor for ever.
20. Have respect unto the covenant for the dark places of the earth are full of the habitations of cruelty.
21. O let not the oppressed return ashamed: let the poor and needy praise thy name.
22. Arise, O God, plead thine own cause: remember how the foolish man reproacheth thee daily.
23. Forget not the voice of thine enemies: the tumult of those that rise up against thee increaseth continually.

Commentary_____

In verses 13-15 the psalmist rehearses to God the history of His manifestation of power on behalf of Israel. The monstrous animals of verses 13 and 14 are emblematic of strong adversaries that only God's power could destroy (Isa. 27:1; Ezk. 29:3). "[T]he people inhabiting the wilderness" refers to the creatures of desert and sea that feasted upon the slain Egyptian soldiers. Verse 15 recalls the water from the smitten rock and the crossing of the Jordan on dry ground.

Verses 16 and 17 acknowledge the work of God in creation. The psalmist is saying to God, "I know that You have been willing in the past to rescue Your people and that You are fully capable of rescuing them at any time."

In the remainder of the psalm, the psalmist points out to God several reasons God should act speedily on behalf of His destitute people. First, it is God, Himself, who has been reproached and blasphemed in the desecration of His holy habitation. Second, God is merciful and His people are as helpless as a dove in a snare. Third, God provides for the poor and needy, and His people are shamefully oppressed. Fourth, God must honor His covenant with Abraham, Isaac, and Jacob. Fifth, God has called out a people for His name. How can they offer praise under these circumstances? Sixth, this is God's cause, and God's enemies are currently prevailing.

Application_____

In Leviticus and Deuteronomy, the Lord fully explained what would bring about the calamity Israel was enduring: they rejected the prophets who were sent to warn them, and they would not learn by instruction so they were forced to learn by experience. Today, are we willing to learn by instruction or must we experience God's chastening hand? "The LORD shall judge His people" (Dt. 32:36; Heb. 10:30; 12:6).

Psalm 75

To the chief Musician, Altaschith, A Psalm *or* Song of Asaph.

1. UNTO THEE, O God, do we give thanks, *unto thee* do we give thanks: for *that* thy name is near thy wondrous works declare.
2. When I shall receive the congregation I will judge uprightly.
3. The earth and all the inhabitants thereof are dissolved: I bear up the pillars of it. Selah.
4. I said unto the fools, Deal not foolishly: and to the wicked, Lift not up the horn:
5. Lift not up your horn on high: speak *not with* a stiff neck.
6. For promotion *cometh* neither from the east, nor from the west, nor from the south.
7. But God *is* the judge: he putteth down one, and setteth up another.
8. For in the hand of the LORD *there is* a cup, and the wine is red; it is full of mixture; and he poureth out of the same: but the dregs thereof, all the wicked of the earth shall wring *them* out, *and* drink *them.*
9. But I will declare for ever; I will sing praises to the God of Jacob.
10. All the horns of the wicked also will I cut off; *but* the horns of the righteous shall be exalted.

Commentary

In verse 1, the psalmist speaks to God on behalf of the congregation; in verses 2 and 3 he speaks to the congregation on behalf of God. In verses 4-8, he addresses the oppressors of Israel on behalf of God. In verse 9 he speaks for himself, and in verse 10, on behalf of God to all people. The entire psalm serves as an answer to the perplexities of 73:2-14 and to the questions of 74:10-11.

The word horn or *horns* is used figuratively four times in Psalm 75 and more than fifty times in twelve different books from Genesis to Revelation. Concerning the tabernacle, and elsewhere, it is used literally with figurative connotations. As is true with most words used metaphorically in the Bible, the figurative meaning has its roots in the Pentateuch. Notice first how the word is used literally (Ex. 21:28-29). Then study the context of verses in which it is obviously used in a figurative sense (Dt. 33:17; 1 Sam. 2:1, 10) and draw connections between the texts. To "have a horn" or to be called "a horn" signifies a usable advantage over another. Think of two cows in a pen with a pile of hay. The one with horns will gorge itself and will not permit the hornless one to eat anything. In a sense, that was Hannah's situation in 1 Samuel 2 before her "horn was exalted in the LORD" (v. 1).

"East," "west," and "south" (v. 6)—the LORD dwells "in the sides of the north" (Ps. 48:2; Isa. 14:13; Ezk. 1:4). If exaltation comes from anywhere else but Him, the horn will be cut off!

Application

Satan doesn't have literal horns, but he certainly has figurative ones. We are "hornless" without the "Horn of Our Salvation" (Ps. 18:2; Lk. 1:69). Antichrist is called a "little horn" in Daniel 8:9. He will have more power to push people around than any other human that has ever lived, but he is "little" compared to our Horn.

Psalm 76

To the chief Musician on Neginoth, A Psalm *or* Song of Asaph.

1. IN JUDAH *is* God known: his name *is* great in Israel.
2. In Salem also is his tabernacle, and his dwelling place in Zion.
3. There brake he the arrows of the bow, the shield, and the sword, and the battle. Selah.
4. Thou *art* more glorious *and* excellent than the mountains of prey.
5. The stout-hearted are spoiled, they have slept their sleep: and none of the men of might have found their hands.
6. At thy rebuke, O God of Jacob, both the chariot and horse are cast into a dead sleep.
7. Thou, *even* thou, *art* to be feared: and who may stand in thy sight when once thou art angry?
8. Thou didst cause judgment to be heard from heaven; the earth feared, and was still,
9. When God arose to judgment, to save all the meek of the earth. Selah.
10. Surely the wrath of man shall praise thee: the remainder of wrath shall thou restrain.
11. Vow, and pay unto the LORD your God: let all that be round about him bring presents unto him that ought to be feared.
12. He shall cut off the spirit of princes: *he is* terrible to the kings of the earth.

Commentary

Psalm 76 is a song of victory that most likely arises from the smiting of 185,000 Assyrian invaders by one heaven-sent angelic being. They were besieging Jerusalem, God's dwelling place on Earth.

The name *Zion* is found thirty-seven times in Psalms and more than 150 times in the Bible. Historically, it was the fortress hill on which King David built his palace (1 Chr. 11:5; 2 Chr. 5:2). When the Ark of the Covenant was moved into Solomon's Temple, Zion became the designation for the Temple Mount, another hill of Jerusalem's mountain complex. Later in Scripture, Zion is Jerusalem. Figuratively, Zion designates the place from which God's authoritative rule emanates.

When the word *mountain* is used figuratively, it means kingdom (Isa. 2:2; Dan. 2:35). The mountains of prey are nations like Assyria which preyed upon other weaker countries.

Verses 3-9 poetically describe a scenario that parallels the account in 2 Kings 19:30-35 which is repeated in Isaiah 37:32-36. (See also 2 Chr. 32:20-23).

The truth of verse 10 is illustrated a number of times in the Bible. Compare the words of Pharoah in Exodus 5:2 with his words in Exodus 9:27. The idolatrous God-hating Philistines glorified God (1 Sam. 6:5). God changed Nebuchadnezzar's proud boast into praise (Dan. 4:30, 37). During the Tribulation, blasphemers will give glory to God (Rev. 11:13).

Application

"Every tongue should confess that Jesus Christ is Lord, to the glory of God the Father (Phil. 2:11). Let us be ever grateful that by the grace of God we have learned to *willingly* bow to His Majesty.

Psalm 77

To the chief Musician, to Jeduthun, A Psalm of Asaph.

1. I CRIED unto God with my voice, *even* unto God with my voice; and he gave ear unto me.
2. In the day of my trouble I sought the Lord: my sore ran in the night, and ceased not: my soul refused to be comforted.
3. I remembered God, and was troubled: I complained, and my spirit was overwhelmed. Selah.
4. Thou holdest mine eyes waking: I am so troubled that I cannot speak.
5. I have considered the days of old, the years of ancient times.
6. I call to remembrance my song in the night: I commune with mine own heart: and my spirit made diligent search.
7. Will the Lord cast off for ever? and will he be favourable no more?
8. Is his mercy clean gone for ever? doth *his* promise fail for evermore?
9. Hath God forgotten to be gracious? hath he in anger shut up his tender mercies? Selah.
10. And I said, This *is* my infirmity: *but I will remember* the years of the right hand of the most High.
11. I will remember the works of the LORD: surely I will remember thy wonders of old.
12. I will meditate also of all thy work, and talk of thy doings.
13. Thy way, O God, *is* in the sanctuary: who *is so* great a God as *our* God?
14. Thou *art* the God that doest wonders: thou hast declared thy strength among the people.
15. Thou hast with *thine* arm redeemed thy people, the sons of Jacob and Joseph. Selah.
16. The waters saw thee, O God, the waters saw thee; they were afraid: the depths also were troubled.
17. The clouds poured out water: the skies sent out a sound: thine arrows also went abroad.
18. The voice of thy thunder *was* in the heaven: the lightnings lightened the world: the earth trembled and shook.
19. Thy way *is* in the sea, and thy path in the great waters, and thy footsteps are not known.
20. Thou leddest thy people like a flock by the hand of Moses and Aaron.

Commentary_____

    The psalmist tells of a past time of deep despair over which he has already had victory when he writes, "I . . . was troubled; I complained, and my spirit was overwhelmed" (v. 3). He was distraught because of the six questions listed in verses 7-9. He couldn't sleep—he couldn't even talk! His root problem came from communing with his own heart instead of with God.

    In verse 10, Asaph recognizes his error. He turns his eyes from his circumstances unto the Most High. This causes him to stop communing with himself and to start meditating on God's Word which told him of God's wondrous work on behalf of Israel. Instead of complaining and questioning God's faithfulness and goodness, he begins to praise God and extol His greatness.

    The Word of God produced the faith necessary for Asaph to believe the promises that the Word proclaimed (Rom. 10:17). Faith has the power to turn the direst of circumstances into eager expectancy of deliverance by God from the circumstances. Notice in verses 11 and 12 that Asaph only supplied the will—the Word supplied everything else. Thus, the despair brought on by thinking about the situation was changed to the expectancy of faith in God's faithfulness.

Application_____

    Jesus said, "In the world ye shall have tribulation." In the same verse, He also said, "be of good cheer" (Jn. 16:33). As long as we are in this world, we should expect to be buffeted by circumstances. It is our tendency to blame God for our plight—and Satan is ever ready to accentuate that proclivity. As long as Asaph questioned God's mercy and goodness, there was no peace for his soul. Trusting in the truth of God's Word brings blessed quietness to the restless soul.

Psalm 78:1-16

Maschil of Asaph.

1. GIVE EAR, O my people, *to* my law: incline your ears to the words of my mouth.
2. I will open my mouth in a parable: I will utter dark sayings of old:
3. Which we have heard and known, and our fathers have told us.
4. We will not hide *them* from their children, shewing to the generation to come the praises of the LORD, and his strength, and his wonderful works that he hath done.
5. For he established a testimony in Jacob, and appointed a law in Israel, which he commanded our fathers, that they should make them known to their children:
6. That the generation to come might know *them, even* the children *which* should be born; *who* should arise and declare *them* to their children:
7. That they might set their hope in God, and not forget the works of God, but keep his commandments:
8. And might not be as their fathers, a stubborn and rebellious generation; a generation *that* set not their heart aright, and whose spirit was not stedfast with God.
9. The children of Ephraim, *being* armed, *and* carrying bows, turned back in the day of battle.
10. They kept not the covenant of God, and refused to walk in his law;
11. And forgat his works, and his wonders that he had shewed them.
12. Marvellous things did he in the sight of their fathers, in the land of Egypt, *in* the field of Zoan.
13. He divided the sea, and caused them to pass through; and he made the waters to stand as an heap.
14. In the daytime also he led them with a cloud, and all the night with a light of fire.
15. He clave the rocks in the wilderness, and gave *them* drink as *out of* the great depths.
16. He brought streams also out of the rock, and caused waters to run down like rivers.

215

Commentary_____

"That the generation to come might know. . . "(v. 6). Adam informed Cain, Abel and then Seth of God's ways. Seth faithfully instructed Enos (Gen. 4:26). However, ten generations after Adam, only Noah instructed his children in the ways of the LORD. Every other father was dooming his progeny to eternal damnation by failing to communicate God's Word to succeeding generations. Mercifully, God intervened by sending the flood, thereby giving the human race a second chance.

When Noah's family walked off the ark, every human being alive knew the way to God. Yet when Abraham came along ten generations after Noah, God had to call him out of idolatry (Josh. 24:2) in order to find a father who would "command his children and his household after him to keep the way of the LORD" (Gen. 18:19).

It is a fearsome sin for a father to beget children into this world and then fail to lead them in the way everlasting. Moses made this responsibility a key issue when he instructed the people of Israel as they entered the Promised Land (Dt. 6:6-9; 11:18-21).

Ephraim became the leading tribe of the northern kingdom of Israel and led the others into idolatry (Hos. 13:1-3). The psalmist therefore singles "the children of Ephraim" out for condemnation (vv. 9-11).

Verse 13, along with Exodus 14:22, 29 and 15:8, proves that the parting of the Red Sea was a miracle of God and could not be explained within the scope of natural laws.

Application_____

The obligation to pass God's message of redemption to succeeding generations is expanded in the New Testament to include spiritual progeny as well as physical progeny. Can you detect four spiritual generations in 2 Timothy 2:2? For how many physical generations does Psalm 78:6 make us responsible?

Psalm 78:17-31

17. And they sinned yet more against him by provoking the most High in the wilderness.
18. And they tempted God in their heart by asking meat for their lust.
19. Yea, they spake against God; they said, Can God furnish a table in the wilderness?
20. Behold, he smote the rock, that the waters gushed out, and the streams overflowed; can he give bread also? can he provide flesh for his people?
21. Therefore the LORD heard *this*, and was wroth: so a fire was kindled against Jacob, and anger also came up against Israel;
22. Because they believed not in God, and trusted not in his salvation:
23. Though he had commanded the clouds from above, and opened the doors of heaven,
24. And had rained down manna upon them to eat, and had given them of the corn of heaven.
25. Man did eat angels' food: he sent them meat to the full.
26. He caused an east wind to blow in the heaven: and by his power he brought in the south wind.
27. He rained flesh also upon them as dust, and feathered fowls like as the sand of the sea:
28. And he let *it* fall in the midst of their camp, round about their habitations.
29. So they did eat, and were well filled: for he gave them their own desire;
30. They were not estranged from their lust. But while their meat *was* yet in their mouths,
31. The wrath of God came upon them, and slew the fattest of them, and smote down the chosen *men* of Israel.

Commentary

The historical events of these verses are taken primarily from Exodus 16 and Numbers 11.

"Corn (grain) of heaven," "angels' food," and "bread of heaven" (Ps. 105:40) are terms God uses to designate the sustenance He provided for Israel in the wilderness. The people called it *manna* (Ex. 16:15) which means "what is it?" It was intended for a wilderness journey of only several months. Upon entering the Promised Land, they were to eat from vineyards and olive trees already producing (Dt. 6:11) as well as from the "old corn (grain) of the land" (Josh. 5:12). At first the people said *manna* tasted like wafers made with honey (Ex. 16:31), but after eating it for forty years they said, "Our soul loathes this light bread" (Num. 21:5).

John 6:30-59 presents the spiritual meaning of *manna*. To feast on *manna* is to meditate on and glory in that which Jesus did for us as the One who came down to Earth. To eat of the "old corn of the land" is to joyously consider that which He is doing in us and through us in His present ministry as our Great High Priest (Heb. 13:20-21).

God miraculously delivered Israel from slavery in Egypt and then met every need in the wilderness. Yet the people refused to trust Him to lead them to victorious conquest of the Promised Land. Then they repeatedly accused God for the discomfort of the arduous wilderness trek that they brought upon themselves. Unbelief, complaints and rebellion brought judgment.

Application

Many believers trust God to deliver them from sin and damnation but fail to trust Him to lead them as warriors in His conquering army. They will spend their lives as wilderness Christians. They'll know nothing of feasting upon "the old corn of the land," losing eternal rewards because they did not fight "a good fight "(2 Tim. 4:7, 8).

Psalm 78:32-44

32. For all this they sinned still, and believed not for his wondrous works.
33. Therefore their days did he consume in vanity, and their years in trouble.
34. When he slew them, they sought him: and they returned and inquired early after God.
35. And they remembered that God *was* their rock, and the high God their redeemer.
36. Nevertheless they flatter him with their mouth, and they lied unto him with their tongue.
37. For their heart was not right with him, neither were they stedfast in his covenant.
38. But he, *being* full of compassion, forgave *their* iniquity, and destroyed *them* not: yea, many a time turned he his anger away, and did not stir up all his wrath.
39. For he remembered that they *were but* flesh; a wind that passeth away, and cometh not again.
40. How oft did they provoke him in the wilderness, *and* grieve him in the desert!
41. Yea, they turned back and tempted God, and limited the Holy One of Israel.
42. They remembered not his hand, *nor* the day when he delivered them from the enemy.
43. How he had wrought his signs in Egypt, and his wonders in the field of Zoan:
44. And had turned their rivers into blood; and their floods, that they could not drink.

Commentary

Notice the contrast in these verses between that which is said about the people and that which is said about God. They sinned, believed not, flattered God, lied to God, failed to keep the covenant, provoked God, grieved God, turned back, tempted (tested) God, limited God, and remembered not God's deliverance. In contrast, God was their Rock, their High God and Redeemer (v. 35). He was full of compassion, forgiving and forbearing (v. 38) and considerate (v. 39).

Their root problem was a heart problem (v. 37; Ps. 95:10). It brought upon them a lifetime of vanity (futility) and trouble (v. 33) and eventually death in the wilderness (v. 34).

". . .[T]hey did flatter him with their mouth . . ."(v. 36). Flattery is not only socially acceptable but a mark of culture in this world. Dale Carnegie's *How to Win Friends and Influence People* swept this country a few decades ago. Businesses set up seminars everywhere. The main theme was "be lavish with praise and profuse with approbation." People love compliments whether or not they are merited, and people will favor those who freely bestow them. ". . .they flatter with their tongue" (Ps. 5:9).

What does God say about flattery? "The LORD shall cut off all flattering lips" (Ps. 12:3); ". . .meddle not with him that flatters with his lips"(Pr. 20:19);". . .a flattering mouth works ruin"(Pr. 26:28). "A man that flatters his neighbor spreads a net for his feet"(Pr. 29:5).

Application

"By Him, therefore, let us offer the sacrifice of praise to God continually, that is the fruit of our lips giving thanks to His name" (Heb. 13:15). To praise God in recognition of His greatness is good. To praise Him for the purpose of gaining His favor is flattery. True praise comes from an overflowing heart of love and gratitude. Flattery comes from the head. You can be sure that God knows the difference.

Psalm 78:45-58

45. He sent divers sorts of flies among them, which devoured them; and frogs, which destroyed them.
46. He gave also their increase unto the caterpillar, and their labour unto the locust.
47. He destroyed their vines with hail, and their sycomore trees with frost.
48. He gave up their cattle also to the hail, and their flocks to hot thunderbolts.
49. He cast upon them the fierceness of his anger, wrath, and indignation, and trouble, by sending evil angels *among them.*
50. He made a way to his anger; he spared not their soul from death, but gave their life over to the pestilence;
51. And smote all the firstborn in Egypt; the chief of *their* strength in the tabernacles of Ham:
52. But made his own people to go forth like sheep, and guided them in the wilderness like a flock.
53. And he led them on safely, so that they feared not: but the sea overwhelmed their enemies.
54. And he brought them to the border of his sanctuary, *even to* this mountain, *which* his right hand had purchased.
55. He cast out the heathen also before them, and divided them an inheritance by line, and made the tribes of Israel to dwell in their tents.
56. Yet they tempted and provoked the most high God, and kept not his testimonies:
57. But turned back, and dealt unfaithfully like their fathers: they were turned aside like a deceitful bow.
58. For they provoked him to anger with their high places, and moved him to jealousy with their graven images.

Commentary_____

In continuing to contrast the greatness and graciousness of God
(vv. 43-55) with the fickleness and obstinacy of His people
(vv. 40-42 and 56-58), the psalmist summarizes (vv. 43-53) the events
recorded in chapters 7-14 of Exodus. Six of the ten plagues God
brought upon Egypt are listed in verses 44-51. The third, fifth, sixth and
ninth plagues are omitted. In a similar listing in Psalm 105:27-36, the
fifth and sixth plagues are also omitted, but the ninth plague is emphasized because the writer places it first. God has His reasons.

The shepherd/sheep relationship between God and His people
(v. 52) is emphasized in several psalms. We will see further develop-
ment of this theme in Psalms 79 and 80.

Does it bother you that God cast out other peoples from their
ancestral homeland to provide a land for His chosen people? If so, perhaps it would be helpful to read Leviticus 18:19-30. The prior inhabitants had become so degraded that there was no hope for their perverted souls. The children they begat were basically fodder for Hell. God
was merciful to their unborn progeny by preventing further procreation
of doomed souls.

"Like a deceitful bow"—one word translated as *sin* in the Bible
means to "miss the mark." God is pictured as a hunter, who with great
care, fashions an arrow. His purpose is to use a finely honed flint and a
highly polished shaft to "hit the mark." However, because the bow is
defective, no amount of craftsmanship or maintenance can make the
arrow accurate. It deceives its owner and misses the mark.

Application_____

In Isaiah 49:2 and 50:4-7, we find prophesies of an arrow which will hit
the mark. Who is this "polished shaft" that would set his "face like flint"? The
bow motivates the arrow as the heart motivates the walk. His heart was
true. If we furnish the true heart, God will polish the arrow, and we will hit
the mark.

Psalm 78:59-72

59. When God heard *this*, he was wroth, and greatly abhorred Israel:
60. So that he forsook the tabernacle of Shiloh, the tent *which* he placed among men;
61. And delivered his strength into capivity, and his glory in the enemy's hand.
62. He gave his people over also unto the sword; and was wroth with his inheritance.
63. The fire consumed their young men; and their maidens were not given to marriage.
64. Their priests fell by the sword; and their widows made no lamentation.
65. Then the Lord awaked as one out of sleep, *and* like a mighty man that shouteth by reason of wine.
66. And he smote his enemies in the hinder parts: he put them to a perpetual reproach.
67. Moreover he refused the tabernacle of Joseph, and chose not the tribe of Epharim:
68. But chose the tribe of Judah, the mount Zion which he loved.
69. And he built his sanctuary like high *palaces*, like the earth which he hath established for ever.
70. He chose David also his servant, and took him from the sheepfolds:
71. From following the ewes great with young he brought him to feed Jacob his people, and Israel his inheritance.
72. So he fed them according to the integrity of his heart; and guided them by the skillfulness of his hands.

Commentary_____

Verses 10-54 of Psalm 78 recounted the events and the relationship between a caring and faithful God and His "stubborn and rebellious" people (v. 8), from their deliverance out of Egypt until their entry into the Promised Land. Verses 55-72 highlight select incidents from the entry into the land until the rule of King David.

Joshua set up a center of worship and government at Shiloh in the territory allotted to the tribe of Ephraim, which was the central and prominent tribe. The Ark of the Covenant, that represented the presence of the LORD among His people, was housed there (Josh. 18 through 1 Sam. 4). Then the Ark was captured by the Philistines. When it was returned to Israel, it was taken to a place in Benjamin and then to Mt. Zion which was located on the border between Benjamin and Judah. David built his palace on the prominence which jutted out from Mt. Zion.

"I have gone astray like a lost sheep" (Ps. 119:176). "All we like sheep have gone astray" (Isa. 53:6). "My sheep hear my voice, and I know them, and they follow me" (Jn. 10:27). "For ye were sheep going astray, but are now returned unto the Shepherd and Bishop of your souls" (1 Pet. 2:25). God's people need a shepherd! David's appointment as shepherd (vv. 70-72) points to the "Son of David" (Lk. 1:32; Mt. 21:9) who will forever be both Israel's shepherd and ours!

Application_____

"Now all these things happened unto them for examples and they are written for our admonition, upon whom the ends of the world are come" (1 Cor. 10:11). They were God's people; we are God's people. When we as His people let our old natures rule, we act towards our loving God as the Israelites did. Thus we need to be admonished as they were!

Psalm 79

A Psalm of Asaph.

1. O GOD, the heathen are come into thine inheritance; thy holy temple have they defiled; they have laid Jerusalem on heaps.
2. The dead bodies of thy servants have they given *to be* meat unto the fowls of the heaven, the flesh of thy saints unto the beasts of the earth.
3. Their blood have they shed like water round about Jerusalem; and *there was* none to bury *them*.
4. We are become a reproach to our neighbors, a scorn and derision to them that are round about us.
5. How long, LORD? wilt thou be angry for ever? shall thy jealousy burn like fire?
6. Pour out thy wrath upon the heathen that have not known thee, and upon the kingdoms that have not called upon thy name.
7. For they have devoured Jacob, and laid waste his dwelling place.
8. O remember not against us former iniquities: let thy tender mercies speedily prevent us: for we are brought very low.
9. Help us, O God of our salvation, for the glory of thy name: and deliver us, and purge away our sins, for they name's sake.
10. Wherefore should the heathen say, Where *is* their God? let him be known among the heathen in our sight *by* the revenging of the blood of thy servants *which is* shed.
11. Let the sighing of the prisoner come before thee; according to the greatness of thy power preserve thou those that are appointed to die;
12. And render unto our neighbors sevenfold into their bosom their reproach, wherewith they have reproached thee, O Lord.
13. So we thy people and sheep of thy pasture will give thee thanks for ever: we will shew forth thy praise to all generations.

Commentary_____

The plaintive lament of verses 1-4 arises from the destruction brought upon Jerusalem by the Babylonians in the year 586BC (2 Ki. 25:8-10). Before Israel entered the Promised Land, the LORD warned that this very calamity would befall His people if they forsook Him and worshipped idols. Compare verse 2 with Deuteronomy 28:26.

"How long, LORD?" (v. 3). This has been the cry of suffering ones throughout the ages. This psalmist joins Job (Job 7:19), David (Ps. 6:3; 13:1, 2; 35:17), Moses (Ps. 90:13), Jeremiah (Jer. 12:4, 47:6), and Habakkuk (Hab. 1:2) in this plea. It was the cry of the angel on behalf of Jerusalem (Zech. 1:12). It continues to be the cry of suffering saints, and it will still be their cry in the future (Rev. 6:10). In times of travail, it seems the LORD is slow to rebuke evil and relieve suffering. "Why doesn't He hurry and do something?" we ask.

In verses 9-13, the psalmist presents to God reasons He should answer the petitions of verses 6-8. It is His holy name that is being reproached. There is a need for His great power to be manifested to the nations. It is His character to show mercy to His sinful people. They are His sheep and the ones who are called to offer thanks and praise unto Him.

"For the glory of Thy name. . .for Thy name's sake"(v. 9). The name of the LORD is infinitely precious to Him though it means so little to most men (Jer. 14:7, Ezk. 36:21-22). Satan is delighted when men profane the holy name of God.

Application_____

Although verse 13 looks forward to Israel's return to God as a nation, the "forever" and "all generations" make it applicable to us as well. A comparison of Jeremiah 13:11 to Ephesians 1:12 makes this evident. It is our privilege and responsibility to thank Him and glorify His name on Earth (1 Pet. 2:9).

Psalm 80

To the chief Musician upon Shoshannim-Eduth, A Psalm of Asaph.

1. GIVE EAR, O Shepherd of Israel, thou that leadest Joseph like a flock; thou that dwellest *between* the cherubims, shine forth.
2. Before Ephraim and Benjamin and Manasseh stir up thy strength, and come *and* save us.
3. Turn us again, O God, and cause thy face to shine; and we shall be saved.
4. O LORD God of hosts, how long wilt thou be angry against the prayer of thy people?
5. Thou feedest them with the bread of tears; and givest them tears to drink in great measure.
6. Thou makest us a strife unto our neighbors: and our enemies laugh among themselves.
7. Turn us again, O God of hosts, and cause thy face to shine; and we shall be saved.
8. Thou hast brought a vine out of Egypt: thou hast cast out the heathen, and planted it.
9. Thou preparedst *room* before it, and didst cause it to take deep root, and it filled the land.
10. The hills were covered with the shadow of it, and the boughs thereof *were like* the goodly cedars.
11. She sent out her boughs unto the sea, and her branches unto the river.
12. Why hast thou *then* broken down her hedges, so that all they which pass by the way do pluck her?
13. The boar out of the wood doth waste it, and the wild beast of the field doth devour it.
14. Return, we beseech thee, O God of hosts: look down from heaven, and behold, and visit this vine;
15. And the vineyard which thy right hand hath planted, and the branch *that* thou madest strong for thyself.
16. *It is* burned with fire, *it is* cut down: they perish at the rebuke of thy countenance.
17. Let thy hand be upon the man of thy right hand, upon the son of man *whom* thou madest strong for thyself.
18. So will not we go back from thee: quicken us, and we will call upon thy name.
19. Turn us again, O LORD God of hosts, cause thy face to shine; and shall be saved.

Commentary

This psalm was most likely written as the Assyrians were besieging Israel just before the ten northern tribes were taken captive (2 Ki. 17:5).

Deriving from the oft repeated Aaronic benediction (Num. 6:22-26), the psalm contains three refrains in the form of a petition (vv. 3, 7, 19). The psalmist progressively adds to the name of God. First, he calls upon Elohim—God in essence, that is, all that He is. Next he invokes the name *Elohim Sabaoth*—God who leads His people. He concludes by beseeching *Yahweh Elohim Sabaoth*—God who comes down and acts on behalf of His people. That is the God who dwells between the cherubim (Ex. 25:20-22).

Verses 4-6 present the plight of the people. Verses 8-11 describe the prosperity of the people under David and Solomon in metaphoric form. For God's own answer to the question of verse 12, and for the reason He does not respond favorably to the plea of verse 14, turn to Isaiah 5:1-7. God had given His special people position (v. 1), provision (v. 2), and privilege (v. 4). Punishment replaces opportunity for productiveness (vv. 5, 6). "For unto whomsoever much is given, of him shall much be required" (Lk. 12:48).

". . .We will call upon Thy name"(v. 18). When the nation of Israel calls upon their true Messiah "all Israel shall be saved," for "out of Zion the Deliverer shall come" (Rom. 11:26).

Application

The New Testament parallels for Isaiah 5:1-7 are John 15:1-6 and Hebrews 6:3-8. Why should God continue to tend a vineyard or cultivate a field that refuses to produce regardless of the care He bestows upon it? The parable of the fig tree in Luke 13:6-9 illustrates this principle.

Psalm 81

To the chief Musician upon Gittith, *A Psalm* of Asaph.

1. SING ALOUD unto God our strength: make a joyful noise unto the God of Jacob.
2. Take a psalm, and bring hither the timbrel, the pleasant harp with the psaltery.
3. Blow up the trumpet in the new moon, in the time appointed, on our solemn feast day.
4. For this *was* a statute for Israel, *and* a law of the God of Jacob.
5. This he ordained in Joseph *for* a testimony, when he went out through the land of Egypt: *where* I heard a language *that* I understood not.
6. I removed his shoulder from the burden: his hands were delivered from the pots.
7. Thou calledst in trouble, and I delivered thee; I answered thee in the secret place of thunder: I proved thee at the waters of Meribah. Selah.
8. Hear, O my people, and I will testify unto thee: O Israel, if thou wilt hearken unto me;
9. There shall no strange god be in thee; neither shalt thou worship any strange god.
10. I *am* the LORD thy God, which brought thee out of the land of Egypt: open thy mouth wide, and I will fill it.
11. But my people would not hearken to my voice; and Israel would none of me.
12. So I gave them up unto their own hearts' lust: *and* they walked in their own counsels.
13. Oh that my people had hearkened unto me, *and* Israel had walked in my ways!
14. I should soon have subdued their enemies, and turned my hand against their adversaries.
15. The haters of the LORD should have submitted themselves unto him: but their time should have endured for ever.
16. He should have fed them also with the finest of the wheat: and with honey out of the rock should I have satisfied thee.

Commentary_____

Throughout the New Testament as well as the Old Testament, biblical singing is a vocal, joyful offering to God
(Ex. 15:1, 21; Acts 16:25; Col. 3:16; Rev. 5:9). If you use a concordance to find verses that contain the words *song, singers* and *singing*, your study will confirm that God has a purpose in music. Notice particularly the special assignments given to singers and the special provision for singers in 2 Chronicles and Nehemiah.

God also uses trumpets, harps and other musical instruments for His purposes. Satan, too, instigates the use of music by God's people to further his purposes (Ex. 32:18; Dan. 3:15). God's people invest little time in discovering what music comes from the heart of God and what derives from the mind of Satan and apparently have little desire to discern the difference.

Verses 5-7 recall the deliverance from slavery in Egypt that God wrought for Israel as recorded in Exodus. In view of that deliverance, what does God ask of His people in verses 8 and 9? How did His people respond to that request (v. 11)? What did their responses cause God to do? (v. 12)? What would God have done for them if their hearts had been right towards Him (vv. 14-16)?

It is rather obvious that figurative language is being used in verse 16. What does it mean spiritually for a believer to be satisfied with "the finest of wheat; and with honey out of the Rock"?

Application_____

The use of music in our worship is important. Our worship should be an offering to God, not a means of self-gratification. As we truly worship Him, He will feed our souls.

Psalm 82

A Psalm of Asaph.

1. GOD STANDETH in the congregation of the mighty; he judgeth among the gods.
2. How long will ye judge unjustly, and accept the persons of the wicked? Selah.
3. Defend the poor and fatherless: do justice to the afflicted and needy.
4. Deliver the poor and needy: rid *them* out of the hand of the wicked.
5. They know not, neither will they understand; they walk on in darkness: all the foundations of the earth are out of course.
6. I have said, Ye *are* gods; and all of you *are* children of the most High.
7. But ye shall die like men, and fall like one of the princes.
8. Arise, O God, judge the earth: for thou shall inherit all nations.

Commentary_____

A good title for this psalm would be "The Judging of the Judges." The psalmist envisions a scene at which those charged with dispensing justice on Earth are summoned before the Judge of all the earth. In verse 2, the Judge points out the error of the earthly judges. In verses 3 and 4, they are told how they should be judging. In verse 5, the psalmist accuses them of disrupting the very foundations of society by their perverseness.

Verse 6 was quoted by the Lord Jesus in John 10:34 when the Jewish religious leaders took up stones to kill Him for blaspheming by claiming to be God.

Why does the psalmist call the judges "gods" in verses 1 and 6? Surely only God can judge. Yet He has ordained that affairs on Earth be administered by human agency. Therefore, when a human being judges, he is exercising a prerogative of deity and acting on behalf of God.

The Bible teaches both that we judge (1 Cor. 6:1-4) and that we judge not (Rom. 14:10). How then am I to know when to judge and when not to judge? I judge when I am involved in a God-given responsibility in the family, church or community. When as a parent I decide not to allow my child to spend the night at a neighbor's home, I am judging my neighbor within the scope of the God-given responsibility of parenthood. If I publicize that same neighbor's sinful television viewing practices, I am judging outside the scope of my God-given responsibility and usurping God's prerogative.

Application_____

The judges of the earth along with the rest of us need to remember that verse 8 of our psalm follows verse 7. We need to ponder 1 John 2:28 as well as Romans 14:10. The nations should carefully consider Isaiah 11:4—"For the Father. . .hath committed all judgment unto the Son" (Jn. 5:22).

Psalm 83

A Song *or* Psalm of Asaph.

1. KEEP NOT thou silence, O God: hold not thy peace, and be not still, O God.
2. For, lo, thine enemies make a tumult: and they that hate thee have lifted up the head.
3. They have taken crafty counsel against thy people, and consulted against thy hidden ones.
4. They have said, Come, and let us cut them off from *being* a nation; that the name of Israel may be no more in remembrance.
5. For they have consulted together with one consent: they are confederate against thee:
6. The tabernacles of Edom, and the Ishmaelites; of Moab, and the Hagarenes;
7. Gebal, and Ammon, and Amalek; the Philistines with the inhabitants of Tyre;
8. Assur also is joined with them: they have holpen the children of Lot. Selah.
9. Do unto them as *unto* the Midianites; as *to* Sisera, as *to* Jabin, at the brook of Kison:
10. *Which* perished at En-dor: they became *as* dung for the earth.
11. Make their nobles like Oreb, and like Zeeb: yea, all their princes as Zebah, and as Zalmunna:
12. Who said, Let us take to ourselves the houses of God in possession.
13. O my God, make them like a wheel; as the stubble before the wind.
14. As the fire burneth a wood, and as the flame setteth the mountains on fire;
15. So persecute them with thy tempest, and make them afraid with thy storm.
16. Fill their faces with shame; that they may seek thy name, O LORD.
17. Let them be confounded and troubled for ever; yea, let them be put to shame, and perish:
18. That *men* may know that thou, whose name alone *is* JEHOVAH, *art* the most high over all the earth.

Commentary_____

A number of episodes in Israel's past could furnish the historical basis for this psalm—for instance, 2 Chronicles 20:1-2 or Nehemiah 4:7. Verses 2-8 certainly are prophetic of the status between Israel and her Arab neighbors in the early twenty-first century. Just before the six-day war of 1967, Nasser, the ruler of Egypt, publicly uttered the very words recorded in verse 4. The nations involved in that war as combatants and/or their supporters inhabited the same geographical area as those listed in verses 6-8. Those words of Nasser are still the theme of Israel's enemies.

According to the psalmist, nations objecting to Israel's occupation of the land promised by God to Jacob's descendents (Gen. 28:13-15) are God's enemies. Joel 3:2 says that one of God's chief complaints against the nations of the world is "they have parted my land." The United Nations as an organization parted His land between Palestinians and Jews in 1948. More than a half century later, they are still insisting on such a partition. During the time of the judges (Jud. 7:12), when a powerful coalition of nations came against Israel, the assailants destroyed each other. A similar incident happened centuries later (2 Chr. 20:22-23). Interestingly, since Israel was re-established as an independent state in 1948, thousands more of its enemies have been killed by each other than by Israelis.

Application_____

Those of us who believe that the Word of God is true, take comfort in knowing that the time will come when verse 18 will be fulfilled. Daniel lets us know when it will happen (Dan. 2:44). We are privileged to willingly bow the knee to such a God before His enemies are forced to do so (Phil. 2:9, 10).

Psalm 84

To the chief Musician upon Gittith, A Psalm for the sons of Korah.

1. HOW AMIABLE *are* thy tabernacles, O LORD of hosts!
2. My soul longeth, yea, even fainteth for the courts of the LORD: my heart and my flesh crieth out for the living God.
3. Yea, the sparrow hath found an house, and the swallow a nest for herself, where she may lay her young, *even* thine altars, O LORD of hosts, my King, and my God.
4. Blessed *are* they that dwell in thy house: they will be still praising thee. Selah.
5. Blessed *is* the man whose strength *is* in thee; in whose heart *are* the ways *of them.*
6. *Who* passing through the valley of Baca make it a well; the rain also filleth the pools.
7. They go from strength to strength, *every one of them* in Zion appeareth before God.
8. O LORD God of hosts, hear my prayer: give ear, O God of Jacob. Selah.
9. Behold, O God our shield, and look upon the face of thine anointed.
10. For a day in thy courts *is* better than a thousand. I had rather be a doorkeeper in the house of my God, than to dwell in the tents of wickedness.
11. For the LORD God *is* a sun and shield: the LORD will give grace and glory: no good *thing* will he withhold from them that walk uprightly.
12. O LORD of hosts, blessed *is* the man that trusteth in thee.

Commentary

This psalm, consisting of three four-verse stanzas, is one of twelve psalms ascribed to the "Sons of Korah." These men held hereditary positions as musicians and watchmen at the Temple of Jerusalem. The psalmist sings a song of praise and appreciation for the privilege of living his entire life at the one place on Earth where the LORD had provided a procedure whereby His people could approach a holy God.

"Tabernacles," "courts," "altars," and "house" are descriptive designations for God's dwelling place. "Soul," "heart," and "flesh" are equivalent to "spirit and soul and body" (1 Th. 5:23). Like the sparrow and the swallow that dwell in the "courts of the LORD" (v. 2, 3), the psalmist appreciates the place, but His deepest desire is to be in the presence of the God of the place.

Throughout the psalm, the speaker uses ten different terms to describe God. He uses the name "LORD of Hosts" three times.

Baca means "weeping" (v. 6). From this verse we derive the expression, "this vale of tears" as a designation for the pilgrim's journey through this spiritually dry world. Those faithful worshipers who traveled through the desert found a spiritual oasis at Zion, which was their name for the Temple mount. The psalmist is grateful for the privilege of living at the oasis. He prefers the lowliest assignment in the work and presence of his God above anything the world has to offer.

Application

It is proper for dedicated believers to sense the special presence of the Lord when we gather at our designated places of worship (Heb. 10:25). However, if our entire being is consumed with a desire for His presence, we may live in the oasis of His provision moment by moment because of what Christ has done for us. If we truly believe the promise of verse 11, we live above the trials of "this vale of tears."

Psalm 85

To the chief Musician, A Psalm for the sons of Korah.

1. LORD, THOU hast been favourable unto thy land: thou hast brought back the captivity of Jacob.
2. Thou hast forgiven the iniquity of thy people, thou hast covered all their sin. Selah.
3. Thou hast taken away all thy wrath: thou hast turned *thyself* from the fierceness of thine anger.
4. Turn us, O God of our salvation, and cause thine anger toward us to cease.
5. Wilt thou be angry with us for ever? wilt thou draw out thine anger to all generations?
6. Wilt thou not revive us again: that thy people may rejoice in thee?
7. Shew us thy mercy, O LORD, and grant us thy salvation.
8. I will hear what God the LORD will speak: for he will speak peace unto his people, and to his saints: but let them not turn again to folly.
9. Surely his salvation *is* nigh them that fear him; that glory may dwell in our land.
10. Mercy and truth are met together; righteousness and peace have kissed *each other.*
11. Truth shall spring out of the earth; and righteousness shall look down from heaven.
12. Yea, the LORD shall give *that which is* good; and our land shall yield her increase.
13. Righteousness shall go before him; and shall set *us* in the way of his steps.

Commentary

The historical basis of this psalm is the return of Israel to the land after the captivity in Babylon. The specific occasion of the writing may have been the revival recorded in Nehemiah 8. The first three verses praise the LORD for bringing His people back to the land. Verses 4-7 express a suitable petition for every devout Israelite from that time and even to "all generations" up to the present time. Verses 8-13 contain ten assuring promises in answer to the petition. We can outline the psalm as follows:

--praise for the past (vv. 1-3)
--petition for the present (vv. 4-7)
--promises for the future (vv. 8-13)

The promise of peace (v. 8) awaits the nation Israel's acceptance of their Messiah (Zech. 12:10).

Notice that the first statement of each verse (vv. 9-13) speaks of the first coming of Christ and has already been fulfilled. Salvation was made "near" (v. 9) to Jew (Mk. 12:34) and Gentile (Eph. 2:13) at Christ's first coming. Mercy and truth met at the Cross. Truth sprang from the Earth in the incarnation at His birth (Isa. 53:2). God gave the ultimate of that which is good when He "came unto His own" (Jn. 1:11; 3:16). The righteous One came and was crucified (Lk. 23:47).

Glory (v. 9) will dwell in the land when "righteousness and peace will kiss each other" (Isa. 32:17). When righteousness reigns (Mt. 6:10), Israel's land will be productive, and its people will walk in His ways.

Application

Although this is not one of the sixteen psalms classified as "Messianic," it speaks of the Messiah. That should alert us to look for the Lord Jesus in every psalm (Lk. 24:44). Although sometimes hidden, Jesus is the subject of the Old Testament as well as the New Testament (Jn. 5:39). The Scriptures that the Bereans searched (Acts 17:11) were the thirty-nine books of the Old Testament.

Psalm 86

A Prayer of David.

1. BOW DOWN thine ear, O LORD, hear me: for I *am* poor and needy.
2. Preserve my soul: for I *am* holy: O thou my God, save thy servant that trusteth in thee.
3. Be merciful unto me, O Lord: for I cry unto thee daily.
4. Rejoice the soul of thy servant: for unto thee, O Lord, do I lift up my soul.
5. For thou, Lord, *art* good, and ready to forgive; and plenteous in mercy unto all them that call upon thee.
6. Give ear, O LORD, unto my prayer; and attend to the voice of my supplications.
7. In the day of trouble I will call upon thee: for thou wilt answer me.
8. Among the gods *there is* none like unto thee, O Lord; neither *are there any works* like unto thy works.
9. All nations whom thou hast made shall come and worship before thee, O Lord; and shall glorify thy name.
10. For thou *art* great, and doest wondrous things: thou *art* God alone.
11. Teach me thy way, O LORD, I will walk in thy truth: unite my heart to fear thy name.
12. I will praise thee, O Lord my God, with all my heart: and I will glorify thy name for evermore.
13. For great *is* thy mercy toward me: and thou hast delivered my soul from the lowest hell.
14. O God, the proud are risen against me, and the assemblies of violent *men* have sought after my soul; and have not set thee before them.
15. But thou, O Lord, *art* a God full of compassion, and gracious, long-suffering, and plenteous in mercy and truth.
16. O turn unto me, and have mercy upon me; give thy strength unto thy servant, and save the son of thine handmaid.
17. Shew me a token for good; that they which hate me may see *it*, and be ashamed: because thou, LORD, hast holpen me, and comforted me.

Commentary

Some Bible prayers are primarily confession (Ezra 9; Ps. 51). Some are principally praise and adoration (I Sam. 2). Others are mostly thanksgiving (1 Chr. 29). Many, including this one, are largely supplication.

There are six petitions in the first four verses, followed by nine more petitions in verses 6, 11, and 16-17. Yet there is still confession in verse 1 and adoration in verses 5, 8-10, and 15. Verses 12 and 13 contain both praise and an aura of thanksgiving.

Four times the psalmist calls upon *Yahweh* (LORD). That is the name of the great God, majestic in essence, as He deigns to look upon His lowly human creature and act on his behalf. Seven times the psalmist invokes the name *Adonai* (Lord). That is the same God, who as the master receives the plea of his servant.

David is beset by an enemy and waivers between distress (vv. 1, 14) and trust (vv. 2, 7). He begins by reciting to Yahweh two reasons He should respond favorably to his petitions. First, he declares himself to be "poor and needy" (v. 1). Then he says, "I am holy" (v. 2). In context, that means he has been set aside for God's purposes and is devoted to Him. (The New Testament parallel for this definition of holiness is Romans 12:1, 2.) David then, in essence, says to his master, "I cry to you daily with a lifted soul and you are merciful to such. Therefore, you should attend to my supplication."

Application

If you believe, as did the psalmist, that your master is a God of compassion, grace, patience, mercy, and truth (v. 15), you should trust Him to give His servant all strength necessary for any situation (v. 16; Phil. 4:13). Your basis for trust is the knowledge that He has helped you and comforted you in the past (v. 17).

Psalm 87

A Psalm *or* Song for the sons of Korah.

1. HIS FOUNDATION *is* in the holy mountains.
2. The LORD loveth the gates of Zion more than all the dwellings of Jacob.
3. Glorious thing are spoken of thee, O city of God. Selah.
4. I will make mention of Rahab and Babylon to them that know me: behold Philistia, and Tyre, with Ethiopia; this *man* was born there.
5. And of Zion it shall be said, This and that man was born in her: and the highest himself shall establish her.
6. The LORD shall count, when he writeth up the people, *that* this *man* was born there. Selah.
7. As well the singers as the players on instruments *shall be there:* all my springs *are* in thee.

Commentary

"For the LORD has chosen Zion; He has desired it for His habitation. This is my rest forever: here will I dwell; for I have desired it" (Ps. 132:13-14). Six times in Deuteronomy 12, before Israel entered into the land, Moses told the people that the LORD would choose a particular place for "His name to dwell." That's the place the LORD told Solomon to build the Temple (2 Chron. 7:12).

"The LORD loveth the gates of Zion" (v. 2). "For out of Zion shall go forth the law, and the Word of the LORD from Jerusalem (Isa. 2:3). "But Zion said, the LORD hath forsaken me" (Isa. 49:14). "Behold, I have engraved you upon the palms of my hands; thy walls are continually before me" (Isa. 49:16). "Thus saith the LORD of hosts; I am jealous for Jerusalem and for Zion with a great jealously" (Zech. 1:14). "Glorious things are spoken of thee, O city of God, Selah" (v. 3). "Great is the LORD, and greatly to be praised in the city of our God, in the mountain of His holiness. Beautiful for situation, the joy of the whole earth, is Mount Zion, on the sides of the north, the city of the great King" (Ps. 48:1-2).

Rahab (v. 4) is a name for Egypt (Isa. 51:9), which is southwest of Jerusalem. Babylon is northeast. Philistia, Tyre and Ethiopia are west, north, and south, respectively. The same countries, from every direction, which historically wanted Israel "cut off from being a nation" (Ps. 83:1-8), will come to Jerusalem to worship the King (Isa. 2:2-3; 56:7; 60:2-3 and Zech. 8:22, 14:16).

They will desire to be considered native citizens of Jerusalem.

Application

"And when He was come near, He beheld the city and wept over it, saying, If thou had known, even thou, at least in this thy day, the things which belong unto peace! But now, they are hidden from thine eyes" (Lk. 19:41-42). There will be no peace on Earth until the Prince of Peace reigns in Jerusalem. Therefore, "pray for the peace of Jerusalem" (Ps. 122:6).

Psalm 88

A Song *or* Psalm for the sons of Korah, to the chief Musician upon Mahalath Leannoth, Maschil of Heman the Ezrahite.

1. O LORD God, of my salvation, I have cried day *and* night before thee:
2. Let my prayer come before thee: incline thine ear unto my cry;
3. For my soul is full of troubles: and my life draweth nigh unto the grave.
4. I am counted with them that go down into the pit: I am as a man *that hath* no strength.
5. Free among the dead, like the slain that lie in the grave, whom thou rememberest no more: and they are cut off from thy hand.
6. Thou hast laid me in the lowest pit, in darkness, in the deeps.
7. Thy wrath lieth hard upon me, and thou hast afflicted *me* with all thy waves, Selah.
8. Thou hast put away mine acquaintance far from me; thou hast made me an abomination unto them: *I am* shut up, and I cannot come forth.
9. Mine eye mourneth by reason of affliction: LORD, I have called daily upon thee, I have stretched out my hands unto thee.
10. Wilt thou shew wonders to the dead? shall the dead arise *and* praise thee? Selah.
11. Shall thy lovingkindness be declared in the grave? *or* thy faithfulness in destruction?
12. Shall my wonders be known in the dark? and thy righteousness in the land of forgetfulness?
13. But unto thee have I cried, O LORD; and in the morning shall my prayer prevent thee.
14. LORD, why castest thou off my soul? *why* hidest thou thy face from me?
15. I *am* afflicted and ready to die from *my* youth up: *while* I suffer thy terrors I am distracted.
16. Thy fierce wrath goeth over me; thy terrors have cut me off.
17. They came round about me daily like water; they compassed me about together.
18. Lover and friend hast thou put far from me, *and* mine acquaintance into darkness.

Commentary

Surely this is the most sorrowful of all the psalms. Not one ray of hope is emitted from its woeful words. Even in David's direst distress, he was able to say, "For in Thee, O LORD, do I hope; Thou wilt hear O Lord, my God" (Ps. 38:15). Though Job was in deep despair, he proclaimed, "I know that I shall be justified" (Job 13:18). In the midst of misery he maintained, "When He hath tried me, I shall come forth as gold" (23:10).

Verses 8, 9, 15 and 18 suggest that the psalmist has suffered from leprosy for many years and is going blind as he approaches the grave. Life on Earth has held neither moments of gladness nor respite from pain, loneliness, rejection and darkness.

Why did God include such a portion in His Word? First, it presents a graphic picture of the earthly plight of countless sufferers. Second, it furnishes a needed contrast. Aren't you more thankful for your lot in life after reading this psalm?

Now let us look at this pitiful being from the eternal perspective. He has placed his trust in the one true God (vv. 1, 9, 13). Thus we can conclude that his God is about to release him from his bonds and bring him into eternal bliss (Job 14:15). Is he not better off than the most fortunate unsaved person that ever lived? Every moment of affliction has produced "a far more exceeding and eternal weight of glory" on his behalf (2 Cor. 4:17). God has all eternity to even things out for him.

Application

An eternal perspective solves every problem for a believer who has learned to trust the promises of God during every circumstance. Two great examples of this are recounted in the New Testament: the apostle Paul, in 2 Corinthians 12: 7-10 and the Lord Jesus Christ, in Hebrews 12:2-3.

Psalm 89:1-18

Maschil of Ethan the Ezrahite.

1. I WILL sing of the mercies of the LORD for ever: with my mouth will I make known thy faithfulness to all generations.
2. For I have said, Mercy shall be built up for ever: thy faithfulness shalt thou establish in the very heavens.
3. I have made a covenant with my chosen, I have sworn unto David my servant.
4. Thy seed will I establish for ever, and build up thy throne to all generations. Selah.
5. And the heavens shall praise thy wonders, O LORD: thy faithfulness also in the congregation of the saints.
6. For who in the heaven can be compared unto the LORD? *who* among the sons of the mighty can be likened unto the LORD?
7. God is greatly to be feared in the assembly of the saints, and to be had in reverence of all *them that are* about him.
8. O LORD God of hosts, who *is* a strong LORD like unto thee? or to thy faithfulness round about thee?
9. Thou rulest the raging of the sea: when the waves thereof arise, thou stillest them.
10. Thou hast broken Rahab in pieces, as one that is slain; thou hast scattered thine enemies with thy strong arm.
11. The heavens *are* thine, the earth also *is* thine: *as for* the world and the fulness thereof, thou hast founded them.
12. The north and the south thou hast created them: Tabor and Hermon shall rejoice in thy name.
13. Thou hast a mighty arm: strong is thy hand, *and* high is thy right hand.
14. Justice and judgment *are* the habitation of thy throne: mercy and truth shall go before thy face.
15. Blessed *is* the people that know the joyful sound: they shall walk, O LORD, in the light of thy countenance.
16. In thy name shall they rejoice all the day: and in thy righteousness shall they be exalted.
17. For thou *art* the glory of their strength: and in thy favour our horn shall be exalted.
18. For the LORD is our defence; and the Holy One of Israel *is* our king.

Commentary_____

The theme of Psalm 89 is God's faithfulness, an attribute which the psalmist desires to spotlight at a time when it appears as though God has forgotten His chosen people. Because of rebellion and idolatry, they have been dispossessed and are held captive in a foreign land.

God's mercy (loving kindness) is extolled in accompaniment with His faithfulness. These two attributes are each mentioned seven times in the psalm. God will show forth these attributes forever to all generations. In verses 3 and 4, the psalmist uses the words of God Himself to confirm the Davidic Covenant (2 Sam. 7:8-16). He highlights the promises God made to David concerning his progeny and his throne. The angelic beings in Heaven will react with praise as they watch the fulfillment of God's promises to David (vv. 5-7) as evidence of His faithfulness.

God is able to perform faithfully because He is omnipotent (vv. 8-13) and therefore sovereign (vv. 9-10, 18). (Rahab is Egypt—see commentary on Psalm 87.) God deserves to be sovereign because He is Creator (vv. 11-12) and because He is just and merciful (v. 14). He is truth personified. Tabor and Herman are prominent mountains.

The figurative use of the word *horn* derives from Hannah's prayer in 1 Samuel 2:1-10. When an individual is said to "be a horn" or "have a horn," he has a usable advantage over another individual, just as a horned animal has over a hornless one.
(See Dt. 33:17 and Ps. 75: 4-5, 10.) The father of John the Baptist speaks of Christ as being the "Horn of our Salvation" (Lk. 1:69).

Application_____

The hymn "Great Is Thy Faithfulness" comes from Psalm 89. If you pay careful attention to the words the composer uses in this hymn, you will enhance your meditation on this psalm.

Psalm 89:19-37

19. Then thou spakest in vision to thy holy one, and saidist, I have laid help upon *one that is* mighty; I have exalted *one* chosen out of the people.
20. I have found David my servant; with my holy oil have I anointed him:
21. With whom my hand shall be established: mine arm also shall strength him.
22. The enemy shall not exact upon him; nor the son of wickedness afflict him.
23. And I will beat down his foes before his face, and plague them that hate him.
24. But my faithfulness and my mercy *shall be* with him: and in my name shall his horn be exalted.
25. I will set his hand also in the sea, and his right hand in the rivers.
26. He shall cry unto me, Thou *art* my father, my God, and the rock of my salvation.
27. Also I will make him *my* firstborn, higher than the kings of the earth.
28. My mercy will I keep for him for evermore, and my covenant shall stand fast with him.
29. His seed also will I make *to endure* for ever, and his throne as the days of heaven.
30. If his children forsake my law, and walk not in my judgments;
31. If they break my statutes, and keep not my commandments;
32. Then will I visit their transgression with the rod, and their iniquity with stripes.
33. Nevertheless my lovingkindness will I not utterly take from him, nor suffer my faithfulness to fail.
34. My covenant will I not break, nor alter the thing that is gone out of my lips.
35. Once have I sworn by my holiness that I will not lie unto David.
36. His seed shall endure for ever, and his throne as the sun before me.
37. It shall be established for ever as the moon, and *as* a faithful witness in heaven. Selah.

Commentary_____

In verses 19-37 of Psalm 89, the LORD Himself speaks again in the first person. In verses 3 and 4, He summarized the covenant He made with David (2 Sam. 7:8-16). In verses 19-37, he presents an exposition of the covenant, expanding the details.

Acts 13:22 makes a reference to the words of verse 20. Hebrews 1:5-6 draws from verses 26 and 27. "Higher than the kings of earth" looks forward to David's greater son, the Messiah. The term "firstborn" denotes position and prerogative rather than order of birth. Among kings, Messiah will have the firstborn position (Ps. 72:11,138:4; Isa. 60:3). He has that same position over God's creation (Col. 1:15), in the resurrection from the dead (Col. 1:18) and over the church (Heb. 12:23).

The references to Messiah qualify Psalm 89 as one of the sixteen Messianic Psalms. These sixteen psalms, in whole or in part, prophesy of the first or second coming of Christ. In addition, various New Testament scriptures document that these psalms refer to Christ.

Verses 28 and 29 reaffirm that the covenant with David is "forever." In verses 30-32, God warns succeeding kings in David's line that disobedience and iniquity will result in disciplinary judgment. At the writing of this psalm, judgment has already fallen, but that does not negate the covenant. It is "forever" (vv. 33-37)!

Application_____

God is loving, kind, and faithful. He is also holy. He will surely keep His covenants; but not without first dealing with the sin of His people. Hebrews 10:26-31 applies this same principle to us—"The Lord shall judge His people." However, He promises, "I will never leave thee, nor forsake thee" (Heb. 13:5).

Psalm 89:38-52

38. But thou hast cast off and abhorred, thou hast been wroth with thine anointed.
39. Thou hast made void the covenant of thy servant: thou hast profaned his crown *by casting it* to the ground.
40. Thou hast broken down all his hedges; thou hast brought his strong holds to ruin.
41. All that pass by the way spoil him: he is a reproach to his neighbours.
42. Thou hast set up the right hand of his adversaries; thou hast made all his enemies to rejoice.
43. Thou hast also turned the edge of his sword, and hast not made him to stand in the battle.
44. Thou hast made his glory to cease, and cast his throne down to the ground.
45. The days of his youth hast thou shortened: thou hast covered him with shame. Selah.
46. How long, LORD? wilt thou hide thyself for ever? shall thy wrath burn like fire?
47. Remember how short my time is: wherefore hast thou made all men in vain?
48. What man *is he that* liveth, and shall not see death? shall he deliver his soul from the hand of the grave? Selah.
49. Lord, where *are* thy former lovingkindnesses, *which* thou swarest unto David in thy truth?
50. Remember, Lord, the reproach of thy servants; *how* I do bear in my bosom *the reproach of* all the mighty people.
51. Wherewith thine enemies have reproached, O LORD; wherewith they have have reproached the footsteps of thine anointed.
52. Blessed *be* the LORD for evermore. Amen, and Amen.

Commentary_____

During the reign of King David, Heman, Aspah, and Ethan were appointed over the music in the worship of the LORD (1 Chr. 15:16-17, 19). For centuries their descendants inherited their positions. The psalms written by the descendants of these men were ascribed to the ancestor from whom they received their offices. Similarly, thrones occupied by descendants of David were considered to be "the throne of David."

In verses 1-37 of Psalm 89, the psalmist was fulfilling his office by leading the people in praise and adoration concerning God's faithfulness. Twice, God Himself spoke through the psalmist, confirming and expanding the covenant He had made with David.

In verses 38-45, the psalmist presents the response of the people. They measure God's promises by their present circumstances. Their king has been deposed, made old in his youth, and covered with shame (vv. 38-39, 44-45). His citadel is destroyed (v. 40). His city has been plundered (v. 41). His enemies are exalted and rejoicing (v. 42). His army has been slaughtered (v. 43). Therefore, the people accuse God of violating His own Word. There is not one word of trust in God or confession of the sin that caused the problem!

In verses 46-51, the psalmist speaks for himself. He presents God with two reasons He should speedily restore His people: first, life is short, and he wants deliverance before he dies; second, the enemy is bringing reproach upon God's king and His people.

Verse 52 is not an integral part of the psalm. Rather, it is the usual benediction at the close of each book (Ps. 41:13; 72:19).

Application_____

Blaming God for adversities is evidence of a lack of faith. A desire to please Him will cure the unbelief (Heb. 11:6). The Holy Spirit will measure out faith to us as we read and trust His Word (Rom. 10:17).

Psalm 90

A Prayer of Moses the man of God.

1. LORD, THOU hast been our dwelling place in all generations.
2. Before the mountains were brought forth, or ever thou hadst formed the earth and the world, even from everlasting to everlasting, thou *art* God.
3. Thou turnest man to destruction; and sayest, Return, ye children of man.
4. For a thousand years in thy sight *are but* as yesterday when it is past, and *as* a watch in the night.
5. Thou carriest them away as with a flood; they are *as* a sleep: in the morning *they are* like grass *which* groweth up.
6. In the morning it flourisheth, and groweth up: in the evening it is cut down, and withereth.
7. For we are consumed by thine anger, and by thy wrath are we troubled.
8. Thou hast set our iniquities before thee, our secret *sins* in the light of thy countenance.
9. For all our days are passed away in thy wrath: we spend our years as a tale *that is told.*
10. The days of our years *are* threescore years and ten; and if by reason of strength *they be* fourscore years, yet *is* their strength labour and sorrow; for it is soon cut off, and we fly away.
11. Who knoweth the power of thine anger? even according to thy fear, *so is* thy wrath.
12. So teach *us* to number our days, that we may apply *our* hearts unto wisdom.
13. Return, O LORD, how long? and let it repent thee concerning thy servants.
14. O satisfy us early with thy mercy; that we may rejoice and be glad all our days.
15. Make us glad according to the days *wherein* thou hast afflicted us, *and* the years *wherein* we have seen evil.
16. Let thy work appear unto thy servants, and thy glory unto their children.
17. And let the beauty of the LORD our God be upon us: and establish the work of our hands upon us; yea, the work of our hands establish thou it.

Commentary

The hymn, "O God Our Help in Ages Past," written by Isaac Watts three centuries ago, is a poetic commentary on Psalm 90. A perusal of the hymn's words will contribute to the understanding of the psalm.

The psalm is one of three songs written by Moses. The first psalm he wrote is a joyous song of redemption, composed after Israel's deliverance from slavery in Egypt (Ex. 15:1-19). Next comes this psalm, written by the weary leader of God's people who needs divine help to successfully finish his earthly sojourn. Moses' third psalm is a song of instruction, written to people about to enter battle to possess the land under new leadership (Dt. 32:1-44).

Psalm 90 consists of three stanzas. Before the psalmist brings his petitions to the LORD (vv. 13-17), he first acknowledges the majesty of the one to whom he prays (vv. 1-6). Next, he confesses what he and his people are before such an awesome one (vv. 7-12). When we adequately express our understanding of the greatness of our God and see ourselves as He sees us, then our petitions will be short, and they will be presented from the right perspective.

In an aura of awe, Moses contrasts the eternality and stability of God with the transitory and sinful nature of man. Because life is so short, Moses desires wisdom so that he may properly utilize every day. He asks for evidence of God's presence so that the days of gladness will equal those of sorrow. He wants the hands of God to guide the work of his own hands.

Application

The three songs of Moses apply to us in the following ways: The song in Exodus parallels the song that flows from every redeemed one who experiences true conversion; Psalm 90 voices the prayer of those in the midst of trial during years of service; The Deuteronomy song is preparation for those launching into the battle. See the comments of Moses about that song in Deuteronomy 32:44-47.

Psalm 91

1. *HE THAT* dwelleth in the secret place of the most High shall abide under the shadow of the Almighty.

2. I will say of the LORD, *He is* my refuge and my fortress: my God; in him will I trust.

3. Surely he shall deliver thee from the snare of the fowler, *and* from the noisome pestilence.

4. He shall cover thee with his feathers, and under his wings shalt thou trust: his truth *shall be thy* shield and buckler.

5. Thou shalt not be afraid for the terror by night; *nor* for the arrow *that* flieth by day;

6. *Nor* for the pestilence *that* walketh in darkness; *nor* for the destruction *that* wasteth at noonday.

7. A thousand shall fall at thy side, and ten thousand at thy right hand; *but* it shall not come nigh thee.

8. Only with thine yes shalt thou behold and see the reward of the wicked.

9. Because thou hast made the LORD, *which is* my refuge, *even* the most High, thy habitation;

10. There shall no evil befall thee, neither shall any plague come nigh thy dwelling.

11. For he shall give his angels charge over thee, to keep thee in all thy ways.

12. Thy shall bear thee up in *their* hands, lest thou dash thy foot against a stone.

13. Thou shalt tread upon the lion and adder: the young lion and the dragon shalt thou trample under feet.

14. Because he hath set his love upon me, therefore will I deliver him: I will set him on high, because he hath known my name.

15. He shall call upon me, and I will answer him: I *will be* with him in trouble; I will deliver him, and honour him.

16. With long life will I satisfy him, and shew him my salvation.

Commentary_____

Verses 1 and 9 tie this psalm to Psalm 90. It was probably composed centuries after Moses' psalm and was arranged for congregational worship following the reading of Psalm 90. The psalmist begins by offering a place of security to each individual who makes the LORD his dwelling place as did Moses. Then in verse 2, the psalmist gives his own witness to his trust in a personal God.

In verses 3-8, he uses the second person singular to impress upon each listener that the promises are individual. Before he continues, he stresses in verse 9 that the promises are meant for those who abide in the LORD.

Verse 11 introduces us to the ministry of guardian angels who are assigned to protect us physically from demonic attack and other dangers that would hinder us from fulfilling God's purposes for us during our earthly sojourn (Dan. 6:22; Mt. 2:13,19; Acts 5:19; Heb. 1:14). In tempting Jesus, Satan quoted from verses 11 and 12, except that he omitted the important phrase "in all thy ways" (Lk. 4:10-11). "Dash thy foot" and "bruise his heel" are figurative expressions; they are used here and elsewhere in Scripture as euphemisms for death (Gen. 3:15, Isa. 53:5, 8).

"I will deliver"; "I will set on high"; "I will answer"; "I will be present"; "I will honor"; "I will satisfy"; "I will show my salvation." In verses 14-16 the LORD Himself speaks through the psalmist in the first person with a seven-fold promise to those who really love Him. In the Old Testament "long life" often means a fully satisfying life rather than additional years of earthly existence.

Application_____

Many Christians quote Proverbs 3:5, 6 as their "life verse." However, in practical living some leave out "in all thy ways." When it comes to marriage, occupation, avocation, possessions and amusement, they want to make choices on their own.

Psalm 92

A Psalm *or* Song for the sabbath day.

1. IT IS a good *thing* to give thanks unto the LORD, and to sing praises unto thy name, O most High:
2. To shew forth thy lovingkindness in the morning, and thy faithfulness every night,
3. Upon an instrument of ten strings, and upon the psaltery; upon the harp with a solemn sound.
4. For thou, LORD, hast made me glad through thy work: I will triumph in the works of thy hands.
5. O LORD, how great are thy works! *and* thy thoughts are very deep.
6. A brutish man knoweth not; neither doth a fool understand this.
7. When the wicked spring as the grass, and when all the workers of iniquity flourish; *it is* that they shall be destroyed for ever:
8. But thou, LORD, *art most* high for evermore.
9. For, lo, thine enemies, O LORD, for, lo, thine enemies shall perish; all the workers of iniquity shall be scattered.
10. But my horn shalt thou exalt like *the horn of* an unicorn: I shall be anointed with fresh oil.
11. Mine eye also shall see *my desire* on mine enemies, *and* mine ears shall hear *my desire* of the wicked that rise up against me.
12. The righteous shall flourish like the palm tree: he shall grow like a cedar in Lebanon.
13. Those that be planted in the house of the LORD shall flourish in the courts of our God.
14. They shall still bring forth fruit in old age; they shall be fat and flourishing;
15. To shew that the LORD *is* upright: *he is* my rock, and *there is* no unrighteousness in him.

Commentary_____

What better interpretation of the first three verses of Psalm 92 could we present than Isaac Watts' classic hymn of the faith:

> How good it is to thank the Lord,
> And praise to You, Most High, accord.
> To show Your love with morning light,
> And tell Your faithfulness each night;
> Yea, good it is Your praise to sing,
> And all our sweetest music bring.

Vocal and instrumental music should be offered to the Lord because it is a gift from the Lord. God graciously provides such a gift even to those who offer Him no thanks for it. Intricate flower blossoms may be admired in a lovely bouquet or in a formal garden, but the source of their beauty is the mind of God. This is true of musical arrangements as well.

The psalmist is made glad, and he triumphs because of the greatness of the LORD's works and the profoundness of His thoughts. Not only are His thoughts "deep" (v. 5), they are very high (Isa. 55:9), "precious" (Ps. 139:17), and numberless (Ps. 139:18). They are "to all generations" (Ps. 33:11) and directed toward us individually (Ps. 40:17).

What kind of thoughts does He have towards me? See Jeremiah 29:11. Wonder of wonders! His thoughts are knowable through His prophets. (See also Amos 3:7, 4:13).

Verse 8 is a high mountain above the valley of verse 7 where we live while the enemy flourishes. When our eyes are upon the mountain, our horns are exalted above the horns of the wicked (Ps. 75:10), and we flourish and bring forth fruit because we are planted in the house of the LORD.

Application_____

Music is a gift from God and should be offered to Him from our hearts. His gracious gift ministers to us as we offer it to Him through our worship.

Psalm 93

1. THE LORD reigneth, he is clothed with majesty; the LORD is clothed with strength, *wherewith* he hath girded himself: the world also is stablished, that it cannot be moved.

2. Thy throne *is* established of old: thou *art* from everlasting.

3. The floods have lifted up, O LORD, the floods have lifted up their voice; the floods lift up their waves.

4. The LORD on high *is* mightier than the noise of many waters, *yea, than* the mighty waves of the sea.

5. Thy testimonies are very sure: holiness becometh thine house, O LORD, for ever.

Commentary_____

The octet of Psalms 93-100 has a common theme—The LORD reigns, therefore sing! This particular psalm highlights four attributes of God which enable Him to manifest absolute sovereignty—His majesty, His omnipotence, His immovability, and His eternality. To be "clothed" with majesty and strength is to possess those qualities to the fullest degree.

Grandeur, splendor, authoritative aura, awesome presence—there are no words adequate to describe the majesty of the LORD! Perhaps His majesty is best understood by the human reactions of those who actually glimpsed it (Isa. 6:1-5; Ezk. 1:28).

The verb *gird* (v. 1), derived from the noun *girdle*, is frequently used figuratively in the Bible. Because the connotation of the word has changed since Bible times, modern translators avoid the use of *girdle* and tend to paraphrase sentences using *gird*. However, this practice can negate the figurative meaning of such phrases as "gird up the loins of your mind" (1 Pet. 1:13). In Bible times the girdle, an important item of male apparel, was tightened so that the individual wearing it could work, run or fight. One who was *girded* was ready, willing and able to do any task.

Jeremiah calls overwhelming military might a "flood" (Jer. 46:7-8, 47:2). Satan has used and will continue to use such a flood in his attempt to destroy Israel (Rev. 12:15). The LORD is ready, willing and able, in His time, to utterly dry up any flood generated by Satan or by the nations of this world.

Application_____

The LORD's testimonies are those parts of Scripture which tell of His personality and His purpose. For instance, He is holy and therefore desires to see holiness exemplified in the members of His household. Since He is immutable, that desire will never cease. If His creatures do not desire to mesh with His purpose, they cannot be a part of His household.

Psalm 94:1-11

1. O LORD God, to whom vengeance belongeth; O God, to whom vengeance belongeth, shew thyself.
2. Lift up thyself, thou judge of the earth: render a reward to the proud.
3. LORD, how long shall the wicked, how long shall the wicked triumph?
4. *How long* shall they utter *and* speak hard things? *and* all the workers of iniquity boast themselves?
5. They break in pieces thy people, O *Lord*, and afflict thine heritage.
6. They slay the widow and the stranger, and murder the fatherless.
7. Yet they say, the LORD shall not see, neither shall the God of Jacob regard *it.*
8. Understand, ye brutish among the people: and *ye* fools, when will ye be wise?
9. He that planted the ear, shall he not hear? he that formed the eye, shall he not see?
10. He that chastiseth the heathen, shall not he correct? he that teacheth man knowledge, *shall not he know?*
11. The LORD knoweth the thoughts of man, that they *are* vanity.

Commentary_____

The one who occupies the throne wears a crown upon his head and holds a scepter in his hand. The crown represents monarchic privilege and prerogative; the scepter represents monarchic obligation and responsibility. A king must judge!

The psalmist is beseeching the Judge to fulfill His responsibility to condemn wickedness and vindicate righteousness. In effect he is saying, "We recognize your right to the crown—now use your scepter! " The wicked boast, they oppress, they murder, and they ignore God. Therefore, the psalmist asks, "Shall not the Judge of all the earth do right?"(Gen. 18:25).

At verse 8, the psalmist recognizes that it is not his job to judge the Judge, but does understand that he should warn the wicked. Thus he addresses them directly, essentially saying, "How foolish and stupid of you to think that the Creator of your ear cannot hear. If He knows enough to design and form something as intricate as your eye, can He not see everything you do? He knows everything that transpires in His creation and will surely bring you to judgment both nationally and individually!"

"The LORD knows the thoughts of man" (v. 11). "But they know not the thoughts of the LORD" (Mic. 4:12). "God is not in all his [the wicked man's] thoughts" (Ps. 10:4). A man may not want to think about God, but that doesn't keep God from knowing the man's thoughts. It just prohibits the man from knowing how God thinks. Unless the wicked heed the warning and repent, they will surely discover how God thinks when it is too late to repent!

Application_____

God knows our thoughts (Ps. 139:2; Lk. 9:47). Do you resent this invasion into your privacy? The spiritual person is comforted that God knows his thoughts and still loves him. Shouldn't I be as concerned about my thought life as God is? "Search me, O God. . .know my thoughts" (Ps. 139:23).

Psalm 94:12-23

12. Blessed *is* the man whom thou chastenest, O LORD, and teachest him out of thy law;

13. That thou mayest give him rest from the days of adversity, until the pit be digged for the wicked.

14. For the LORD will not cast off his people, neither will he forsake his inheritance.

15. But judgment shall return unto righteousness: and all the upright in heart shall follow it.

16. Who will rise up for me against the evildoers? *or* who will stand up for me against the workers of iniquity?

17. Unless the LORD *had been* my help, my soul had almost dwelt in silence.

18. When I said, My foot slippeth; thy mercy, O LORD, held me up.

19. In the multitude of my thoughts within me thy comforts delight my soul.

20. Shall the throne of iniquity have fellowship with thee, which frameth mischief by a law?

21. They gather themselves together against the soul of the righteous, and condemn the innocent blood.

22. But the LORD is my defence; and my God *is* the rock of my refuge.

23. And he shall bring upon them their own iniquity, and shall cut them off in their own wickedness; *yea,* the LORD our God shall cut them off.

Commentary

The theme of the psalm now changes from vengeance (v.1) to blessedness (v. 12). What brought about the change? "Law" in this context denotes all that God has revealed in Scriptures. Being admonished by God's Word, the psalmist leaves the timing of vengeance upon the wicked to the LORD. He now rests in the promises given to God's people in the Word. "Rest in the LORD, and wait patiently for Him; fret not thyself because of. . .the man who brings wicked devices to pass" (Ps. 37:7).

This psalmist suffered from the same malady (v. 18) as did Asaph (Ps. 73:2) until he found refuge in the knowledge of his God (Ps. 73:17). His cry was the same as Habakkuk's (Hab. 1:2) until that prophet took his eyes off the wicked and placed them upon the LORD (Hab. 2:1). He put his trust in God's promises (Hab. 2:14).

Comparing verse 3 to verse 19, notice the marked change in the psalmist's perspective as he rests in God's promises. He is still fully aware of the evil that is perpetrated by godless governments (vv. 20-21). But he sees it all from his safe refuge—the LORD, his rock.

"For their rock is not as our Rock; even our enemies themselves being judges" (Deut. 32:31). The wicked have no refuge, and they know it. The devil knows that his time is short and therefore is venting his wrath upon God's people through his control over the nations of the world.

Leave it to the LORD our God. He will "cut them off in their own wickedness" (v.23).

Application

The tumult of the nations is typified by the tossing waves of the sea (Ps. 65:7; Isa. 17:12, 13; Lk. 21:25). When Jesus walked upon the tumultuous sea (Mt. 14:22-36), Peter did also as *long* as he kept his eyes upon the Lord. When distracted by the boisterous sea, Peter sank. When you are overwhelmed by the turmoil of the times, meditate upon Psalm 37:1-10.

Psalm 95

1. O COME, let us sing unto the LORD: let us make a joyful noise to the rock of our salvation.

2. Let us come before his presence with thanksgiving, and make a joyful noise unto him with psalms.

3. For the LORD *is* a great God, and a great King above all gods.

4. In his hand *are* the deep places of the earth: the strength of the hills *is* his also.

5. The sea *is* his, and he made it: and his hands formed the dry *land*.

6. O come, let us worship and bow down: let us kneel before the *LORD* our maker.

7. For he *is* our God; and we *are* the people of his pasture, and the sheep of his hand. Today if ye will hear his voice,

8. Harden not your heart, as in the provocation, *and* as *in* the day of temptation in the wilderness:

9. When your fathers tempted me, proved me, and saw my work.

10. Forty years long was I grieved with *this* generation, and said, It *is* a people that do err in their heart, and they have not known my ways:

11. Unto whom I sware in my wrath that they should not enter into my rest.

Commentary

Verses 1 and 2 exhort the LORD's people to gather in praise and thanksgiving unto Him. Verses 3-5 present the reasons He should be extolled. Verse 6 is a call to worship the LORD, and verse 7 gives the reasons He should be worshipped. The remaining verses warn against the type of error that kept the first generation of redeemed Israelites from enjoying the blessings God intended for them.

Singing, joyful shouts, expressions of thanksgiving and recitation of psalms are received by the Lord as pleasing and acceptable sacrifices from our lips (Ps. 69:30-31; Heb. 13:15). Such sacrifices should be offered because the LORD is a great God and the coming King of Kings (Rev. 19:16). He is worthy of praise because He is the creator of all (Rev. 4:11).

Three proper postures are given for worship. The word translated *worship* means "to prostrate oneself." Bowing and kneeling are also acceptable. We should worship the LORD because He is our own God and our dear shepherd (Heb. 13:20).

The warning begins with the last line of verse 7. The word *today* makes the warning applicable to the psalmist's generation. The warning is quoted in its entirety in Hebrews 3:7-11 and made applicable to our generation. The passage is then expounded upon in Hebrews 3:12-4:11.

The LORD's people in any generation can miss the blessing of the Promised Land and spend their lives wandering in the wilderness by failing to trust Him to lead them after they have trusted Him for deliverance.

Application

"As ye have, therefore, received Christ Jesus the Lord, so walk ye in Him" (Col. 2:6). Either a walk of faith or a walk of faithlessness follows the initial step of faith that saved us from a life of slavery to sin. It is a matter of whether or not we have "a heart" for our God and His ways.

Psalm 96

1. O SING unto the LORD a new song: sing unto the LORD, all the earth.
2. Sing unto the LORD, bless his name; shew forth his salvation from day to day.
3. Declare his glory among the heathen, his wonders among all people.
4. For the LORD *is* great, and greatly to be praised: he *is* to be feared above all gods.
5. For all the gods of the nations *are* idols: but the LORD made the heavens.
6. Honour and majesty *are* before him: strength and beauty *are* in his sanctuary.
7. Give unto the LORD, O ye kindreds of the people, give unto the LORD glory and strength.
8. Give unto the LORD the glory *due unto* his name: bring an offering, and come into his courts.
9. O worship the LORD in the beauty of holiness: fear before him, all the earth.
10. Say among the heathen *that* the LORD reigneth: the world also shall be established that it shall not be moved: he shall judge the people righteously.
11. Let the heavens rejoice, and let the earth be glad; let the sea roar, and the fulness thereof.
12. Let the field be joyful, and all that *is* therein: then shall all the trees of the wood rejoice.
13. Before the LORD: for he cometh, for he cometh to judge the earth: he shall judge the world with righteousness, and the people with his truth.

Commentary_____

In the Septuagint (early Greek) translation of the Hebrew scriptures, there are two superscriptions above Psalm 96—"A Psalm of David" and "When the house was being built after the captivity." The following is the most logical of several explanations that have been offered.

1 Chronicles 15:25-16:6 describes a gala procession and celebration that occurred when King David brought the Ark of the Covenant to Jerusalem: "Then on that day David delivered first this psalm, to thank the LORD, into the hand of Asaph and his brethren" (1 Chron. 16:7). Verses 8-36 of chapter 16 recite that psalm. Verses 8-22 are in the psalter as Psalm 105:1-15.

Verses 34-36 are a part of Psalm 106. Verses 23-33 are repeated as Psalm 96 with some additions: for instance, a threefold "sing unto the LORD" replaces the single "sing unto the LORD" at the beginning of David's psalm. The final verse of Psalm 96 includes a double "for He cometh." These and other minor additions were included for liturgical purposes at a celebration occurring centuries after David lived.

Psalm 96 may be divided into four stanzas. Verses 1-3 are a call to all nations to praise the LORD and proclaim His glory. Next is a declaration of His worthiness to be praised (vv. 4-6). Stanza 3 (vv. 7-9) is a series of earnest pleas to all the Earth to acknowledge the greatness of the LORD by worshipping Him. The final stanza is a call to all nations, the heavens and all of creation to joyfully celebrate the coming One who will usher in a government of righteousness and truth.

Application_____

The answer to the calls and pleas of Psalm 96 will not come "until the times of the Gentiles be fulfilled" (Lk. 21:24), nor until Israel as a nation says, "Blessed is He who cometh in the name of the Lord" (Lk. 13:35). But we can be very sure that "for yet a little while, and He that shall come will come, and will not tarry" (Heb. 10:37). "Amen, even so come, Lord Jesus" (Rev. 22:20).

Psalm 97

1. THE LORD reigneth; let the earth rejoice; let the multitude of isles be glad *thereof.*
2. Clouds and darkness *are* round about him: righteousness and judgment *are* the habitation of his throne.
3. A fire goeth before him, and burneth up his enemies round about.
4. His lightenings enlightened the world: the earth saw, and trembled.
5. The hills melted like wax at the presence of the LORD, at the presence of the Lord of the whole earth.
6. The heavens declare his righteousness, and all the people see his glory.
7. Confounded be all they that serve graven images, that boast themselves of idols: worship him, all *ye* gods.
8. Zion heard, and was glad; and the daughters of Judah rejoiced because of his judgments, O LORD.
9. For thou, LORD, *art* high above all the earth: thou art exalted far above all gods.
10. Ye that love the LORD, hate evil: he preserveth the souls of his saints; he delivereth them out of the hand of the wicked.
11. Light is sown for the righteous, and gladness for the upright in heart.
12. Rejoice in the LORD, ye righteous; and give thanks at the remembrance of his holiness.

Commentary_____

Psalm 97 contains a considerable amount of figurative language. This is our understanding of the imagery in verses 1-8 of the KJV. "Isles" (for coasts) is frequently used in the Old Testament prophetic books to designate the far-flung inhabited places on Earth (Isa. 41:5; Jer. 31:10). "Clouds, darkness, fire, and lightning" used together indicate the manifestation of God towards Earth in His judgment of sin (Ex. 19:16; Heb. 12:18; Rev. 8:5). "Hills" is figurative for nations (Isa. 2:2, 40:4). "Zion" is Jerusalem as the place from which God's true government emanates (Isa. 2:3). "Daughters of Judah" denotes the inhabited places around Jerusalem (Isa. 37:22; Ezk. 16:53). In verse 1, the LORD is ready to manifest, as Messiah, His right to reign on Earth. Verses 2-5 speak of the judgment upon the government of this world preceding Messiah's enthronement at Jerusalem. The Hebrew word translated "gods," used in this way over 250 times in the Old Testament, means any personages that receive the homage due to the true God.

One way to measure an individual's love for God is his hatred for that which God calls evil. The wicked are all those who disregard their Creator's right to allegiance. Lovers of God, called saints, the righteous and upright in heart, are promised protection, deliverance, light, and gladness. That should evoke rejoicing, thanksgiving, and remembrance of His holiness.

Application_____

Verse 8 makes it clear that this psalm is primarily designed to sustain the people of Israel in trying times—particularly in the "time of Jacob's trouble" (Jer. 30:7), an Old Testament denotation of "the Great Tribulation." The marvel of God's Word is that He can communicate a specific message to a particular people for a particular time and yet the words are fully applicable to all of His people in any time (1 Cor. 10:11).

Psalm 98

A Psalm.

1. O SING unto the LORD a new song; for he hath done marvellous things: his right hand, and his holy arm, hath gotten him the victory.
2. The LORD hath made known his salvation: his righteousness hath he openly shewed in the sight of the heathen.
3. He hath remembered his mercy and his truth toward the house of Israel: all the ends of the earth have seen the salvation of our God.
4. Make a joyful noise unto the LORD, all the earth: make a loud noise, and rejoice, and sing praise.
5. Sing unto the LORD with the harp; with the harp, and the voice of a psalm.
6. With trumpets and sound of cornet make a joyful noise before the LORD, the King.
7. Let the sea roar, and the fulness thereof; the world, and they that dwell therein.
8. Let the floods clap *their* hands: let the hills be joyful together
9. Before the LORD; for he cometh to judge the earth: with righteousness shall he judge the world, and the people with equity.

Commentary_____

Isaac Watt's interpretation of Psalm 98 is "Joy to the World," written in 1719. We sing this favorite Christmas carol in celebration of Christ's first coming. However, both the psalm and the carol speak of a time when "earth receives her king," and "the savior reigns." The carol looks forward to a time when sin and sorrow will cease and when the curse will be removed from the Earth (Rom. 8:19-22).

The singing of "a new song" is mentioned six times in Psalms, once in Isaiah and twice in Revelation. A "new song" is the proper response whenever the LORD does new "marvelous things." In Psalm 96, 98, and 149, that marvelous act is the enthronement of Messiah.

Verses 1-3 speak of Messiah, the Deliverer, and the sword by which He delivers His people and defeats the Antichrist (Isa. 11:4; 2 Thes. 2:8; Rev. 19:15).

Verses 4-6 sing of Messiah, the King, and His crown, which symbolizes His right to the throne. He will be extolled with singing, joyful shouts, rejoicing, praise and musical instruments.

Verses 7-9 focus on Messiah, the Judge (ruler), and His scepter which symbolizes His authority and capability to restore dominion as the "man" of Isaiah 32:1, 2. (See also Heb. 2:8, 9). "Sea," "floods," and "hills" summarize the physical creation. Symbolically, they can represent peoples and nations as well as the realm of nature (Rev. 17:15). Verse 9 summarizes Isaiah 11:1-5 which describes the righteous rule of Messiah's millennial kingdom.

Application_____

We, as members of the present Body of Christ on Earth, are watching for the appearance of the Morning Star, which precedes the rising of the Sun of Righteousness in the East (Mal. 4:2; Rev. 22:16). We also rejoice now for those who, in the future, will come out of the Tribulation at the establishment of the millennial kingdom.

Psalm 99

1. THE LORD reigneth; let the people tremble: he sitteth *between* the cherubims; let the earth be moved.
2. The LORD *is* great in Zion; and he *is* high above all the people.
3. Let them praise thy great and terrible name; *for* it *is* holy.
4. The king's strength also loveth judgment; thou dost establish equity, thou executest judgment and righteousness in Jacob.
5. Exalt ye the LORD our God, and worship at his footstool; *for* he *is* holy.
6. Moses and Aaron among his priests, and Samuel among them that call upon his name; they called upon the LORD, and he answered them.
7. He spake unto them in the cloudy pillar: they kept his testimonies, and the ordinance *that* he gave them.
8. Thou answeredst them, O LORD our God: thou wast a God that forgavest them, though thou tookest vengeance of their inventions.
9. Exalt the LORD our God, and worship at his holy hill; for the LORD our God *is* holy.

Commentary_____

Psalm 99 consists of three stanzas of different lengths, each ending with a declaration of the holiness of the LORD our God (vv. 3, 5, 9). Verses 1-5 and verse 9 present the LORD seated upon His throne—particularly focusing on His millennial reign. Verses 6-8 tell of His sovereign acts of the past. Each stanza conveys the same message: The LORD reigns as king over all people. Let them tremble at His awesome presence because He is holy. Let His subjects exalt and worship Him.

In the Bible, "holy" is the most frequently stressed attribute of God. The Hebrew word means "set apart" or "distinct from." Consider two aspects of the holiness of God: first, he is absolutely perfect morally; second, as Creator and Sovereign, He is "high above all the peoples" (v. 2).

"Be ye holy for I am holy" (Lev. 11:45; 1 Pet. 1:16). "For Thou only art holy" (Rev.15:4). Since only God is holy, how can I fulfill His directive to be holy? Before God, I am holy positionally because I am in Christ and partake of His absolute moral perfection. Practically, I am holy to the extent that I follow His steps (1 Pet. 2:21-23).

Application_____

"I do always those things that please Him" (Jn. 8:29). I please the Father in regards to practical holiness when I properly conduct myself as a child of that Father, a student of the Teacher, a servant of the Master, a subject of the Sovereign, a creature of the Creator, and a worshipper of the True God.

Psalm 100

A Psalm of praise.

1. MAKE A joyful noise unto the LORD, all ye lands.
2. Serve the LORD with gladness: come before his presence with singing.
3. Know ye that the LORD he *is* God: *it is* he *that* hath made us, and not we ourselves; *we are* his people, and the sheep of his pasture.
4. Enter into his gates with thanksgiving, *and* into his courts with praise: be thankful unto him, *and* bless his name.
5. For the *LORD is* good: his mercy *is* everlasting; and his truth *endureth* to all generations.

Commentary_____

This short psalm of praise and thanksgiving is the most memorized psalm in the psalter except for Psalm 23. It is a song for all ages of any age. Yet several phrases point especially to the earthly reign of Messiah. "All ye lands," "before His presence," and "enter into His gates. . .and into His courts" all suggest millennial conditions.

The psalm contains seven exhortations to publicly praise, extol, and thank the King upon His throne. To "make a joyful noise" means to gather together with joyful shouting. "Serve the LORD with gladness" signifies that we should worship Him with smiling countenances. "Come before His presence" suggests that we should approach Him in joyous song. "Know. . .the Lord" implies that the worshipper with a full under-standing of how God loves, thinks, and acts towards us will come to Him with spontaneous and profuse praise. The phrase "enter into" indi-cates that a truly thankful heart is effervescent with praise. To "be thankful" is to live moment by moment in a state of overflowing thankful-ness. "Bless His name" means sound out good things about Him.

Verse 3 gives three reasons we should joyfully offer praise to the LORD—He made us, we belong to Him, and He provides for us. Verse five gives three additional reasons for praise—He is good, He will always be merciful, and He will forever be true. The word *truth* in verse five connotes fidelity more than verity as in "he is a true friend."

Application_____

Scripture memorization is not as prevalent in Sunday schools and youth groups as it was when the King James Version was the predomi-nant English text. Some of the modern versions tend towards para-phrase rather than translation. Does that make them less conducive to memorization? Many wondrous promises have been given to those who hide the Word in their hearts (Ps. 1:2-3, 119: 11, 99).

Psalm 101

A Psalm of David.

1. I WILL sing of mercy and judgment: unto thee, O LORD, will I sing.
2. I will behave myself wisely in a perfect way. O when wilt thou come unto me? I will walk within my house with a perfect heart.
3. I will set no wicked thing before mine eyes: I hate the work of them that turn aside; *it* shall not cleave to me.
4. A froward heart shall depart from me: I will not know a wicked *person*.
5. Whoso privily slandereth his neighbour, him will I cut off: him that hath an high look and a proud heart will not I suffer.
6. Mine eyes *shall be* upon the faithful of the land, that they may dwell with me: he that walketh in a perfect way, he shall serve me.
7. He that worketh deceit shall not dwell within my house: he that telleth lies shall not tarry in my sight.
8. I will early destroy all the wicked of the land; that I may cut off all wicked doers from the city of the LORD.

Commentary_____

Through the centuries, Psalm 101 has been read at coronations. It expresses the high purposes and noble aspirations of a ruler upon his accession to the throne. It is suitable for anyone who undertakes a position of authority. It is best understood when it is divided into two stanzas—each with four verses. The first stanza presents the proper heart purpose of a leader for his own conduct. The second stanza presents his intent for his realm.

The psalmist's preeminent desire is to live a life that exalts a LORD of mercy and judgment; he then desires to model such a lifestyle before others. He wants a constant sense of God's presence with him so that his way will be one of wisdom. He is concerned with his walk and with what he sets before his eyes (vv. 2,3). He purposes to avoid wickedness and to separate himself from evil doers.

In stanza two the psalmist resolves to seek out companions who are free from falsehood, pride and injustice. His heart's desire is that the City of the LORD will be a holy city worthy of its designation.

When God spoke of David as "a man after my own heart, who will do all my will" (Acts 13:22), He graciously looked beyond David's fleshly failures to his heart purpose, as recorded in this psalm. When the heart is right, the LORD Himself undertakes the task of molding and chastening until the actions match the intents and purposes (Heb. 12:7,11).

Application_____

Even a babysitter who has the oversight of two little children for two hours can be a positive influence on them. But first she must have established a standard of conduct for herself. Then there is something to model for the children. Therefore, my heart's cry should be "search me, O God and know my heart: try me and know my thoughts; and see if there be any wicked way in me and lead me in the way everlasting" (Ps. 139:23-24).

Psalm 102:1-14

A Prayer of the afflicted, when he is overwhelmed, and poureth out his complaint before the LORD.

1. HEAR MY prayer, O LORD, and let my cry come unto thee.
2. Hide not thy face from me in the day *when* I am in trouble; incline thine ear unto me: in the day *when* I call answer me speedily.
3. For my days are consumed like smoke, and my bones are burned as an hearth.
4. My heart is smitten, and withered like grass; so that I forgot to eat my bread.
5. By reason of the voice of my groaning my bones cleave to my skin.
6. I am like a pelican of the wilderness: I am like an owl of the desert.
7. I watch, and am as a sparrow alone upon the house top.
8. Mine enemies reproach me all the day; *and* they that are mad against me are sworn against me.
9. For I have eaten ashes like bread, and mingled my drink with weeping.
10. Because of thine indignation and thy wrath: for thou hast lifted me up, and cast me down.
11. My days *are* like a shadow that declineth; and I am withered like grass.
12. But thou, O LORD, shalt endure for ever; and thy remembrance unto all generations.
13. Thou shalt arise, *and* have mercy upon Zion: for the time to favour her, yea, the set time, is come.
14. For thy servants take pleasure in her stones, and favour the dust thereof.

Commentary_____

Verses 1-11 present the plaintive plea of one overwhelmed by his distressful situation. He complains that his life is being snuffed out like vanishing smoke or like wood being consumed by fire. He is so heartsick that he can't eat. He feels all alone while being oppressed by his enemies. His God seems unconcerned about him.

The words describing his plight are remarkably like those describing the suffering Savior in Psalm 22:1-15. Expressions like "hide thy face," "the day I am in trouble," and "my heart is smitten" along with images like "wilderness," "desert," "reproach," "weeping, "indignation," and "wrath," suggest that God is using the psalmist's affliction to depict the plight of Israel in our present age.

In Deuteronomy 29:24-28, the LORD warns Israel of a time of wrath and great indignation. Ezekiel 21:31 and 22:31 let us know that the time of indignation began with the captivity in Babylon. The indignation will culminate in a future time called the "time of Jacob's trouble" (Jer. 30:7) and "great tribulation (Mt. 24:21). The "set time" for Israel's deliverance (Isa. 26:20; Dan. 8:19) will be the coming of her Messiah.

In verses 12-14 the perspective of the psalmist changes when he centers his mind on the LORD's eternality and faithfulness as well as on the coming of the "set time" when the LORD will no longer "hide His face" (Dt. 31:18).

Application_____

Remember, this psalmist did not have the comfort of knowing that a Savior had paid his sin debt at Calvary. He knew nothing of a risen Savior seated at the right hand of God as his intercessor. He had none of the New Testament promises or an indwelling Holy Spirit. We have both a comforting hope (1 Th. 4:18) and a "blessed hope" (Ti. 2:13) while we wait!

Psalm 102:15-28

15. So the heathen shall fear the name of the LORD, and all the kings of the earth thy glory.
16. When the LORD shall build up Zion, he shall appear in his glory.
17. He will regard the prayer of the destitute, and not despise their prayer.
18. This shall be written for the generation to come: and the people which shall be created shall praise the LORD.
19. For he hath looked down from the height of his sanctuary; from heaven did the LORD behold the earth;
20. To hear the groaning of the prisoner; to loose those that are appointed to death;
21. To declare the name of the LORD in Zion, and his praise in Jerusalem;
22. When the people are gathered together, and the kingdoms, to serve the LORD.
23. He weakened my strength in the way; he shortened my days.
24. I said, O my God, take me not away in the midst of my days: thy years *are* throughout all generations.
25. Of old hast thou laid the foundation of the earth: and the heavens *are* the work of thy hands.
26. They shall perish, but thou shalt endure: yea, all of them shall wax old like a garment; as a vesture shalt thou change them, and they shall be changed:
27. But thou *art* the same, and thy years shall have no end.
28. The children of thy servants shall continue, and their seed shall be established before thee.

Commentary

When the psalmist elevated his prayer by acknowledging the eternality of God and His faithfulness to all generations (v. 12), the LORD gave him the privilege of prophesying about the kingdom of the coming Messiah (vv. 13-22). The LORD also gave him the spiritual insight to know that the time about which he wrote was for a future generation (v. 18; 1 Pet. 1:10-12).

The psalmist failed, however, to realize the magnitude of that privilege and resumed his complaint (vv. 23-24). His words could be paraphrased in this way: You have taken away my strength at an age when I should be strong. Why are you shortening my life? You are eternal. Why are you doing this to me?

Verses 25-27 are quoted in Hebrews 1:10-12 and are applied to God the Son. They are among seven Old Testament passages cited in Hebrews 1:5-13 as proof of the deity of Jesus Christ, our Great High Priest. This quotation presents the Son's preeminence as Creator (Col. 1:16-19). It also points out the Son's eternality and immutability.

Verse 28 also speaks of the Son and His servants, who are counted as His progeny. Isaiah 53:8 says prophetically, "He [Jesus Christ] was cut off out of the land of the living." Then verse 10 states, "He shall see His seed." Psalm 22:30 declares, "A seed shall serve Him; it shall be accounted to the Lord for a generation [progeny]."

Application

During his lifetime, the psalmist may have never known that he was prophesying about his Savior as well as his eternal King. When you see him in Heaven, surely he will have no complaints about his brief trouble-filled life on Earth. What a privilege was his to impact lives for centuries through his authorship of the psalm. We too will be in awe when we know the eternal impact of that which the Lord was pleased to do through each of us during our sojourn here.

Psalm 103

A Psalm of David.

1. BLESS THE LORD, O my soul: and all that is within me, *bless* his holy name.
2. Bless the LORD, O my soul, and forget not all his benefits:
3. Who forgiveth all thine iniquities; who healeth all thy diseases;
4. Who redeemeth thy life from destruction; who crowneth thee with lovingkindness and tender mercies;
5. Who satisfieth thy mouth with good *things; so that* thy youth is renewed like the eagle's.
6. The LORD executeth righteousness and judgment for all that are oppressed.
7. He made known his ways unto Moses, his acts unto the children of Israel.
8. The LORD *is* merciful and gracious, slow to anger, and plenteous in mercy.
9. He will not always chide: neither will he keep *his anger* for ever.
10. He hath not dealt with us after our sins; nor rewarded us according to our iniquities.
11. For as the heaven is high above the earth, *so* great is his mercy toward them that fear him.
12. As far as the east is from the west, *so* far hath he removed our transgressions from us.
13. Like as a father pitieth *his* children, *so* the LORD pitieth them that fear him.
14. For he knoweth our frame; he remembereth that we *are* dust.
15. *As for* man, his days *are* as grass: as a flower of the field, so he flourisheth.
16. For the wind passeth over it, and it is gone; and the place thereof shall know it no more.
17. But the mercy of the LORD *is* from everlasting to everlasting upon them that fear him, and his righteousness unto children's children;
18. To such as keep his covenant, and to those that remember his commandments to do them.
19. The LORD hath prepared his throne in the heavens; and his kingdom ruleth over all.
20. Bless the LORD, ye his angels, that excel in strength, that do his commandments, hearkening unto the voice of his word.
21. Bless ye the LORD, all *ye* his hosts; ye ministers of his, that do his pleasure.
22. Bless the LORD, all his works in all places of his dominion: bless the LORD, O my soul.

Commentary

David begins this song of unmitigated praise by admonishing himself to bless the LORD and His holy name with his entire being. To "bless" is to "sound out favorable words." He further admonishes himself not to forget all the benefits bestowed upon him by the LORD. In verses 3-5 he enumerates those benefits. In verses 6-11, David tells how the LORD has dealt with His people in the past. Notice how he magnifies the attributes of God.

The distance from north to south is finite. You can go no farther in either of those directions than the pole. East and west are infinite. When God casts your sins behind His back (Isa. 38:17), He is facing you forevermore while your sins speed away behind His back into oblivion and are blotted out (Isa. 43:25, 44:22). He remembers them "no more" (Jer. 31:34) because they are in the sea of His forgetfulness (Mic. 7:19). Who then shall bring a charge against God's elect (Rom. 8:33)?

In contrast to our sinfulness, the LORD is everlasting and righteous in His dealings with His children. He keeps His promises to those who regard Him. One of those promises is given in verse 19.

David began the psalm speaking to himself, and he ends it in the same manner. But first, in verses 20-22, he addresses all of creation. He calls upon the angelic beings in Heaven to bless the LORD and His works everywhere in His universal domain.

Application

Why is it that many who are glad to publicly proclaim the goodness of God, seldom publicly exalt the name of the Lord Jesus Christ? Is it because almost everyone believes in some sort of god but the name of our blessed Savior is a reproach?

Psalm 104:1-13

1. BLESS THE LORD, O my soul. O LORD my God, thou art very great; thou art clothed with honour and majesty.
2. Who coverest *thyself* with light as *with* a garment: who stretchest out the heavens like a curtain:
3. Who layeth the beams of his chambers in the waters: who maketh the clouds his chariot: who walketh upon the wings of the wind.
4. Who maketh his angels spirits; his ministers a flaming fire:
5. *Who* laid the foundations of the earth, *that* it should not be removed for ever.
6. Thou coverest it with the deep as *with* a garment: the waters stood above the mountains.
7. At thy rebuke they fled; at the voice of thy thunder they hasted away.
8. They go up by the mountains; they go down by the valleys unto the place which thou hast founded for them.
9. Thou hast set a bound that they may not pass over; that they turn not again to cover the earth.
10. He sendeth the springs into the valleys, *which* run among the hills.
11. They give drink to every beast of the field: the wild asses quench their thirst.
12. By them shall the fowls of the heaven have their habitation, *which* sing among the branches.
13. He watereth the hills from his chambers: the earth is satisfied with the fruit of thy works.

Commentary

Psalm 104 is, in a sense, a sequel to 103, which glorifies the LORD for His benefits to His people. This hymn of praise glorifies the LORD's greatness as manifested in His creation. In general, but not precisely, the psalm follows the sequence of Genesis 1, with verses 1 and 2 singing of day 1, and 3 and 4 of day 2, etc.

"Honor" in verse 1 means awe-inspiring splendor. "Majesty" is grandeur. The LORD is clothed (enveloped) in light. Light dwells with God (Dan. 2:22). God dwells in light (1 Tim. 6:16). God is light (1 Jn. 1:5). Light is as eternal as is God. In Genesis 1:3, light was manifested on Earth.

Although "angels" can be translated "messengers" and spirits can be translated "winds," we know that verse 4 is speaking of heavenly angelic beings because of the quotation of the verse in Hebrews 1:7. Also, there is a connection to Psalm 103:20, 21.

Verses 6-9 are not a reference to Noah's flood. They speak of the condition described in Genesis 1:2 and God's actions in Genesis 1:9, 10, when He spoke and the waters "fled," revealing the mountains. After Noah's flood, the waters receded over a period of several months. God's promise of Genesis 9:11 is not in view here in verse 9, which is one of several passages that proclaim God's sovereign determination of the boundary between land and sea. (Job 38:8-11; Prov. 8:29; Jer. 5:22).

Application

"Therefore with joy shall ye draw water out of the wells of salvation (Isa. 12:3). The psalmist glorifies the LORD for providing life-giving physical water for His earthly creatures (vv. 10-13). Let us glorify Him for providing eternal life—for giving spiritual water for His people (Jn. 4:14).

Psalm 104:14-23

14. He causeth the grass to grow for the cattle, and herb for the service of man: that he may bring forth food out of the earth;

15. And wine *that* maketh glad the heart of man, *and* oil to make *his* face to shine, and bread *which* strengtheneth man's heart.

16. The trees of the LORD are full *of sap;* the cedars of Lebanon, which he hath planted;

17. Where the birds make their nests: *as for* the stork, the fir trees *are* her house.

18. The high hills *are* a refuge for the wild goats; *and* the rocks for the conies.

19. He appointed the moon for seasons: the sun knoweth his going down.

20. Thou makest darkness, and it is night: wherein all the beasts of the forest do creep *forth*.

21. The young lions roar after their prey, and seek their meat from God.

22. The sun ariseth, they gather themselves together, and lay them down in their dens.

23. Man goeth forth unto his work and to his labour until the evening.

Commentary_____

The verbs in verses 5-9 are in the past tense. In poetic form, the psalmist is retelling what God did as recorded in Genesis 1:2-10. The verbs in verses 10-23 are in the present tense. The psalmist is applying that which is recorded in Genesis 1:11-31 to the ecology of his day. He wants to emphasize that the LORD his God not only created, but He also watches over and administers His creation.

The combination of wine, oil and grain (or its product) is often used in the Old Testament to symbolize prosperity. Moses used it in describing to Israel the abundance of the Promised Land before the conquest (Dt. 7:13, 11:14, 14:23, 28:51). Some see a spiritual application in these symbols. Wine speaks of the joy of the Spirit (Jud. 9:13). Only Jesus turns water into wine. Oil symbolizes the empowering of the Spirit, and bread represents spiritual sustenance.

In verses 16-18, the psalmist takes us for a nature walk so that together we might glory in the LORD's wondrous creation and His providential care of His creatures. Verses 19 and 20 are the psalmist's comment on day 4 of the creation story (Gen. 1:14-19). Having already mentioned the birds of day 5, he moves on to comment on day 6 in verses 21-23.

Application_____

According to Psalm 19:1-4 and Romans 1:19-20, the manifest action of God through His creation speaks to every human being. The observable creation says, "There is a God who made you and all that surrounds you. Seek His face." Human society ignores the message given by the Creator. Some will receive the saving gospel message. Therefore, we proclaim Christ Jesus the Savior!

Psalms 104:24-35

24. O LORD, how manifold are thy works! in wisdom hast thou made them all: the earth is full of thy riches.
25. *So is* this great and wide sea, wherein *are* things creeping innumerable, both small and great beasts.
26. There go the ships: *there is* that leviathan, *whom* thou hast made to play therein.
27. These wait all upon thee; that thou mayest give *them* their meat in due season.
28. *That* thou givest them they gather: thou openest thine hand, they are filled with good.
29. Thou hidest thy face, they are troubled: thou takest away their breath, they die, and return to their dust.
30. Thou sendest forth thy spirit, they are created: and thou renewest the face of the earth.
31. The glory of the LORD shall endure for ever: the LORD shall rejoice in his works.
32. He looketh on the earth, and it trembleth: he toucheth the hills, and they smoke.
33. I will sing unto the LORD as long as I live: I will sing praise to my God while I have my being.
34. My meditation of him shall be sweet: I will be glad in the LORD.
35. Let the sinners be consumed out of the earth, and let the wicked be no more. Bless thou the LORD, O my soul. Praise ye the LORD.

Commentary

Our society teaches children to disregard the Creator and to regard His creation, which we call Mother Nature (Rom. 1:25). Not so with the psalmist. He considers the observable results of creation and lifts his voice in praise to the Creator (v. 24). After he resumes his contemplation of day 6 of creation (vv. 25-30), he closes his song of creation with unrestrained adoration of the Creator (vv. 31-34).

Leviathan means "sea monster." Verse 26 says it was a creature made by the LORD. In His own words, the LORD gives a detailed description of leviathan in Job 41. He was similar to a mammoth-sized crocodile and is now extinct. In the past, it pleased God to make a creature that could spew enough fire out of its mouth to light a coal (Job 41:21). In the future, God will cause enough fire to spew from the mouths of two men to defeat all their enemies (Rev. 11:5). It pleased God to bring an end to leviathan and use him to symbolize enemies so powerful that only the omnipotent God can destroy them (Ps. 74:14; Isa. 27:1; Ezek. 29:3).

His contemplation of God's creation and the greatness of the Creator causes the psalmist to make a resolve that is to continue for the rest of his life (vv. 33, 34).

In verse 35, the psalmist looks forward to the time when "the wicked will be no more." Only then will all the Earth bless and praise the LORD as Creator.

Application

"I will sing unto the LORD"; "I will be glad in the LORD." When my contemplation of the Creator and His creation is in the right perspective, then my singing will be "unto the LORD." When my meditation upon the LORD is sweet, I will be glad in the LORD. Then with the psalmist I will say, "How sweet are Thy words unto my taste! Yea, sweeter than honey to my mouth" (Ps. 119:103).

Psalm 105:1-12

1. O GIVE thanks unto the LORD; call upon his name: make known his deeds among he people.

2. Sing unto him, sing psalms unto him: talk ye of all his wondrous works.

3. Glory ye in his holy name: let the heart of them rejoice that seek the LORD.

4. Seek the LORD, and his strength: seek his face evermore.

5. Remember his marvelous works that he hath done; his wonders, and the judgments of his mouth;

6. O ye seed of Abraham his servant, ye children of Jacob his chosen.

7. He *is* the LORD our God: his judgments *are* in all the earth.

8. He hath remembered his covenant for ever, the word *which* he commanded to a thousand generations.

9. Which *covenant* he made with Abraham, and his oath unto Isaac;

10. And confirmed the same unto Jacob for a law, and to Israel *for* an everlasting covenant:

11. Saying, Unto thee will I give the land of Canaan, the lot of your inheritance:

12. When they were *but* a few men in number; yea, very few, and strangers in it.

Commentary_____

In Genesis 12:2-3, the LORD made a seven-fold promise to Abraham. In chapters 13-22, He repeated and expanded upon the promise several times. In chapter 15 the LORD put the promise in the form of a unilateral, unconditional, permanent covenant. The covenant was confirmed to Isaac (Gen. 26:3, 4) and then to Jacob and his descendants (Gen 28:13, 14).

Psalm 105 is a tribute to the LORD for His faithfulness in keeping His covenant to the descendants of Abraham, Isaac and Jacob. Though the covenant was unconditionally forever, each generation was to meet certain requirements if it was to enjoy the blessings of the covenant (Lev. 26:3,14). The first five verses of Psalm 105 list twelve of these conditions:

1.Give thanks unto the LORD.
2.Call upon the name of the LORD
3.Make His deeds known to other nations.
4.Sing unto the LORD.
5.Talk about His wondrous works (miracles).
6.Glory in His holy name.
7.Seek the LORD with a rejoicing heart.
8.Seek the LORD's strength.
9.Seek His face continually.
10. Remember His works.
11.Remember His wonders.
12.Remember His words.

Application_____

Review the above list to see how many of the twelve apply to you in living a life that pleases your Lord. Which ones could you omit and still follow the instructions of Colossians 3:17 – "And whatsoever ye do in word or deed, do all in the name of the Lord Jesus, giving thanks to God the Father by Him"?

Psalm 105:13-25

13. When they went from one nation to another, from *one* kingdom to another people;
14. He suffered no man to do them wrong: yea, he reproved kings for their sakes;
15. *Saying,* Touch not mine anointed, and do my prophets no harm.
16. Moreover he called for a famine upon the land: he brake the whole staff of bread.
17. He sent a man before them; *even* Joseph, *who* was sold for a servant:
18. Whose feet they hurt with fetters: he was laid in iron:
19. Until the time that his word came: the word of the LORD tried him.
20. The king sent and loosed him; *even* the ruler of the people, and let him go free.
21. He made him lord of his house, and rule of all his substance:
22. To bind his princes at his pleasure; and teach his senators wisdom.
23. Israel also came into Egypt; and Jacob sojourned in the land of Ham.
24. And he increased his people greatly; and made them stronger than their enemies.
25. He turned their heart to hate his people, to deal subtilly with his servants.

Commentary_____

Soon after King David established his government in Jerusalem, he brought the Ark of the Covenant there with great ceremony (I Chr. 16:1-7). He delivered a medley of psalms to his chief musician, Asaph, for use in the celebration. The medley is recorded in I Chronicles 16:8-36. It is comprised of Psalm 105:1-15, followed by Psalm 96 and three verses from Psalm 106. So these passages may be read in the context of the Psalter or in the context of the historical account.

Abraham, Isaac, and Jacob never settled permanently; instead, they moved their tents from place to place. Through all of their journeys, they were under the special providential care of the LORD. Hebrews 11:9-16 furnishes an interesting and helpful commentary on their wanderings.

Verses 16-22 give a brief summary of the history of Joseph as recorded in Genesis chapters 37-50. Verse 18 gives a detail of the suffering Joseph endured during the years he was imprisoned in Egypt. The historical account (Gen. 39:21-40:23) doesn't tell us Joseph was placed in irons.

Verses 23-25 summarize the history recorded in Exodus 1. Egypt supplied all that God's people needed for physical well being, but it supplied no sustenance for the spirit. Eventually, Egypt brought sorrow, slavery, and despair.

Application_____

Satan, as "the god of this world" (2 Cor. 4:4), has established a system designed to allure and then ensnare. That system promises pleasures, gratification, and material prosperity. It supplies that sufficiently enough to entice us. The Bible warns, "There is a way which seemeth right unto a man, but the end thereof are the ways of death" (Pr. 14:12). Egypt, under Pharaoh, typifies that way of death.

Psalm 105:26-36

26. He sent Moses his servant; *and* Aaron whom he had chosen.
27. They shewed his signs among them, and wonders in the land of Ham.
28. He sent darkness, and made it dark; and they rebelled not against his word.
29. He turned their waters into blood, and slew their fish.
30. Their land brought forth frogs in abundance, in the chambers of their kings.
31. He spake, and there came divers sorts of flies, *and* lice in all their coasts.
32. He gave them hail for rain, *and* flaming fire in their land.
33. He smote their vines also and their fig trees; and brake the trees of their coasts.
34. He spake, and the locusts came, and caterpillars, and that without number,
35. And did eat up all the herbs in their land, and devoured the fruit of their ground.
36. He smote also all the firstborn in their land, the chief of all their strength.

Commentary_____

It is interesting to compare this passage with Psalm 78:44-51, which also presents a partial list of the ten plagues of Egypt as recorded in Exodus 7-11. Psalm 78 omits the following plagues: lice (3), death of livestock (5), boils (6), and darkness (9). Psalm 105 also omits livestock (5) and boils (6) but lists darkness (9) first. Several explanations have been offered for the selection of certain plagues and the order of listing, which differ from the historical account in Exodus. Most explanations involve the use of extra-biblical Egyptian history--especially concerning the many gods of Egypt. For instance, first place is supposedly given to darkness in 105:28 because it demonstrates that *Ra*, the sun god, is powerless when confronted by the omnipotent LORD God of the Israelites. *Ra* was the chief deity of the Egyptians.

Even among the plagues that are mentioned by both psalmists, different comments are made about those plagues. When the water was turned to blood, Psalm 78 points out that the Egyptians were deprived of drinking water; Psalm 105 says they were deprived of fish. Psalm 78 says the frogs "destroyed them"; Psalm 105 comments that the frogs filled "the chambers of the kings". Psalm 105:33 says the hail and fire "smote their vines and fig trees"; Psalm 78:47 emphasizes vines and sycamore trees. Psalm 78 devotes three long verses to the tenth plague; Psalm 105 uses only one short verse.

Application_____

God used four human authors to present the totality of what He is pleased to reveal concerning the earthly sojourn of Jesus Christ. Each of the four Gospels contributes different elements to the account. Here God uses two psalmists to comment on one subject. Each compliments the other in presenting all that God wants to say to us on that subject. We need to be students of the entire Bible if we wish to understand all that God has revealed about any single subject.

Psalm 105:37-45

37. He brought them forth also with silver and gold: and *there was* not one feeble *person* among their tribes.
38. Egypt was glad when they departed: for the fear of them fell upon them.
39. He spread a cloud for a covering; and fire to give light in the night.
40. *The people* asked, and he brought quails, and satisfied them with the bread of heaven.
41. He opened the rock, and the waters gushed out; they ran in the dry places *like* a river.
42. For he remembered his holy promise, *and* Abraham his servant.
43. And he brought forth his people with joy, *and* his chosen with gladness:
44. And gave them the lands of the heathen: and they inherited the labour of the people;
45. That they might observe his statutes, and keep his laws. Praise ye the LORD.

Commentary

In these verses the psalmist recounts seven ways in which the LORD provided for the descendants of Abraham, Isaac, and Jacob in faithfulness to His promises to them. First, He provided the material needs as prophesied by Moses (Ex. 3:21, 22) and later fulfilled (Ex. 12:35, 36). These provisions were their wages for the years of slavery. Second, the LORD gave the physical soundness needed for their journey. Third, He gave them the cloud by day for a covering from the heat of the desert sun, for a guide, and for assurance of the LORD's presence among them. It became a pillar of fire by night for light and protection (Ex. 14:20, 21; 40:34-38). Fourth, He provided manna for bread and fifth, quail for meat (Ex. 16:13, 32). Sixth, pure, cool water flowed from a rock in the desert at the command of Moses (Ex. 17:6).

The LORD provided in this miraculous manner as they journeyed to the Promised Land. Yet that generation perished in the wilderness because they failed to trust the LORD to conquer the adversaries in the Land. Forty years later, when Moses was preparing the second generation for entry into the Land, God promised them a seventh provision. They would live in houses they didn't build, eat from trees they didn't plant, and drink from wells they didn't dig (Dt. 6:10-11). Years later, Joshua reminded the people that the LORD had fulfilled the promise spoken by Moses (Josh. 24:13).

Application

Psalm 105 ends with a reminder of why God has a special people on Earth for whom He provides. He has given written instructions concerning Himself and His purposes. He wants a people on Earth who will carefully study those instructions and then make it their purpose to fulfill His purpose on Earth. As His people fulfill His purpose, He wants them to "praise the LORD."

Psalm 106:1-15

1. PRAISE YE the LORD. O give thanks unto the LORD; for *he is* good: for his mercy *endureth* for ever.
2. Who can utter the mighty acts of the LORD? *who* can shew forth all his praise?
3. Blessed *are* they that keep judgment, *and* he that doeth righteousness at all times.
4. Remember me O LORD, with the favour *that thou bearest unto* thy people: O visit me with thy salvation;
5. That I may see the good of thy chosen, that I may rejoice in the gladness of thy nation, that I may glory with thine inheritance.
6. We have sinned with our fathers, we have committed iniquity, we have done wickedly.
7. Our fathers understood not thy wonders in Egypt; they remembered not the multitude of thy mercies; but provoked *him* at the sea, *even* at the Red sea.
8. Nevertheless he saved them for his name's sake, that he might make his mighty power to be known.
9. He rebuked the Red sea also, and it was dried up: so he led them through the depths, as through the wilderness.
10. And he saved them from the hand of him that hated *them,* and redeemed them from the hand of the enemy.
11. And the waters covered their enemies: there was not one of them left.
12. Then believed they his words; they sang his praise.
13. They soon forgat his works; they waited not for his counsel:
14. But lusted exceedingly in the wilderness, and tempted God in the desert.
15. And he gave them their request; but sent leanness into their soul.

Commentary_____

This psalm is a prayer of national confession. When the nation of Israel digressed into spiritual declension, the LORD raised up leaders of spiritual stature to publicly glorify God and confess the nation's sin. First, the psalmist calls for praise and thanksgiving in acknowledgement of the goodness, mercy, and might of the One whom he is petitioning.

The psalmist is confident the Lord will forgive and bestow the promised blessings upon His penitent people (2 Chr. 7:14). In verses 4 and 5, he pleads to be present at that time.

"We have sinned with our fathers" (v. 6). "Pardon our iniquity and our sin" (Ex. 34:9). "Our iniquities are increased over our heads" (Ezra 9:6). "We have sinned against thee" (Neh. 1:6). "We have sinned, and have committed iniquity" (Dan. 9:5). The confessor identifies himself with the sinning people regardless of his own state.

The word "sinned" indicates that the people failed to meet God's required standard of righteousness. The phrase "committed iniquity" means that they did that which is inherently wrong whether or not there is a law concerning those actions. The phrase "done wickedly" identifies the nature of their deeds as the opposite of godliness.

Verse 7 refers to Exodus 14:11-12. God saved them for Himself (v. 8). He led them miraculously (v. 9). He saved them from the adversary by redemption (v. 10).

Verse 12 speaks of the song of victory recorded in Exodus 15:1-21. Verses 13 and 14 refer to the complaining and rebelling concerning God's provision of water and food in Exodus chapters 15-17.

Application_____

"He gave them their request, but sent leanness into their souls" (v. 15). Sometimes the Lord grants His people their petitions even when He knows the results will be to their detriment. That's the only way some of us learn to *not* ask selfishly. We should ask Him to search our hearts before we make the petition (Ps. 139:23-24).

Psalm 106:16-31

16. They envied Moses also in the camp, *and* Aaron the saint of the LORD.
17. The earth opened and swallowed up Dathan, and covered the company of Abiram.
18. And a fire was kindled in their company; the flame burned up the wicked.
19. They made a calf in Horeb, and woshipped the molten image.
20. Thus they changed their glory into the similitude of an ox that eateth grass.
21. They forgat God their saviour, which had done great things in Egypt;
22. Wondrous works in the land of Ham, *and* terrible things by the Red sea.
23. Therefore he said that he would destroy them, had not Moses his chosen stood before him in the breach, to turn away his wrath, lest he should destroy *them*.
24. Yea, they despised the pleasant land, they believed not his word:
25. But murmured in their tents, *and* hearkened not unto the voice of the LORD.
26. Therefore he lifted up his hand against them, to overthrow them in the wilderness:
27. To overthrow their seed also among the nations, and to scatter them in the lands.
28. They joined themselves also unto Baal-peor, and ate the sacrifices of the dead.
29. Thus they provoked *him* to anger with their inventions: and the plague brake in upon them.
30. Then stood up Phinehas, and executed judgment: and *so* the plague was stayed.
31. And that was counted unto him for righteousness unto all generations for evermore.

Commentary_____

Psalm 105 summarized the early history of the nation of Israel from the standpoint of the LORD's faithfulness in keeping His covenant promises to Abraham, Isaac, Jacob and their descendants. Psalm 106 summarizes that history from the viewpoint of Israel's rebellion and unfaithfulness. The selected episodes of history in chapter 106 are not precisely chronological. Those in verses 7-12 are from Exodus 14 and 15. Verses 14-33 are from Exodus and Numbers.

"Then believed they his words; they sang his praise" (v.12); "they believed not his word, but murmured" (vv. 24-25). Trust in the word of the LORD brought them out of Egypt and through the Red Sea. Singing and praise follow faith. A lack of trust in the word of the LORD barred them from the blessings of the Promised Land. Murmuring and complaining follow faithlessness. Faith in the promises of the LORD gave the next generation the lands of the nations (Ps. 105:44). Faithlessness scattered subsequent generations among the nations (Ps. 106: 27).

"They do always err in their heart" (Heb. 3:10); "they could not enter in because of unbelief" (Heb. 3:19). "Today, if ye will hear my voice, harden not your hearts" (Heb. 4:7). The book of Hebrews takes the experiences of Israel as presented in Psalms 105 and 106 and applies them to Christians who trust God for salvation but fail to trust Him to lead them into a life of fruitful service.

Application_____

"Now all these things happened unto them for ensamples and they are written for our admonition, upon whom the ends of the world are come" (1 Cor. 10:11). "As ye have therefore received Christ Jesus the Lord, so walk ye in Him" (Col. 2:6). Lyricist John H. Yates reminds us that "faith is the victory" over the penalty of sin; so also is it the victory over the power of the sin of unbelief in the Christian walk.

Psalm 106:32-48

32. They angered *him* also at the waters of strife, so that it went ill with Moses for their sakes:

33. Because they provoked his spirit, so that he spake unadvisedly with his lips.

34. They did not destroy the nations, concerning whom the LORD commanded them:

35. But were mingled among the heathen, and learned their works.

36. And they served their idols: which were a snare unto them.

37. Yea, they sacrificed their sons and their daughters unto devils,

38. And shed innocent blood, *even* the blood of their sons and of their daughters, whom they sacrificed unto the idols of Canaan: and the land was polluted with blood.

39. Thus were they defiled with their own works, and went a-whoring with their own inventions.

40. Therefore was the wrath of the LORD kindled against his people, insomuch that he abhorred his own inheritance.

41. And he gave them into the hand of the heathen; and they that hated them ruled over them.

42. Their enemies also oppressed them, and they were brought into subjection under their hand.

43. Many times did he deliver them; but they provoked *him* with their counsel, and were brought low for their iniquity.

44. Nevertheless he regarded their affliction, when he heard their cry:

45. And he remembered for them his covenant, and repented according to the multitude of his mercies.

46. He made them also to be pitied of all those that carried them captives.

47. Save us, O LORD our God, and gather us from among the heathen, to give thanks unto thy holy name, *and* to triumph in thy praise.

48. Blessed *be* the LORD God of Israel from everlasting to everlasting: and let all the people say, Amen. Praise ye the LORD.

83

Commentary

Verses 32 and 33 refer to an episode recorded in Numbers 20:2-13. The smiting of the rock by Moses with the rod of God (Ex. 17:6) was a picture of the smiting of Christ at Calvary (1 Cor. 10:4). The flow of water from the rock depicts the outflow of the life-giving Spirit that brings everlasting life (Jn. 7:37-39). Striking the rock more than once is comparable to putting Christ on the cross again (Heb. 6:6) and spoils the picture of the sufficiency of the Lord's "once for all" sacrifice (Heb. 10:10-14).

Moses' disobedience, prompted by his provoked spirit, cost him the privilege and blessing of the Promised Land. His own testimony about the incident is recorded in Deuteronomy 3:23-27.

Verses 35-45 summarize the history of the people of Israel during the time of the judges. It was a continual cycle of rebellion, retribution, repentance and restoration. Judges 2:10-19 gives a preview of those times and facilitates the understanding of this portion of the psalm. Moses had warned the Israelites of the danger of mixing with the heathen who would even lead them to sacrifice their own children to false gods (Dt. 12:29-31).

Verse 46 and the petition of verse 47 not only speak of past captivities and re-gatherings but also ultimately look forward to that final re-gathering when Israel will receive her Messiah and will say, "Blessed is he that cometh in the name of the LORD" (Lk. 13:35).

The benediction of verse 48 is a proper closing for both Psalm 106 and the fourth book of Psalms.

Application

Moses' service to God's people produced the results they desired, but his method was detrimental to God's purposes. He brought attention to his God-given authority rather than to the gracious provision of the Lord, thereby robbing God of the honor and glory due Him. May we be admonished to do His work in His way.

Psalm 107:1-16

1. O GIVE thanks unto the LORD, for *he is* good: for his mercy *endureth* for ever.
2. Let the redeemed of the LORD say *so*, whom he hath redeemed from the hand of the enemy;
3. And gathered them out of the lands, from the east, and from the west, from the north, and from the south.
4. They wandered in the wilderness in a solitary way; they found no city to dwell in.
5. Hungry and thirsty, their soul fainted in them.
6. Then they cried unto the LORD in their trouble, *and* he delivered them out of their distresses.
7. And he led them forth by the right way, that they might go to a city of habitation.
8. Oh that *men* would praise the LORD *for* his goodness, and *for* his wonderful works to the children of men!
9. For he satisfieth the longing soul, and filleth the hungry soul with goodness.
10. Such as sit in darkness and in the shadow of death, *being* bound in affliction and iron;
11. Because they rebelled against the words of God, and contemned the counsel of the most High:
12. Therefore he brought down their heart with labour; they fell down, and *there was* none to help.
13. Then they cried unto the LORD in their trouble, *and* he saved them out of their distresses.
14. He brought them out of darkness and the shadow of death, and brake their bands in sunder.
15. Oh that *men* would praise the LORD *for* his goodness, and *for* his wonderful works to the children of men!
16. For he hath broken the gates of brass, and cut the bars of iron in sunder.

Commentary_____

Although Psalms 105 and 106 are in Book IV and Psalm 107 is in Book V, they should be considered a trilogy. Notice that each begins with a call to thanksgiving followed by an exhortation to make known to other nations the wondrous works of the Lord. Also note the sequential order of 105:44, 106:27, 106:47, and 107:3.

The three psalms summarize the history of Israel from three different perspectives. Psalm 107 reviews Israel's past history and also extends the view to the present and the future. Though there have been limited re-gatherings in the past, verse three looks to the ultimate re-gathering when all Israelites will return to the Promised Land from everywhere (Isa. 43:5-6; Jer. 31:8-10; Ezk. 39:27-28). This return will answer the prayer of Psalm 106:47.

Verses 4-9 picture Israel as a wanderer in a spiritual wilderness, alone and homeless. The passage contains a plight (v. 5), a plea (v. 6), a provision (v. 7), and a praise (vv. 8-9).

Verses 10-16 present a second picture. Israel is a prisoner in a dungeon being punished for rebellion against her God. No one is concerned about her sad state. Again, we see the same sequence—a plight, a plea, a provision, and a praise. Notice that verse 13 is a repetition of verse 6. The story is the same; however, the second verse of praise is changed to fit the second picture. The fulfillment of verses 9 and 16 awaits the coming of Messiah.

Application_____

"If my people, which are called by my name, shall humble themselves, and pray, and seek my face, and turn from their wicked ways; then will I hear from heaven, and will forgive their sin, and will heal their land" (2 Chr. 7:14). This verse and this entire psalm apply particularly to Israel, but they are also applicable to our own nation and our personal lives.

Psalm 107:17-32

17. Fools because of their transgression, and because of their iniquities, are afflicted.
18. Their soul abhorreth all manner of meat; and they draw near unto the gates of death.
19. Then they cry unto the LORD in their trouble, *and* he saveth them out of their distresses.
20. He sent his word, and healed them, and delivered *them* from their destructions.
21. Oh that *men* would praise the LORD *for* his goodness, and *for* his wonderful works to the children of men!
22. And let them sacrifice the sacrifices of thanksgiving, and declare his works with rejoicing.
23. They that go down to the sea in ships, that do business in great waters;
24. These see the works of the LORD, and his wonders in the deep.
25. For he commandeth, and raiseth the stormy wind, which lifeth up the waves thereof.
26. They mount up to the heaven, they go down again to the depths: their soul is melted because of trouble.
27. They reel to and fro, and stagger like a drunken man, and are at their wit's end.
28. Then they cry unto the LORD in their trouble, and he bringeth them out of their distresses.
29. He maketh the storm a calm, so that the waves thereof are still.
30. Then they are glad because they be quiet; so he bringeth them unto their desired haven.
31. Oh that *men* would praise the LORD *for* his goodness, and *for* his wonderful works to the children of men!
32. Let them exalt him also in the congregation of the people, and praise him in the assembly of the elders.

Commentary_____

In Psalm 107:4-32, four word pictures poetically tell the plight of Israel when it is in rebellion and out of fellowship with its God. The first depiction (vv. 4-5) is that of a wilderness wanderer without home or friend on Earth. The second image pictures Israel as a prisoner in a dungeon (vv. 10-11). The Israelites are imprisoned because they rejected the "counsel of the Most High"(v. 11).

The third poetic picture (vv. 17-18) is that of an individual who is so sick and so debilitated that he can't eat and lies at death's door. A fool is one who attempts to run his life without regard for God's Word (Jer. 10:23). Transgression is conduct against the law. Iniquity is that which is inherently wrong whether or not there is a law against it—cruelty, arrogance, unfaithfulness and bigotry are examples. In both the Old Testament and the New Testament, thanksgiving is a pleasing sacrifice to the Lord (v. 22; Ps. 50:14; Heb. 13:15).

The fourth depiction (vv. 23-27) is that of a seaman perishing in a storm-tossed sea. For Israel, the sea is the world of Gentile dominance (Ps. 65:7; Isa. 17:12-13; Lk. 21:25). Israel has been tossed by that sea since the destruction of Jerusalem is 586 BC and will continue to be tossed by that sea "until the times of the Gentiles be fulfilled" (Lk. 21:24). At that time, Messiah "bringeth them unto their desired haven" (Ps. 107:30). Then they will "exalt Him also in the congregation of the people, and praise Him in the assembly of the elders" (v. 32).

Application_____

Before salvation in Christ Jesus, we were in Israel's plight. We were wandering in the wilderness, walking "according to the course of this world" (Eph. 2:2). We were bound in "chains of darkness" (2 Pet. 2:4) and lying at death's door. As hymnist H.E. Smith wrote, we were tossed about in the sea of a godless society, "sinking deep in sin." Now, like Noah and his family, we are in the ark of safety while the world perishes. "Oh, give thanks unto the LORD" (v.1).

Psalm 107:33-43

33. He turneth rivers into a wilderness, and the watersprings into dry ground;
34. A fruitful land into barreness, for the wickedness of them that dwell therein.
35. He turneth the wilderness into a standing water, and dry ground into watersprings.
36. And there he maketh the hungry to dwell, that they may prepare a city for habitation;
37. And sow the fields, and plant vineyards, which may yield fruits of increase.
38. He blesseth them also, so that they are multiplied greatly; and suffereth not their cattle to decrease.
39. Again, they are minished and brought low through oppression, affliction, and sorrow.
40. He poureth contempt upon princes, and causeth them to wander in the wilderness, *where there is* no way.
41. Yet setteth he the poor on high from affliction, and maketh *him* families like a flock.
42. The righteous shall see *it*, and rejoice: and all iniquity shall stop her mouth.
43. Whoso *is* wise, and will observe these *things*, even they shall understand the lovingkindness of the LORD.

Commentary

The LORD, through Moses, promised to bring the children of Israel into a productive land "flowing with milk and honey" (Ex. 3:8). That generation failed to trust God to deliver the Promised Land to them. Forty years later, Moses renewed the promise to the second generation, just before they entered the land under Joshua (Dt. 11:9). He promised it would be a land of abundant rain from heaven (Dt. 11:11-15). He also warned that if they turned from the LORD God to worship idols that the LORD would "shut up the Heaven, that there would be no rain" (Dt. 11:16-17). The psalmist recalls that warning in verses 33-34.

When King Ahab slew the prophets of God and established Baal worship in Israel, the LORD caused the rain to cease for three and a half years. Almost 3,000 years later, the Promised Land still has not fully recovered from that drought.

In verses 35-38, the psalmist assures Israel that their God controls the climate and is able to make the land unbelievably fruitful again. ". . . the desert shall rejoice, and blossom as the rose" (Isa. 35:1). "And the parched ground shall become a pool, and the thirsty land springs of water" (Isa. 35:7).

Verses 39 and 40 describe the plight of Israel since the Messiah was rejected almost 2,000 years ago, but the promises of verses 41 and 42 will surely come.

Application

The psalmist is reminding the LORD's people that He has complete control of their situation on Earth; however, their conduct influences how He chooses to control their situation. We are as much in need of the admonition of verse 43 as those who first read this psalm. We have the wisdom and understanding of God to the extent that we observe His Word and are admonished (1 Cor. 10:11).

Psalm 108

A Song *or* Psalm of David.

1. O GOD, my heart is fixed; I will sing and give praise, even with my glory.
2. Awake, psaltery and harp: I *myself* will awake early.
3. I will praise thee, O LORD, among the people: and I will sing praises unto thee among the nations.
4. For thy mercy *is* great above the heavens: and thy truth *reacheth* unto the clouds.
5. Be thou exalted, O God, above the heavens: and thy glory above all the earth;
6. That thy beloved may be delivered: save *with* thy right hand, and answer me.
7. God hath spoken in his holiness; I will rejoice, I will divide Shechem, and mete out the valley of Succoth.
8. Gilead *is* mine; Manasseh *is* mine: Ephraim also *is* the strength of mine head; Judah *is* my lawgiver;
9. Moab *is* my washpot; over Edom will I cast out my shoe; over Philistia will I triumph.
10. Who will bring me into the strong city? who will lead me into Edom?
11. *Wilt* not *thou*, O God, *who* hast cast us off? and wilt not thou, O God, go forth with our hosts?
12. Give us help from trouble: for vain *is* the help of man.
13. Through God we shall do valiantly: for he *it is that* shall tread down our enemies.

Commentary_____

Psalm 108 is a compilation from portions of two psalms written at an earlier time. The first five verses of praise, exaltation and glorification to the Lord repeat Psalm 57:7-11. The superscription over that psalm places the historical occasion at a time when David "fled from Saul in a cave." The first four verses of Psalm 57 record a plea to his God from one in desperate circumstances. The plea turns to praise when faith overcomes fear as David relies upon promises previously given him by God.

Psalm 108:6-13 repeats the last eight verses of Psalm 60. The super-scription over that psalm gives the historical setting as "when Joab returned, and smote of Edom in the Valley of Salt twelve thousand." This occurred later, when David was king. David's armies had suffered defeat by Edom, and Psalm 60 is his prayer for God's help as he prepares to conquer Edom. Verse 6 of Psalm 108 continues the prayer of Psalm 60.

Verses 7 and 8 name six locations in the Promised Land according to its boundaries at the time David began his reign over Israel. God proclaims that all of that land is His. Verse 9 names three nations surrounding David's kingdom. He was in the process of subjugating them when he prayed the prayer of Psalm 60. His plea is that he is trusting in God alone. Notice in verse 13 that David claimed victory before the battle began. God does not deny that kind of faith.

Application_____

Faith not only conquers fear, it also brings "the peace of God, which passeth all understanding" (Phil. 4:7). The formula for that kind of peace is outlined in Colossians 3:15-17. First, be thankful. Second, "let the word of Christ dwell in you richly." Third, "in all wisdom" teach and admonish one another. Fourth, sing "psalms and hymns and spiritual songs" to the Lord. Finally, "whatever ye do in word or deed, do all in the name of the Lord Jesus, giving thanks to God and the Father by Him."

Psalm 109:1-10

To the chief Musician, A Psalm of David.

1. HOLD NOT thy peace, O God of my praise;
2. For the mouth of the wicked and the mouth of the deceitful are opened against me: they have spoken against me with a lying tongue.
3. They compassed me about also with words of hatred; and fought against me without a cause.
4. For my love they are my adversaries: but I *give myself unto* prayer.
5. And they have rewarded me evil for good, and hatred for my love.
6. Set thou a wicked man over him: and let Satan stand at his right hand.
7. When he shall be judged, let him be condemned: and let his prayer become sin.
8. Let his days be few; *and* let another take his office.
9. Let his children be fatherless, and his wife a widow.
10. Let his children be continually vagabonds, and beg: let them *seek their bread* also out of their desolate places.

Commentary

Except for the last two verses, Psalm 109 is a petition. The first twenty verses are imprecatory—the psalmist is calling upon God to exercise vengeance upon his enemies. David proved early in his life that he understood he was not to avenge himself, but that vengeance belongs to God (Dt. 32:35). For instance, he abstained from avenging himself against both Saul and Nabal (1 Sam. 24:4-7; 25:32-34; 26:8-10).

Verses 1-5 tell us that David was being maligned by people who were wicked, deceitful liars and haters. He had shown particular kindness to them, but they "hated him without a cause" (Ps. 69:4; Jn. 15:25). He was being treated like his greater Son, Jesus, would be treated a thousand years later.

In verses 6-19, the "they" is changed to "he" as David calls upon God to judge and condemn the leader of his adversaries. In verse 6, *Satan* is a word usually translated "adversary" or "accuser." However, it is rendered *Satan* in 1 Chronicles 21:1, Job 1:6 and Zechariah 3:1—in each of these verses the accuser is Satan. (See also Rev. 12:9-10). Here in Psalm 109, the KJV translators deduced that Satan was the real perpetrator of the evil against David.

In Acts 1:16-20, the apostle Peter quotes from verse 8 and from Psalm 69:25. He tells us that ultimately the maledictions of verses 7-10 are against Judas Iscariot and that the Holy Spirit was directing the words of David. Luke 22:3 informs us that the betrayal by Judas was instigated by Satan.

Application

It is true that in this world children suffer for the sins of their fathers (Dt. 5:9; Josh. 7:24; Dan. 6:24). However, condemnation and eternal destiny are determined according to each one's individual works (Dt. 24:16; Ezk. 18:20; Rev. 20:12). In the eternal perspective, justice will be done. "Shall not the Judge of all the earth do right?" (Gen. 18:25)

Psalm 109:11-20

11. Let the extortioner catch all that he hath; and let the strangers spoil his labour.
12. Let there be none to extend mercy unto him: neither let there be any to favour his fatherless children.
13. Let his posterity be cut off; *and* in the generation following let their name be blotted out.
14. Let the iniquity of his fathers be remembered with the LORD; and let not the sin of his mother be blotted out.
15. Let them be before the LORD continually, that he may cut off the memory of them from the earth.
16. Because that he remembered not to shew mercy, but persecuted the poor and needy man, that he might even slay the broken in heart.
17. As he loved cursing, so let it come unto him: as he delighted not in blessing, so let it be far from him.
18. As he clothed himself with cursing like as with his garment, so let it come into his bowels like water, and like oil into his bones.
19. Let it be unto him as the garment *which* covereth him, and for a girdle wherewith he is girded continually.
20. *Let* this *be* the reward of mine adversaries from the LORD, and of them that speak evil against my soul.

Commentary_____

Did it please the Lord for His servant to pray such a vindictive prayer? David was anointed by God to be king over His people. David recognized the importance of his assignment in God's program on Earth. He had a heart's desire to perform in a way pleasing to God, and he communed with God regularly.

Evil men who had no respect for God or God's anointed king were impeding God's work. David was perplexed—how could an almighty, righteous God allow mere men to sabotage His work? He wanted God to avenge Himself and His king so the work of God could proceed. Since David was contemplating vengeance, it was better to pray about his thoughts than to act upon them. From that standpoint, God was pleased.

Because David had a teachable heart, God could use the prayer to help him better understand how God thinks and acts. Also God had a purpose in recording this prayer for future generations. New Testament passages, like Romans 15:4 and 2 Timothy 3:16-17, assure us that God had us in mind when He made this prayer a part of Scripture. If David had never prayed the prayer, God could not have used it in Acts 1:20.

When our hearts are right towards God, He can use even an improper prayer for His purposes! However, such prayers do not alter His methods of dealing with His enemies. Those actions were determined and settled before the foundation of the world.

Application_____

"Fret not thyself because of evildoers"; "rest in the LORD, and wait patiently for Him"; "for evildoers shall be cut off: but those that wait upon the LORD, they shall inherit the earth" (Ps. 37: 1, 7, 9). The most difficult assignment for the Lord's servants is waiting for Him to deal with wickedness in His way and at His time.

Psalm 109: 21-31

21. But do thou for me, O God the Lord, for thy name's sake: because thy mercy *is* good, deliver thou me.
22. For I *am* poor and needy, and my heart is wounded within me.
23. I am gone like the shadow when it declineth: I am tossed up and down as the locust.
24. My knees are weak through fasting; and thy flesh faileth of fatness.
25. I became also a reproach unto them: *when* they looked upon me they shaked their heads.
26. Help me, O LORD my God: O save me according to thy mercy:
27. That they may know that this *is* thy hand; *that* thou, LORD, hast done it.
28. Let them curse, but bless thou: when they arise, let them be ashamed; but let thy servant rejoice.
29. Let mine adversaries be clothed with shame, and let them cover themselves with their own confusion, as with a mantle.
30. I will greatly praise the LORD with my mouth; yea, I will praise him among the multitude.
31. For he shall stand at the right hand of the poor, to save *him* from those that condemn his soul.

Commentary_____

At verse 21, David's prayer changes markedly. It is as though the Lord said, "David, you're on the wrong track. I'll handle your accusers--you're the one who needs my attention now." By fretting about his adversaries, David had brought himself to a state of exhaustion: mentally, emotionally, spiritually and physically. While he is praying, God has made him aware of his own desperate need. Thus he cries out to GOD the Lord, "Deliver me! Help me!" He bases his plea both on God's reputation before men and God's mercy to His servants. He asks God to act on his behalf in such a way that his enemies will know that his God has manifested Himself.

David's attitude now is, "Let them curse--just demonstrate that Your blessing is upon me." In verse 28 and 29, he is not asking for vengance as he did previously. He is drawing a contrast between what the future for his enemies will be and what his own future will be. While he is rejoicing, they will be enveloped in the confusion and the shame they brought upon themselves.

In verse 30, David shows that he has claimed the victory over his enemies! He resolves to spend his time on Earth publicly praising the LORD instead of fretting about his enemies. In verse 31, the Lord is at David's right hand because he has confessed that he is poor and needy. The Lord is always merciful to those who acknowledge their helpless state. In contrast, Satan is at the right hand of David's cheif adversary (v. 6). Who, therefore, stands in the better place?

Application_____

What have we learned from Psalm 109? First, if we feel vengeful, it is better to pray than to act. Second, fretting over the evil deeds of the wicked will make us sick--body and soul. It will also make us ineffective in God's purpose for us. Third, the purpose of prayer is not to get God to act on our behalf; its purpose is to make us more usable to God. Fourth, the Lord is at the right hand of those who see themselves as poor and needy.

Psalm 110

A Psalm of David.

1. THE LORD said unto my Lord, Sit thou at my right hand, until I make thine enemies thy footstool.
2. The LORD shall send the rod of thy strength out of Zion: rule thou in the midst of thine enemies.
3. Thy people *shall be* willing in the day of thy power, in the beauties of holiness from the womb of the morning: thou hast the dew of thy youth.
4. The LORD hath sworn, and will not repent, Thou *art* a priest for ever after the order of Melchizedek.
5. The Lord at thy right hand shall strike through kings in the day of his wrath.
6. He shall judge among the heathen, he shall fill *the places* with the dead bodies; he shall wound the heads over many countries.
7. He shall drink of the brook in the way: therefore shall he lift up the head.

Commentary

In the New Testament, there are more quotes from and references to Psalm 110 than any other chapter of the Old Testament—more than twenty-five from verse 1 alone. Jesus quoted from verse 1 (Mt. 22:44) to prove to Jewish leaders that the Messiah must be both David's son and David's Lord, both man and God. Peter quoted the verse (Acts 2:34-35) to prove that the resurrection of Jesus Christ was "according to the Scriptures" (1 Cor. 15:4). The writer of Hebrews uses the verse to prove the deity of Christ as the Great High Priest (Heb. 1:13).

"The LORD (*Yahweh*) said unto my Lord (*Adonai*), sit thou at my right hand." That was fulfilled at our Lord's ascension (Lk. 24:51; Heb. 1:3). The ultimate fulfillment of "until I make thine enemies thy footstool" will occur at the end of the Millennial reign of Messiah (1 Cor. 15:24-25).

Verse 2 speaks of that coming day when the God of Heaven sends the Messiah to be God with His people on Earth (Joel 3:16; Rev. 19:11-16). Israel will receive Jesus as Messiah and become a nation born in a day (v. 3). See also Isaiah 66:8 and Zechariah 12:10.

The chief characteristics of a priest "after the order of Melchizedek" are the following: 1) He is a priest upon a throne, meaning he is both priest and king. 2) His priesthood is eternal. Aaron met neither of these requirements.

Verse 5 and 6 prophesy of Armageddon, when the Lord Jesus will manifest Himself as Messiah by destroying this world's system and establishing His kingdom on Earth (Dan. 2:44). Verse 7 portrays the kingdom as the time of "refreshing" and "restitution" (Acts. 3:19-21).

Application

Melchizedek is a remarkable Bible personality introduced in Genesis 14:18. After he is mentioned there, he is further described in Hebrews 7:1-4. Hebrews 7:5-28 contrasts his priesthood with that of Aaron and explains how Melchizedek typifies our Great High Priest, Jesus Christ. He is a fascinating subject for your personal study.

Psalm 111

1. PRAISE YE the LORD. I will praise the LORD with *my* whole heart, in the assembly of the upright, and *in* the congregation.
2. The works of the LORD *are* great, sought out of all them that have pleasure therein.
3. His work *is* honourable and glorious: and his righteousness endureth for ever.
4. He hath made his wonderful works to be remembered: the LORD *is* gracious and full of compassion.
5. He hath given meat unto them that fear him: he will ever be mindful of his covenant.
6. He hath shewed his people the power of his works, that he may give them the heritage of the heathen.
7. The works of his hands *are* verity and judgment; all his commandments *are* sure.
8. They stand fast for ever and ever, *and are* done in truth and uprightness.
9. He sent redemption unto his people: he hath commanded his covenant for ever: holy and reverend is his name.
10. The fear of the LORD *is* the beginning of wisdom: a good understanding have all they that do *his commandments:* his praise endureth for ever.

Commentary_____

In the Hebrew text, Psalm 111 is a twenty-two line acrostic poem. After an introductory "Praise the LORD" (*Hallelujah*), each line begins with a different letter of the Hebrew alphabet successively. The psalmist is announcing that he will praise the LORD in public assembly for His attributes as manifested by His wondrous works. His works are proclaimed to be "great" (v. 2), "honorable and glorious" (v. 3), "wonderful" (v. 4), powerful (v. 6), and "verity and judgment"—true and just (v. 7).

Because of the magnitude of His works, those who take pleasure in them seek them out, that is, ponder them. What the LORD does arises from what He is—righteous, gracious, and full of compassion. He will be like that forever. Because of His attributes, that which He communicates to us is forever sure, true, and right.

The greatest manifestation of the LORD on behalf of His own is redemption. He has purchased out from slavery those who were already rightfully His by creation. His people are doubly His. He made them for Himself. Then He found His own in the slave market of sin. He redeemed us not with silver and gold but "with the precious blood of Christ, as of a lamb without blemish and without spot" (1 Pet. 1:19). Our redemption is made possible through a covenant of blood and endures forever; therefore, we regard His holy name with reverence and awe.

Application_____

If I apply verse 10 to myself, I will purpose to regard the awesome Lord with the respect and honor due Him. When I do that, He will be pleased to impart to me His own wisdom and understanding through His Word. The world in which I live is devoid of such wisdom and understanding in its quest for knowledge and possessions. I will praise Him here and now and forevermore.

Psalm 112

1. PRAISE YE the LORD. Blessed *is* the man *that* feareth the LORD, *that* delighteth greatly in his commandments.
2. His seed shall be mighty upon the earth: the generation of the upright shall be blessed.
3. Wealth and riches *shall be* in his house: and his righteousness endureth for ever.
4. Unto the upright there ariseth light in the darkness: *he is* gracious, and full of compassion, and righteous.
5. A good man sheweth favour, and lendeth: he will guide his affairs with discretion.
6. Surely he shall not be moved for ever: the righteous shall be in everlasting remembrance.
7. He shall not be afraid of evil tidings: his heart is fixed, trusting in the LORD.
8. His heart *is* established, he shall not be afraid, until he see *his desire* upon his enemies.
9. He hath dispersed, he hath given to the poor; his righteousness endureth for ever; his horn shall be exalted with honour.
10. The wicked shall see *it,* and be grieved; he shall gnash with his teeth, and melt away: the desire of the wicked shall perish.

Commentary_____

By reading Psalm 111:10 and 112:1, we see that this psalm is a sequel to Psalm 111 which extols the awesome LORD God who is to be feared. Psalm 112 presents the blessedness of the one who fears that awesome God. The structure of the two psalms is the same. The first verse is translated from the first three lines of a Hebrew poem, each line beginning with the first three letters of the Hebrew alphabet in successive order. In verse 10, the last three letters are used to begin the last three lines of the Hebraic twenty-two line poem. Verses 2-9 contain the main theme of each psalm, utilizing the remaining sixteen letters of the Hebrew alphabet in successive order.

Both Abraham (Gen. 22:12) and Job (Job 1:1, 8) feared God, who declared both men righteous (Gen. 15:6; Job 1:1). Both were men of great material wealth. That wealth was temporal, but their "righteousness endureth forever" (v. 9). Now compare Psalm 111:3-5 with Psalm 112:3-5. Those who "fear the LORD" acquire His attributes. The measure of one's fear of the LORD is his lack of fear of "evil tidings" (v.7) and of enemies (v. 8; Ps. 56:11; Mt. 10:28).

The first part of verse 9 is quoted in 2 Corinthians 9:9 and is applied to Christians in 2 Corinthians 9:10-15. Our principle obligation is to see that the seed of the Gospel is sown. When we minister to those who sow the seed, we supply their material needs and generate much prayer and thanksgiving to God on both their part and ours.

Application_____

Hannah's horn was "exalted in the LORD" (1 Sam. 2:1). Messiah's horn will be exalted when the LORD thunders out of Heaven to judge the ends of the earth (1 Sam. 2:10; Joel 3:16). Before that could come to pass, it was necessary that He become "the horn of our salvation," our Savior (2 Sam. 22:3; Lk. 1:69).

Psalm 113

1. PRAISE YE the LORD. Praise, O ye servants of the LORD, praise the name of the LORD.

2. Blessed be the name of the LORD from this time forth and for evermore.

3. From the rising of the sun unto the going down of the same the LORD'S name *is* to be praised.

4. The LORD *is* high above all nations, *and* his glory above the heavens.

5. Who *is* like unto the Lord our God, who dwelleth on high,

6. Who humbleth *himself* be behold *the things that are* in heaven, and in the earth!

7. He raiseth up the poor out of the dust, *and* lifteth the needy out of the dunghill;

8. That he may set *him* with princes, *even* with the princes of his people.

9. He maketh the barren woman to keep house, *and to be* a joyful mother of children. Praise ye the LORD.

Commentary

This psalm is the pinnacle of the hallelujah (praise) psalms because in it the psalmist purposes to put into words the magnitude of God's greatness and the height of His position. Through the ages, the people of Israel have sung this psalm at the ordained annual festivals. Along with Psalm 114, it is recited at the Passover *Seder* before the meal is eaten.

"From the rising of the sun unto the going down of the same" is a poetic reference to "everyone, everywhere on Earth" (Ps. 50:1; Isa. 59:19; Mal. 1:11). The realization of verse 3 will not occur until Messiah is enthroned at Jerusalem. Not until then will everyone on Earth confess, "The LORD is high above all nations, and His glory above the Heavens" (v. 4).

The psalmist is not entirely successful in his purpose because there are no words sufficient to fully describe the LORD our God. Neither can the finite mind grasp His fullness. The best the psalmist can do is to ask the question of verse 5 so that it can be pondered.

The Infinite One must look down from His heights even to minister to the inhabitants of Heaven. Yet He descends to tend to the very lowliest on Earth! Each individual who calls upon Him without reservation will be among the princely group who reign with Him. The prime example of verse 9 is Hannah (1 Sam. 1:10, 17).

Application

The LORD God has been pleased to reveal much about Himself through creation, the written word, and the person of His Son (Heb. 1:1-4, 10). As we yield to the ministration of the indwelling Holy Spirit, He uses God's revelation to increase our comprehension of His person and purposes. The time will come when those who now "know in part" shall "know even as we are know" (1 Cor. 13:12).

Psalm 114

1. WHEN ISRAEL went out of Egypt, the house of Jacob from a people of strange language;
2. Judah was his sanctuary, *and* Israel his dominion.
3. The sea saw *it,* and fled: Jordan was driven back.
4. The mountains skipped like rams, *and* the little hills like lambs.
5. What *ailed* thee, O thou sea, that thou fleddest? thou Jordan, *that* thou was driven back?
6. Ye mountains, *that* ye skipped like rams; *and* ye little hills, like lambs?
7. Tremble, thou earth, at the presence of the Lord, at the presence of the God of Jacob;
8. Which turned the rock *into* a standing water, the flint into a fountain of waters.

Commentary

Psalm 114 is an excellent example of the Hebrew form of poetic expression known as "synonymous parallelism." Each verse is a couplet in which the second line repeats the thought of the first and complements it with additional information. One purpose of the psalm is to conform to the instructions of Deuteronomy 4:9-10. In every devout Hebrew home, the children would hear and sing this psalm on many occasions. It summarizes the miraculous works the LORD performed for Israel during the first forty years of its history—from its departure from Egypt to the entry into the Promised Land (Exodus 13 through Joshua 3).

The LORD brought Israel out of Egypt to be a "kingdom of priests" (Ex. 19:6). His purpose was to establish His sanctuary among them. He would be their God, and they would be His special people (Lev. 26:11-13).

In verses 3-6, the psalmist personifies the mountains, the sea, and the river. The Israelites were amazed and awestruck in the presence of One who could set aside the natural laws that governed them. They beheld what their Creator could do in order to keep His covenant with Jacob. (See Exodus 19:18 for the historical background of verse 4, and see Exodus 17:6 and Numbers 20:11 for the background of verse 8). The first issuance of water from the rock was at the beginning of the forty year period. The second instance of this miracle was near the end of that period.

Application

For those of us now on Earth, verse 7 points to a great shaking yet to come. Here are just a few of the many scriptures that prophesy of it: Joel 3:15-16; Matthew 24:29; Hebrews 12:26; Revelation 6:12-17. Praise God, before that terrible day arrives, our Lord Jesus will come for His own (Jn. 14:3; 1 Th. 4:16-18), to "deliver us from the wrath to come" (1 Th. 1:10). "So shall we ever be with the Lord" (1 Th. 4:18). "Even so, come, Lord Jesus" (Rev. 22:20).

Psalm 115

1. NOT UNTO us, O LORD, not unto us, but unto thy name give glory, for thy mercy, *and* for thy truth's sake.
2. Wherefore should the heathen say, Where *is* now their God?
3. But our God *is* in the heavens: he hath done whatsoever he hath pleased.
4. Their idols *are* silver and gold, the work of men's hands.
5. They have mouths, that they speak not: eyes have they, but they see not:
6. They have ears, but they hear not: noses have they, but they smell not:
7. They have hands, but they handle not: feet have they, but they walk not: neither speak they through their throat.
8. They that make them are like unto them; *so is* every one that trusteth in them.
9. O Israel, trust thou in the LORD: he *is* their help and their shield.
10. O house of Aaron, trust in the LORD, he *is* their help and their shield.
11. Ye that fear the LORD, trust in the LORD: he *is* their help and their shield.
12. The LORD hath been mindful of us: he will bless *us;* he will bless the house of Israel; he will bless the house of Aaron.
13. He will bless them that fear the LORD, *both* small and great.
14. The LORD shall increase you more and more, you and your children.
15. Ye *are* blessed of the LORD which made heaven and earth.
16. The heaven, *even* the heavens, *are* the LORD'S: but the earth hath he given to the children of men.
17. The dead praise not the LORD, neither any that go down into silence.
18. But we will bless the LORD from this time forth and for evermore. Praise the LORD.

Commentary_____

The first verse of this worship psalm is addressed to the LORD in the hearing of an assembled audience. The listeners are not gathered to glorify men but to give glory to the true God. After denouncing the gods of the heathen people around them (vv. 2-8), the worship leader exhorts his listeners to trust the LORD (vv. 9-11), receive His blessings (vv. 12-16), and in return, praise Him(vv. 17-18).

The God of heaven does whatever pleases Him because He is omnipotent. The idols of the heathen can do nothing! It should be obvious that anything made is inferior to its maker. Therefore, an idol worshipper trusts a god that is inferior to its worshipper. The absurdity of this is satirized in a number of Bible passages. See Isaiah 44:9-20 for one of the best examples.

The threefold exhortation to trust the LORD (vv. 9-11) is fortified by a threefold assurance that He is trustworthy, as a help and a shield to all who fear the LORD. The God of heaven, who is able to do as He pleases, is mindful of His people and is pleased to bless them, whether they be great or small. The One who is pleased to bless is the One who made the heavens and the earth as well as the One who placed man in charge of the earth (Ps. 8:4-6). The ungodly want to make their own objects of worship in an effort to control heaven and earth as evidenced in the story of Babel (Gen. 11:4).

Application_____

The LORD receives no praise on Earth from bodies in the grave (v. 17); therefore, we should praise Him while we have breath! When we are raised from the grave and are present with the Lord, we will need no exhortation. In this reluctant body, I need to be exhorted unto praise—"from this time forth" (v. 18). To "bless the LORD" is to extol Him vocally and publicly both for His attributes and His wonderful works toward us.

Psalm 116:1-14

1. I LOVE the LORD, because he hath heard my voice *and* my supplications.
2. Because he hath inclined his ear unto me, therefore will I call upon *him* as long as I live.
3. The sorrows of death compassed me, and the pains of hell gat hold upon me: I found trouble and sorrow.
4. Then called I upon the name of the LORD; O LORD, I beseech thee, deliver my soul.
5. Gracious *is* the LORD, and righteous; yea, our God *is* merciful.
6. The LORD preserveth the simple: I was brought low, and he helped me.
7. Return unto thy rest, O my soul; for the LORD hath dealt bountifully with thee.
8. For thou hast delivered my soul from death, mine eyes from tears, *and* my feet from falling.
9. I will walk before the LORD in the land of the living.
10. I believed, therefore have I spoken: I was greatly afflicted:
11. I said in my haste, All men *are* liars.
12. What shall I render unto the LORD *for* all his benefits toward me?
13. I will take the cup of salvation, and call upon the name of the LORD.
14. I will pay my vows unto the LORD now in the presence of all his people.

Commentary_____

The use of the first person singular throughout this psalm assures us that it is the personal testimony of the psalmist. He proclaims his love for the LORD who has delivered him from a life-threatening malady. His testimony mirrors that of everyone who has received Christ as Savior. Compare this psalm with the following New Testament passages about salvation:

Verse 3—"You hath he quickened (made alive) who were dead in trespasses and sins" (Eph. 2:1).

Verse 4—"For whosoever shall call upon the name of the LORD shall be saved" (Rom. 10:13).

Verse 5—"For by grace are ye saved through faith; and that not of yourselves: it is the gift of God--" (Eph. 2:8).

Verse 6—"Humble yourselves in the sight of the Lord, and he shall lift you up" (Jas. 4:10).

Verse 7—"Come unto me, all ye that labor and are heavy laden, and I will give you rest" (Mt. 11:28).

Verse 8—"For the wages of sin is death; but the gift of God is eternal life through Jesus Christ, our Lord" (Rom. 6:23).

Verse 9—"As ye have therefore received Christ Jesus the Lord, so walk ye in Him" (Col. 2:6).

Verse 10—"I believed, and therefore have I spoken; we also believe, and therefore speak (2 Cor. 4:13). "For I have delivered unto you first of all that which I also received" (1 Cor. 15:3).

Application_____

The evidence that we received salvation is that we deliver that which we received. The testimony of the Apostle Paul was "I received. . . I delivered. . . you received. . . you're saved. . .you stand" (1 Cor. 15:1). Delivering what we have received is the answer to the question posed in Psalm 116:12.

Psalm 116:15-19

15. Precious in the sight of the LORD *is* the death of his saints.
16. O LORD, truly I *am* thy servant; I *am* thy servant, *and* the son of thine handmaid: thou hast loosed my bonds.
17. I will offer to thee the sacrifice of thanksgiving, and will call upon the name of the LORD.
18. I will pay my vows unto the LORD now in the presence of all his people,
19. In the courts of the LORD'S house, in the midst of thee, O Jerusalem. Praise ye the LORD.

Psalm 117

1. O PRAISE the LORD, all ye nations: praise him, all ye people.
2. For his merciful kindness is great toward us: and the truth of the LORD *endureth* for ever. Praise ye the LORD.

Commentary

Verse 15 is great comfort for those approaching death and those bereaved by another's death. The Lord does not take the death of His own lightly. He has made full preparations for the transition beforehand (Jn. 14:2, Rev. 14:13).

Three of the complaints the LORD makes against Israel in Isaiah 43:22-24 are the following: "thou hast not called upon me"; "neither hast thou honored me with thy sacrifices"; "thou hast made me to serve with thy sins. . . [and] wearied me with thine iniquities." In verse 4 of this psalm, the psalmist declares that he had called upon the LORD for deliverance. Three times he vows to continue calling upon the LORD (vv. 2, 13, 17). Twice he vows to offer the thanksgiving sacrifice (Lev. 7:12) in the presence of the LORD's people at the temple court (vv. 14, 18). He will thus serve the LORD free of sin and iniquity.

The uniqueness of Psalm 117 is three-fold. It is the shortest of the 1189 chapters of the Bible. It is also the middle chapter—549 chapters precede it, and 549 chapters follow it. The psalm has another distinctive characteristic. Romans 15:4 assures us that the Holy Spirit had present day saints in mind when He authored the Old Testament. Verses 9-12 of Romans 15 quote from each of the four divisions of the Old Testament (Law, History, Poetry, Prophecy) to prove that it was written for both Gentile and Jew. Romans 15:9 quotes from 2 Samuel 22:50, Romans 15:10 from Deuteronomy 32:43, Romans 15:11 from Psalm 117:1, and Romans 15:12 from Isaiah 11:1, 2. Little Psalm 117 was chosen to represent the entire poetic section of the Old Testament!

Application

The Lord wants us to call upon Him (Jer. 33:3; Rom. 10:12). If you want to be "meet" (fit) for the master's use, and prepared unto every good work" with "righteousness, faith, love, and peace," then "call on the Lord out of a pure heart" (2 Tim. 2:22). "Let us offer the sacrifice of praise to God continually, that is, the fruit of our lips, giving thanks to his name" (Heb.13:15).

Psalm 118:1-14

1. O GIVE thanks unto the LORD; for *he is* good: because his mercy *endureth* for ever.
2. Let Israel now say, that his mercy *endureth* for ever.
3. Let the house of Aaron now say, that his mercy *endureth* for ever.
4. Let them now that fear the LORD say, that his mercy *endureth* for ever.
5. I called upon the LORD in distress: the LORD answered me, *and set me* in a large place.
6. The LORD *is* on my side; I will not fear: what can man do unto me?
7. The LORD taketh my part with them that help me: therefore shall I see *my desire* upon them that hate me.
8. *It is* better to trust in the LORD than to put confidence in man.
9. *It is* better to trust in the LORD than to put confidence in princes.
10. All nations compassed me about: but in the name of the LORD will I destroy them.
11. They compassed me about; yea, they compassed me about: but in the name of the LORD I will destroy them.
12. They compassed me about like bees; they are quenched as the fire of thorns: for in the name of the LORD I will destroy them.
13. Thou hast thrust sore at me that I might fall: but the LORD helped me.
14. The LORD *is* my strength and song, and is become my salvation.

Commentary_____

The arrangement of this psalm reflects its purpose—antiphonal singing that celebrates events such as the laying of the foundation of the rebuilt temple (Ezra 3:11). This psalm was used as a processional for worshippers ascending to Mt. Zion during annual feasts. Leaders sounded out the first part of each verse; the rest of the worshippers responded with the second part. Verse 1 begins several other psalms such as 106 and 107. Compare the first four verses of Psalm 118 with the structure of Psalm 136, which is also an example of an antiphonal processional.

"Let Israel," "the house of Aaron," "them who fear the LORD"—compare these phrases with Psalm 115:9-13. Trust in the LORD followed by blessings from the LORD began with the nation of Israel, led by its priestly family. Looking forward, Messiah's kingdom will extend to all people in every nation who "fear the LORD." Then everyone will say, "His mercy endureth forever."

Verse 5 certainly depicts the present plight of Israel. They are "in distress" (dire straits). Messiah will surely "enlarge their borders (Ex. 34:24; Dt. 19:8).

Hebrews 13:6 quotes verse 6 and applies it to present day believers.

It is better to trust the LORD than to trust the chiefest of men because only the LORD can determine an individual's eternal destiny.

Verses 10-13 expand upon verse 5. At Armageddon, the LORD will solve the plight of Israel.

Application_____

Verse 14 is extracted from the song of Moses (Ex. 15:2), which was the victory song of a people saved from Pharaoh's grasp. It will be Israel's song of victory in the coming Messianic Kingdom (Isa. 12:2). It will be the song of victory for the Tribulation saints (Rev. 15:3), and finally, it will be the song of all nations (Rev. 15:4). It should be our song both now and forevermore.

Psalm 118:15-29

15. The voice of rejoicing and salvation *is* in the tabernacles of the righteous: the right hand of the LORD doeth valiantly.

16. The right hand of the LORD is exalted: the right hand of the LORD doeth valiantly.

17. I shall not die, but live, and declare the works of the LORD.

18. The LORD hath chastened me sore: but he hath not given me over unto death.

19. Open to me the gates of righteousness: I will go into them, *and* I will praise the LORD:

20. This gate of the LORD, into which the righteous shall enter.

21. I will praise thee: for thou hast heard me, and art become my salvation.

22. The stone *which* the builders refused is become the head *stone* of the corner.

23. This is the LORD'S doing; it *is* marvelous in our eyes.

24. This *is* the day *which* the LORD hath made; we will rejoice and be glad in it.

25. Save now, I beseech thee, O LORD: O LORD, I beseech thee, send now prosperity.

26. Blessed *be* he that cometh in the name of the LORD: we have blessed you out of the house of the LORD.

27. God *is* the LORD, which hath shewed us light: bind the sacrifice with cords, *even* unto the horns of the altar.

28. Thou *art* my God, and I will praise thee: *thou art* my God, I will exalt thee.

29. O give thanks unto the LORD; for *he is* good: for his mercy *endureth* for ever.

Commentary_____

Martin Luther declared Psalm 118 to be the dearest to his own heart of all the scriptures that he treasured. No doubt, through the centuries, verse 24 has been the most quoted portion of God's Word. Verse 22 is quoted six times in the New Testament. Remarkably, the same can be said for the first half of verse 26, which looks forward to the first coming of Christ (Mt. 21:9) and also to the second coming (Mt. 23:39).

The word *rock* is used metaphorically throughout Scripture for Christ (1 Cor. 10:4) as is the word *stone* (Acts 4:11). Particularly to the Church, Christ is the Chief Cornerstone. This truth is declared by the apostle Paul in Ephesians 2:19-22 and further expounded upon by the apostle Peter in 1 Peter 2:4-6. Peter continues his exposition of the subject by identifying Christ as the "stone of stumbling" to the Jewish nation in its present stance (1 Pet. 2:8).

Daniel prophesied a "smiting stone" which would destroy the Gentile world powers at the end of this age (Dan. 2:34). In other words, our Lord Jesus Christ, who was, in the past, the "stumbling stone" to the Jew is now the "Cornerstone" to the Church. In the future, He will become the "smiting stone" to the Gentile. "This is the LORD's doing; it is marvelous in our eyes" (Ps. 118:23).

Application_____

Notice the psalm ends with the same admonition with which it begins. We would thank Him more for His goodness and His mercy if we reached the same conclusion about Him as the psalmist did. "Thou art my God, and I will praise Thee: thou art my God, I will exalt Thee" (v. 28).

Psalm 119:1-8

ALEPH.

1. BLESSED ARE the undefiled in the way, who walk in the law of the LORD.
2. Blessed *are* they that keep his testimonies, *and that* seek him with the whole heart.
3. They also do no iniquity: they walk in his ways.
4. Thou hast commanded *us* to keep thy precepts diligently.
5. O that my ways were directed to keep thy statutes!
6. Then shall I not be ashamed, when I have respect unto all thy commandments.
7. I will praise thee with uprightness of heart, when I shall have learned thy righteous judgments.
8. I will keep thy statutes: O forsake me not utterly.

Commentary

With 176 verses, Psalm 119 is by far the longest chapter in the Bible. It is also the most elaborate of the acrostic psalms. Each of the eight verses in each of the twenty-two sections begins with the same Hebrew letter. In the ALEPH section each verse begins with the first letter of the Hebrew alphabet. Each verse in the BETH section begins with the second letter, and this pattern continues through all twenty-two letters of the Hebrew alphabet.

In the context of this psalm, the "law" of the LORD consists of all the instructions He has given to mankind. His "testimonies" are His own witness concerning His person, purposes, and pronouncements. His "ways" speak of the manner in which He acts and the manner in which He wants His people to act. His ways are different than our ways (Isa. 55:8, 9).

The first three verses are addressed to the reader. Beginning at verse 4, the psalm is addressed to the LORD. His "precepts" are authoritative principles by which His children are to live. His "statutes" are written rules of conduct. His "commandments" are specific directives, and His "judgments" are judicial decisions.

In these eight verses the psalmist utilizes seven different Hebrew words to designate God's revelation to man. If our walk—our hour-to-hour conduct—continues to be undefiled, we will be blessed. Seeking Him with a whole heart, we will do no iniquity because we will be walking in His ways. We will not be ashamed; rather, we will praise Him with an upright heart and continue to learn from His law, testimonies, ways, precepts, statutes, commandments, and judgments.

Application

The key word in the ALEPH section of Psalm 119 is "keep" (vv. 2, 4, 5, 8). It means "to continually observe" in the sense that one would say, "he keeps his word," "she keeps a clean house" or "we keep in touch with one another."

Psalm 119:9-16

BETH.

9. Wherewithal shall a young man cleanse his way? by taking heed *thereto* according to thy word.
10. With my whole heart have I sought thee: O let me not wander from thy commandments.
11. Thy word have I hid in mine heart, that I might not sin against thee.
12. Blessed *art* thou, O LORD: teach me thy statutes.
13. With my lips have I declared all the judgments of thy mouth.
14. I have rejoiced in the way of thy testimonies, as *much as* in all riches.
15. I will meditate in thy precepts, and have respect unto thy ways.
16. I will delight myself in thy statutes: I will not forget thy word.

Commentary_____

In section BETH we find the same seven designations for God's word used by the psalmist in section ALEPH. He adds an eighth one and uses it three times. The Hebrew word translated "word" connotes the total revelation of God to man. It is the sum of the other seven designations. The exaltation of the Word of God is the theme of Psalm 119.

The psalmist asks a question and then answers it (v. 9). He makes two requests of the LORD (vv. 10, 12). He recounts to the LORD four ways in which he has conducted his life in the past: 1) he has sought the LORD with his whole heart in conformity to his observation in verse 2; 2) in obedience to the command in verse 4, he has memorized God's Word; 3) he has publicly declared God's message; 4) rejoicing in God's ways has been more important than riches to him.

The psalmist tells the LORD how he purposes to conduct himself in the future: 1) he will take time to meditate upon God's Word and thereby show due respect to the ways of the LORD; 2) he will keep God's words in constant remembrance by finding his delight in heeding God's Word.

In verse 15, the psalmist introduces a key theme that is developed in later verses--the benefits that accrue to those who meditate upon God's Word. Think upon the wondrous promises in Psalm 1:2, 3 for those who meditate.

Application_____

The psalmist has given us a pattern for a proper relationship with our God. We should ask Him questions and seek to find the answers in His Word. He is pleased when we make requests like "let me not wander" and "teach me thy statutes." It is good to evaluate with Him our past conduct in respect to our relationship with Him and His Word. Then we need to declare to Him our intentions and desires concerning the future of our relationship.

Psalm 119:17-24

GIMEL.

17. Deal bountifully with thy servant, *that* I may live, and keep thy word.
18. Open thou mine eyes, that I may behold wondrous things out of thy law.
19. I *am* a stranger in the earth: hide not thy commandments from me.
20. My soul breaketh for the longing *that it hath* unto thy judgments at all times.
21. Thou hast rebuked the proud *that are* cursed, which do err from thy commandments.
22. Remove from me reproach and contempt; for I have kept thy testimonies.
23. Princes also did sit *and* speak against me: *but* thy servant did meditate in thy statutes.
24. Thy testimonies also *are* my delight *and* my counsellors.

Commentary_____

In each of the eight verses of section GIMEL, the psalmist employs one of the eight designations for God's Word. But he doesn't use all eight of the Hebrew nouns. "Ways" and "precepts" are omitted; "commandments" and "testimonies" are used twice.

"Deal bountifully"—the psalmist is asking that he be classified among the blessed ones of verse 2. Except for the spiritual sight and insight given by the Lord, it is not possible for earth dwellers to behold the wondrous truths in God's Word (Jn. 3:3, 1 Cor. 2:9-12). Like Abraham, we must consider ourselves "strangers and pilgrims on the earth" if we are to see and embrace the promises and deep truths of God's Word (Heb. 11:13). We must "at all times" (v. 20) have a longing for His Word that can only be sated by a Spirit-supplied knowledge of His wonders.

In this world people who "err from [His] commandments" (v. 21) reproach and have contempt for anyone who keeps His testimonies. Since God has rebuked such individuals and condemned them, the psalmist asks to be separated from them. Even though he has been verbally abused by the leaders of society, he continues to keep God's testimonies.

In verses 15 and 16, the psalmist announced his intent to meditate and delight in God's Word. In verses 23 and 24, meditation and delight have become both his pattern of life and his counselors.

Application_____

As I hide God's Word in my heart (v. 11), He will open my eyes that I may behold wondrous things (v. 18). As I meditate on it and take delight in it, I will become unconcerned about those who hold me in contempt and speak against me. They are blind leaders of the blind (Mt. 15:14), and they will all fall into the ditch of eternal damnation.

Psalm 119:25-32

DALETH.

25. My soul cleaveth unto the dust: quicken thou me according to thy word.
26. I have declared my ways, and thou heardest me: teach me thy statutes.
27. Make me to understand the way of thy precepts: so shall I talk of thy wondrous works.
28. My soul melteth for heaviness: strengthen thou me according unto thy word.
29. Remove from me the way of lying: and grant me thy law graciously.
30. I have chosen the way of truth: thy judgments have I laid *before me*.
31. I have stuck unto thy testimonies: O LORD, put me not to shame.
32. I will run the way of thy commandments, when thou shall enlarge my heart.

Commentary_____

In the first half of this DALETH section, the psalmist sends to the LORD four petitions—"quicken (enliven) me," "teach me," "make me to understand," and "strengthen me." He also makes four statements that give us insight into his personal life. By adding the information in these four verses to that given in verses 22 and 23, we deduce the following: after suffering reproach, contempt and malediction from people in high office, he experienced dire bodily affliction. He speaks more of his affliction later in the psalm. He has spoken to the LORD about his deep despair and is confident the LORD heard his plea. Although he has physical and emotional relapses (vv. 25, 28), he is growing spiritually by calling upon his LORD and trusting in His Word.

In verse 29, the psalmist asks to be separated from those who have chosen the path of lies and to receive from God grace to live by His law. He has chosen the way of truth and follows that path by constantly keeping in his mind the LORD's judgments (ordinances). During his time of trial, the psalmist has tenaciously clung to the LORD's testimonies. He asks the LORD for vindication. Verse 32 lets us know that he is on the road to victory and that he has regained his confidence. He is up and running on the right path with an enlarged heart.

Application_____

What are your thoughts about what it means to have an enlarged heart? The psalmist believes that such a heart can only come from God. What does verse 32 say one will do when the LORD enlarges His heart?

Psalm 119:33-40

HE.

33. Teach me, O LORD, the way of thy statutes; and I shall keep it *unto* the end.
34. Give me understanding, and I shall keep thy law; yea, I shall observe it with *my* whole heart.
35. Make me to go in the path of thy commandments; for therein do I delight.
36. Incline my heart unto thy testimonies, and not to covetousness.
37. Turn away mine eyes from beholding vanity; *and* quicken thou me in thy way.
38. Stablish thy word unto thy servant, who is *devoted* to thy fear.
39. Turn away my reproach which I fear: for thy judgments *are* good.
40. Behold, I have longed after thy precepts: quicken me in thy right-eousness.

Commentary_____

In these eight verses (section HE), the psalmist requests nine petitions of the LORD (two in verse 37). "Teach me, O LORD"—twice before we have heard the psalmist utter this plea (vv. 12, 26). This time he pledges to observe that which he is taught for the remainder of his life. In the previous section, he followed his plea to be taught with a request for understanding, in order that he might be effective in proclaiming the wondrous works of the LORD to others. Here he asks for understanding of the teaching so that he can observe the law of God wholeheartedly. It is one thing to receive instructions but another to comprehend the teaching sufficiently to be able to use it. That comprehension comes through meditation (vv. 15, 23).

The requests of verses 33 and 34 pertain to the activity of the mind. Verse 35 is a plea that the feet walk in the right pathway. The petition of verse 36 speaks of the heart—the innermost desires. The first petition of verse 37 seeks direction for the use of the eyes. The second asks for fervor of spirit on life's journey.

The psalmist wants the Word so established in his being that he will fear God rather than the reproaches of man. Since the judgments and precepts of the LORD are good, he longs for the life-giving righteousness they produce in one's life.

Application_____

Notice the order in which the psalmist presents his petitions. That which enters our minds occupies our thinking, which in turn determines our walk. Our heart's desires determine what we will covet. That which we see with our eyes attracts us to the vanities of this world. The establishment of the Word in our beings produces the righteousness that is a reproach unto man but a delight unto God (v. 11).

Psalm 119:41-48

VAU.

41. Let thy mercies come also unto me, O LORD, *even* thy salvation, according to thy word.
42. So shall I have wherewith to answer him that reproacheth me: for I trust in thy word.
43. And take not the word of truth utterly out of my mouth; for I have hoped in thy judgments.
44. So shall I keep thy law continually for ever and ever.
45. And I will walk at liberty: for I seek thy precepts.
46. I will speak of thy testimonies also before kings, and will not be ashamed.
47. And I will delight myself in thy commandments, which I have loved.
48. My hands also will I lift up unto thy commandments, which I have loved; and I will meditate in thy statutes.

Commentary_____

In each of the forty verses already considered in Psalm 119, we have seen at least one of the eight synonyms used to designate the Word. Except for three or four verses late in the psalm, that pattern continues. Here in the VAU section, verses 43 and 48 each have two; thus, a total of ten are present in the entire section.

Notice how the psalmist's experience in verses 41 and 42 parallels our own salvation. It is from the LORD's mercy (Tit. 3:5), by God's Word (1 Pet. 1:23), and through faith (trust) in the Word (Eph. 2:8). The psalmist trusts in the Word (v. 42), hopes in the Word (v. 43), and seeks the Word (v. 45) because he loves the Word (v. 47). He resolves to observe the Word continually forever and ever (v.44). As a result, he will walk at liberty. That is, his path will be free from the stumbling stones of a sinful life. He will also have the boldness to proclaim God's Word and meditate therein.

Six times in this psalm, the writer speaks of his delight in God's Word. I was saved by the Word. I am very grateful for the Word. I know that I grow by the Word and need to feed upon the Word each day. I revere the Word because of whose Word it is. I am cognizant of the instruction and admonition I receive from the Word. I sense the comfort the Word brings into my life. I trust and have hope in the promises of the Word. Now here is the question: do I delight in the Word? One definition of the word *delight* is "enraptured attention."

Application_____

The Bible instructs us to hear the Word, read the Word, study the Word, memorize the Word, and meditate upon the Word. How pleased our Lord would be if we did all of this in an aura of enraptured attention to His Word.

Psalm 119:49-56

ZAIN.

49. Remember the word unto thy servant, upon which thou hast caused me to hope.
50. This *is* my comfort in my affliction: for thy word hath quickened me.
51. The proud have had me greatly in derision: *yet* have I not declined from thy law.
52. I remembered thy judgments of old, O LORD; and have comforted myself.
53. Horror hath taken hold upon me because of the wicked that forsake thy law.
54. Thy statutes have been my songs in the house of my pilgrimage.
55. I have remembered thy name, O LORD, in the night, and have kept thy law.
56. This I had, because I kept thy precepts.

Commentary

The glad message of section ZAIN is that through God's word there is comfort in times of affliction. "For whatever things were written aforetime were written for our learning, that we, through patience and comfort of the scriptures might have hope" (Rom. 15:4). "Thou hast caused me to hope" (v. 49). "I have hoped in thy word" (v. 74). Hope is appropriated by trusting the promises of God in His Word—"in hope of eternal life, which God, who cannot lie, promised before the world began" (Tit. 1:2). Hope in the Bible is not the hope of which we speak in everyday conversation: "My lawn is dying—I hope it rains today," or "I hope to pass this exam." Those are wishes that may or may not come to pass. Scriptural hope is the present appropriation of a future joyous certainty—"which hope we have as an anchor of the soul, both sure and steadfast" (Heb. 6:19).

Think of a seven-year-old girl ten days before Christmas. She sees her name on a package from her grandmother. She doesn't wait until Christmas to become elated—she exults every day in anticipation. Hope is *about* the future, but it is *for* the present. We are "looking for that blessed hope, and the glorious appearing of the great God and our Savior, Jesus Christ" (Tit. 2:13). "Wherefore, comfort one another with these words" (1 Th. 4:18). The apostle Paul called all of his afflictions "light" and "for a moment" (2 Cor. 4:17). He was taking comfort in the trustworthiness of God's promises. "Now the God of hope fill you with all joy and peace in believing, that ye may abound in hope" (Rom. 15:13).

Application

Hope is not for enjoyment in Heaven, for there all hope will have become reality. There certainly is no hope in Hell. Hope is to be enjoyed *now*. If you are not appropriating, in this life, your share of hope by rejoicing in the certainty of God's promises, you are missing this great provision from God.

Psalm 119:57-64

CHETH.

57. *Thou art* my portion, O LORD: I have said that I would keep thy words.
58. I entreated thy favour with *my* whole heart: be merciful unto me according to thy word.
59. I thought on my ways, and turned my feet unto thy testimonies.
60. I made haste, and delayed not to keep thy commandments.
61. The bands of the wicked have robbed me: *but* I have not forgotten thy law.
62. At midnight I will rise to give thanks unto thee because of thy righteous judgments.
63. I *am* a companion of all *them* that fear thee, and of them that keep thy precepts.
64. The earth, O LORD, is full of thy mercy: teach me thy statutes.

Commentary

To begin section CHETH, the psalmist repeats the first part of David's pronouncement in Psalm 16:5, which derives from Numbers 18:20. When the Promised Land was divided among the families of Israel, Aaron's descendants were to receive no portion. As the LORD's personal representatives on Earth, they were to look directly to Him for present sustenance and future security.

In verses 57-61, the psalmist reflects upon events that brought him to the point of proclaiming, "Thou are my portion, O LORD." In effect he was saying, "The LORD is all I need. My life is completely wrapped up in Him."

At a certain point in his life, he came to the realization that he was not walking according to God's Word. He made an "about face" by resolving to keep God's Word and pled with his whole heart for God's mercy. Evidently, he had been recently robbed of his earthly possessions (v. 61). However, that will not deter him from his resolve to live by God's Word.

Verses 62 and 63 explain how that resolve will govern his future. When he awakes in the night, he will take the opportunity to arise and thank his God for the righteousness the Word has produced in his life. He won't need sleeping pills! He'll sleep when the LORD provides sleep and occupy himself with thanksgiving when he can't sleep. He will seek like-minded companions with whom he will praise the LORD, and he will be taught by Him.

Application

Like the prodigal son of Luke 15:17-20, the psalmist was received with open arms by a forgiving father when he "thought on [his] ways and turned [his] feet" unto the LORD's way (v. 59). When we stray, hopefully we will think and turn before we fall into total degradation and bring reproach upon our Father as did the prodigal son.

Psalm 119:65-72

TETH.

65. Thou hast dealt well with thy servant, O LORD, according unto thy word.
66. Teach me good judgment and knowledge: for I have believed thy commandments.
67. Before I was afflicted I went astray: but now have I kept thy word.
68. Thou *art* good, and doest good; teach me thy statutes.
69. The proud have forged a lie against me: *but* I will keep thy precepts with *my* whole heart.
70. Their heart is a fat as grease; *but* I delight in thy law.
71. *It is* good for me that I have been afflicted; that I might learn thy statutes.
72. The law of thy mouth *is* better unto me than thousands of gold and silver.

Commentary_____

Section TETH advances two themes that we have been following in Psalm 119—the desire of the psalmist to be taught and the subject of his affliction. The word *judgment* in verse 66 means "discernment." It is not related to the word *judgments* used eighteen times in Psalm 119 as one of the eight designations for God's Word. In sections DALETH and HE, the psalmist asked to be taught so that he could understand God's ways. This would enable him to "talk of His wondrous works" (v. 27) and "run the way of His commandments" (v. 32). His thirst for teaching sprang from a desire to use knowledge with discernment.

It was affliction that brought the psalmist a desire for learning (v. 71). Therefore, it was good for him to be afflicted. What he received because of affliction is better "than thousands of gold and silver" (v.72).

Consider the "work" of affliction in the lives of the following individuals: Because Joseph was afflicted, he preserved a posterity for a nation (Gen. 45:7, Acts 7:10). Because Hannah was afflicted, she was exalted in the LORD and gave birth to Samuel, judge and prophet. Because Job was afflicted, the LORD gave him "twice as much as he had before" (Job 42:10). Because Paul was afflicted, his "strength was made perfect in weakness (2 Cor. 12:7-10). Because our Lord Jesus Christ was afflicted (Isa. 53:4-7), we have life "purchased by His own blood" (Acts 20:28).

Application_____

It is a great day in each of our lives when we truly learn that every affliction "worketh for us a far more exceeding and eternal weight of glory" (2 Cor. 4:17). We will then say with the psalmist, "It is good for me that I have been afflicted" (v. 71). We will say with Paul, "I take pleasure in infirmities, in reproaches, in necessities, in persecutions, in distresses for Christ's sake" (2 Cor. 12:10).

Psalm 119:73-80

JOD.

73. Thy hands have made me and fashioned me: give me understanding, that I may learn thy commandments.
74. They that fear thee will be glad when they see me; because I have hoped in thy word.
75. I know, O LORD, that thy judgments *are* right, and *that* thou in faithfulness hast afflicted me.
76. Let, I pray thee, thy merciful kindness be for my comfort, according to thy word unto thy servant.
77. Let thy tender mercies come unto me, that I may live: for thy law *is* my delight.
78. Let the proud be ashamed; for they dealt perversely with me without a cause: *but* I will meditate in thy precepts.
79. Let those that fear thee turn unto me, and those that have known thy testimonies.
80. Let my heart be sound in thy statutes; that I be not ashamed.

Commentary_____

Once in section CHETH (v. 63) and twice in JOD, the psalmist speaks of his relationship with those who fear the LORD. He wants their companionship and they want His.

The psalmist was severely afflicted. The affliction turned him to God's Word for comfort (v. 50). The Word showed him that he had gone astray (v. 67), and that the LORD, in righteous judgment, had brought the affliction upon him (v. 75). He realized that his chastisement was a manifestation of God's faithfulness to His own attributes of righteousness and justice. It also manifested God's faithfulness as a loving Father (Heb. 12:6, 7).

In Deuteronomy 10:12, Moses instructed the LORD's people that they were required "to *fear* the LORD thy God, to *walk* in all His ways, and to *love* Him, and to *serve* the LORD thy God with all thy heart and with all thy soul." The sequence is important.

The affliction brought to the psalmist the fear of the LORD. It also brought him a desire to be taught by God's Word. From the Word he learned that the God of righteousness is also a forgiving God of merciful kindness. He requested to be a recipient of God's tender mercies, citing to the LORD his delight in His Word as evidenced by his meditation on God's precepts. His further request was that the proud ones, who dealt with him perversely without cause, be brought to the shame they brought upon him, while his heart is made sound by the LORD' statutes.

Application_____

A dedicated Christian should fear the Lord and love the Lord. The two attitudes are essential and inseparable. Fear prevents love from degenerating into presumptuous familiarity. Without love, fear would result in cringing dread. Neither of these would be pleasing to God.

Psalm 119:81-88

CAPH.

81. My soul fainteth for thy salvation: *but* I hope in thy word.
82. Mine eyes fail for thy word, saying, When wilt thou comfort me?
83. For I am become like a bottle in the smoke; *yet* do I not forget thy statutes.
84. How many *are* the days of thy servant? when wilt thou execute judgment on them that persecute me?
85. The proud have digged pits for me, which *are* not after thy law.
86. All thy commandments *are* faithful: they persecute me wrongfully; help thou me.
87. They had almost consumed me upon earth; but I forsook not thy precepts.
88. Quicken me after thy lovingkindness; so shall I keep the testimony of thy mouth.

Commentary

"My soul fainteth" (v. 81); "mine eyes fail" (v. 82); "they persecute me" (v. 86); "help thou me" (v. 86)—these are the words of one who is deeply depressed by sore oppression. Here in the CAPH section, the psalmist appears to have reached a low point. "When wilt thou comfort me?" he asks in verse 82. In other words, "I may not have many days left to serve You, so when will You execute judgment upon my persecutors?" His faith is wavering because he sees no action upon his oppressors from the LORD.

Actually, the psalmist is on the way up. Though his reactions to oppression are pulling him down, his course of action will lift him up. His hope is founded on the Word. He is seeking comfort from "the Father of mercies, and the God of all comfort, Who comforteth us in all our tribulation" (2 Cor. 1:3, 4). He is calling to memory that which he has read in God's Word. He is proclaiming God's faithfulness and His loving-kindness, while continuing to observe His precepts and testimonies.

The psalmist is in greater need of having his faith stabilized than he is in need of seeing judgment upon his persecutors. The Word in which he delights and upon which he meditates (vv. 77, 78) will produce that faith for him (Rom. 10:17). Faith will permit him to "see" that which is not visible. Then he will find rest unto his soul (Ps. 37:7, Mt. 11:29). His prayers will be answered to his complete satisfaction, although not according to his thinking.

Application

It is a work of the indwelling Holy Spirit to bring us to our knees when we have a pressing need. However, the supply from the loving Father may not be that for which we petitioned Him. There may be a more urgent need that we did not comprehend. He will supply according to that need (Phil. 4:19).

Psalms 119:89-96

LAMED.

89. For ever, O LORD, thy word is settled in heaven.
90. Thy faithfulness *is* unto all generations: thou hast established the earth, and it abideth.
91. They continue this day according to thine ordinances: for all *are* thy servants.
92. Unless thy law *had been* my delights, I should then have perished in mine affliction.
93. I will never forget thy precepts: for with them thou hast quickened me.
94. I *am* thine, save me; for I have sought thy precepts.
95. The wicked have waited for me to destroy me: *but* I will consider thy testimonies.
96. I have seen an end of all perfection: *but* thy commandment *is* exceeding broad.

Commentary_____

Section LAMED is the first in which we find a verse that doesn't employ one of the eight designations for God's Word. However, the word *faithfulness* in verse 90 is translated "truth" in verse 30 and frequently elsewhere. Verses 89 and 90 inform us that our generation has equal opportunity to know God's perfect truth as did the generation living when the original text was written. See also Psalms 100:5 and 117:2 where this word is used. Psalm 33:11 teaches the same truth. How can we be sure that God's perfect Word is available to us, and how does God accomplish this?

We are aware that God used imperfect servants to translate His Word into the language we speak and that no translation is perfect in every detail. Verse 89 states that God's Word is "settled"—established, preserved, held firmly—"in Heaven," not on Earth. God has sent the perfect Author of His perfect Word to dwell within us as our teacher and guide (Jn. 14:26, 16:13). If we trust Him, He will guide us to the best translation available in our language and use it to the extent that we are yielded both to Him and to His direction of our lives. In John 7:17, Jesus presents a promise preceded by a condition. The problem is that we want the benefit of the promise without fully meeting the condition. We have our own preferences of translations and interpreters and make little attempt to get the mind of the Spirit through total submission to Him for direction.

Application_____

Here are some questions for dedicated believers willing to do a little self-examination: How much prayer effort did I expend in selecting the translation I use? How much Spirit direction do I seek in choosing speakers and writers that interpret God's Word? How much do I depend upon the Holy Spirit's enlightenment of Scriptures?

Psalm 119:97-104

MEM.

97. O how love I thy law! It *is* my meditation all the day.
98. Thou through thy commandments hast made me wiser than mine enemies: for they *are* ever with me.
99. I have more understanding than all my teachers: for thy testimonies *are* my meditation.
100. I understand more than the ancients, because I keep thy precepts.
101. I have refrained my feet from every evil way, that I might keep thy word.
102. I have not departed from thy judgments: for thou hast taught me.
103. How sweet are thy words unto my taste! *yea, sweeter* than honey to my mouth!
104. Through thy precepts I get understanding: therefore I hate every false way.

Commentary_____

This, the MEM section, is the first in which the psalmist asks nothing of God—there are no petitions. Also, he will begin emphasizing the word love to describe his dedication to God's Word. Look again at Deuteronomy 10:12. Heretofore, he has been centering on "to fear the LORD" in order "to walk in all His ways." The Word of God next teaches him "to love Him" in order "to serve the LORD thy God with all thy heart and with all thy soul."

Love of the Word is evidenced by continual meditation upon it. Through meditation, the psalmist entered into the benefits, as well as the obligations, of the Word. He became more focused on the promises in the Word than upon the afflictions by his enemies because meditation made him wiser than his enemies.

Teachers of the Word are needful in gaining knowledge, but one gains insight and understanding through meditation. Long life brings a degree of understanding and wisdom through experience. But experience is a hard schoolmaster. Obtaining understanding and wisdom is sweet like honey when there is a love relationship with the Word. "Thy words were found, and I did eat them, and Thy Word was unto me the joy and rejoicing of mine heart" (Jer. 15:16). "More to be desired are they than gold, yea, than much fine gold; sweeter also than honey and the honeycomb. Moreover, by them is Thy servant warned; and in keeping of them there is great reward" (Ps. 19:10,11).

Application_____

Is there a way to acquire spiritual understanding other than by meditation upon God's Word? Is it possible to meditate without first hiding the Word in the heart? Can a cow chew its cud without first eating something?

Psalm 119:105-112

NUN.

105. Thy word *is* a lamp unto my feet, and a light unto my path.
106. I have sworn, and I will perform *it,* that I will keep thy righteous judgments.
107. I am afflicted very much: quicken me, O LORD, according unto thy word.
108. Accept, I beseech thee, the freewill offerings of my mouth, O LORD, and teach me thy judgments.
109. My soul *is* continually in my hand: yet I do not forget thy law.
110. The wicked have laid a snare for me: yet I erred not from thy precepts.
111. Thy testimonies have I taken as an heritage for ever: for they *are* the rejoicing of my heart.
112. I have inclined mine heart to perform thy statutes alway, *even unto* the end.

Commentary_____

In the NUN section, the psalmist confirms his vow to perform according to the LORD's righteous judgments and His statutes, always—to the end of his life. Neither the darkness of the way, nor affliction, nor dangers to his life, nor the snares of the wicked will deter him. He will walk in darkness of night with the light of God's Word. With a rejoicing heart, he will offer praise and thanksgiving as his sacrifice to God (Ps. 50:14, 54:6, 107:22). He will not forget God's law nor err from His precepts.

"O, LORD, I know that the way of man is not in himself; it is not in man that walketh to direct his steps"(Jer. 10:23). We walk in a world of spiritual darkness. Without the light of God's Word, we will surely join the sinning angels and the false prophets in chains of darkness forever (2 Pet. 2:4, 17). God has given us Bible prophecy as a "light that shineth in a dark place, until the day dawn and the day star arise in our hearts" (2 Pet. 1:19). As we walk on the pathway of life towards that light, it "shineth more and more unto the perfect day" (Pr. 4:18). But we need lights along the way to guide us to that perfect light. We also need a lamp (lantern) to show us where to place each footstep to avoid stumbling on the stones in the pathway. The Word is both of those lights.

Application_____

For Israel as a nation, the light of Bible prophecy is the promise of the dawning of the millennial day when Messiah appears on the eastern horizon as the "Sun of Righteousness" (Isa. 60:1-3, Mal. 4:2). For the church, the morning star will appear before the dawning of that day (Rev. 22:16). That is the blessed hope already shining in our hearts (Tit. 2:13).

Psalm 119:113-120

SAMECH.

113. I hate *vain* thoughts: but thy law do I love.
114. Thou *art* my hiding place and my shield: I hope in thy word.
115. Depart from me, ye evildoers: for I will keep the commandments of my God.
116. Uphold me according unto thy word, that I may live: and let me not be ashamed of my hope.
117. Hold thou me up, and I shall be safe: and I will have respect unto thy statutes continually.
118. Thou hast trodden down all them that err from thy statutes: for their deceit *is* falsehood.
119. Thou puttest away all the wicked of the earth *like* dross: therefore I love thy testimonies.
120. My flesh trembleth for fear of thee; and I am afraid of thy judgments.

Commentary_____

"I hate." "I love." "I hope." "I am afraid." In the SAMECH section, the psalmist lets us know that he is a person of emotions. Twice in the eight verses, he describes his emotion towards God's Word as one of love. Does God have emotions? He loves (Jn. 3:16). Love is an element of His essence (1 Jn. 4:8). He is love, He loves, and He is able to bestow His ability to love (1 Jn. 4:19). "The God of Love" is one of His names (2 Cor. 13:11).

The psalmist expresses his hatred for every false way (v. 104), for wrong thinking (v. 113), and for lying (v. 163). Does God hate? The Bible tells of many things God hates. Seven are listed in Proverbs 6:16-19. But never in Scriptures is He called "the God of Hate."

Another name for God is "the God of Hope" (Rom. 15:13). Then, does God hope? He has no more need to hope than will we when we go to be with Him. Hope is the *present* appropriation of a *future* joyous certainty—it is a gift from God for us "to lay hold upon" in this life (Heb. 6:18-20). There is no need for hope in Heaven—all will be realized.

The psalmist also possesses the emotion of fear. Is that good? When we are properly in awe of God and revere His Word, we need not fear anything else. When considering the emotion of fear, we should keep in mind the promise of 1 John 4:18. There is a fear that complements love to keep us in a right relationship with God, and there is a fear that torments.

Application_____

We are creatures of emotion. Only the Holy Spirit through the Word of God can properly channel those emotions. The psalmist expresses emotions such as "delight" and "love" towards God's Word. We must frequently take inventory of our emotions towards Him and His Word.

Psalm 119:121-128

AIN.

121. I have done judgment and justice: leave me not to mine oppressors.
122. Be surety for thy servant for good: let not the proud oppress me.
123. Mine eyes fail for thy salvation, and for the word of thy righteousness.
124. Deal with thy servant according unto thy mercy, and teach me thy statutes.
125. I *am* thy servant; give me understanding, that I may know thy testimonies.
126. *It is* time for *thee,* LORD, to work: *for* they have made void thy law.
127. Therefore I love thy commandments above gold; yea, above fine gold.
128. Therefore I esteem all *thy* precepts *concerning* all *things to be* right; *and* I hate every false way.

Commentary_____

Some suggest that "judgment" in verses 84 and 121 as well as "faithfulness" in verse 90 do not designate the Word of God. Clearly, verses 122 and 132 contain no synonym for the Word. Otherwise, every verse in Psalm 119 names God's Word in some form.

A major portion of the psalm consists of petitions asking for the LORD's ministry on behalf of the psalmist. There are six such petitions in verses 121-125 of this, the AIN section. Verse 122, however, is the only place in the psalm in which the psalmist asks the LORD to be surety for him. A surety is one who assumes the obligation or failure in duty of another (Pr. 6:1). God is perfect. His righteousness does not permit Him to require less (Mt. 5:48). At the cross, Jesus made full payment to God for my obligation to God. As my surety, He paid for my default. If my true heart's desire is to please God, He will receive my imperfect service because Jesus Christ, my mediator, makes up for my inadequacy day by day (Heb. 7:22, 8:6).

Often in Psalm 119, the psalmist submits to God reasons that his petitions should be answered. He does this three times in verses 121-125. The LORD should grant his petitions because of his rectitude, because of God's mercy, and because, as a servant, he is entitled to be taught knowledge with understanding.

The psalmist knows that the LORD will certainly deal with those who live as though there were no word from God. From observation, he believes the time has come for God to act.

Application_____

From our present day vantage, we conclude with the psalmist that the world has "made void Thy law" (v. 126), and that it is time for God to act. Until He does, we should follow the example of the psalmist—loving His commandments more than riches and esteeming His precepts, while hating every false way.

Psalm 119:129-136

PE.

129. Thy testimonies *are* wonderful: therefore doth my soul keep them.
130. The entrance of thy words giveth light; it giveth understanding unto the simple.
131. I opened my mouth, and panted: for I longed for thy commandments.
132. Look thou upon me, and be merciful unto me, as thou usest to do unto those that love thy name.
133. Order my steps in thy word: and let not any iniquity have dominion over me.
134. Deliver me from the oppression of man: so will I keep thy precepts.
135. Make thy face to shine upon thy servant; and teach me thy statutes.
136. Rivers of waters run down mine eyes, because they keep not thy law.

Commentary_____

In the second half of the psalm, more and more, the psalmist used the word *love* in expressing his regard for God's Word. In verses 113, 119, and 127 he continued to tell of his love for that which God says. But it is not until here in section PE that we see the word *love* applied to God Himself. The "name of God" includes all that He has revealed about Himself. It represents the totality of what can be known of Him. God is zealous concerning His name. It is not to be used lightly or in vain (Ex. 20:7). The psalmist still appears to be hesitant to express his love for the LORD, but he wants to be identified with those who love His name.

"Order my steps in Thy Word." The psalmist knows that he is not capable of directing his own steps (Jer. 10:23). However, he also knows the source of the light that prevents iniquity from having dominion over him. The light of understanding enters his soul through his intense thirst for God's Word, giving the direction he needs.

"Make Thy face to shine." These words derive from the Aaronic benediction of Numbers 6:24-26. They are quoted several times in Psalms, including three times in Psalm 80. The psalmist is saying, "Deal favorably with me concerning my request."

Compare verse 136 with Jeremiah 9:1, 13:17, 14:17. The psalmist wept over the plight of those who disregard God's Word. So did Jeremiah. So did Jesus (Lk. 19:41). When was the last time you observed anyone shedding tears for the lost?

Application_____

Many Christians who would not think of deliberately using God's name in vain, nevertheless fall into the habit of using exclamations that are substitutes for His Holy name. If the expressions begin with a *g* or a *j*, they should be avoided. The hearer may not distinguish it from the divine name from which it derives.

Psalm 119:137-144

TZADDI.

137. Righteous *art* thou, O LORD, and upright *are* thy judgments.
138. Thy testimonies *that* thou hast commanded *are* righteous and very faithful.
139. My zeal hath consumed me, because mine enemies have forgotten thy words.
140. Thy word *is* very pure: therefore thy servant loveth it.
141. I *am* small and despised: *yet* do not I forget thy precepts.
142. Thy righteousness *is* an everlasting righteousness, and thy law *is* the truth.
143. Trouble and anguish have taken hold on me: *yet* thy commandments *are* my delight.
144. The righteousness of thy testimonies *is* everlasting: give me understanding, and I shall live.

Commentary_____

The Hebrew word for righteous begins with the letter TZADDI. Therefore, it is not surprising that the TZADDI section begins with "righteous" and that the theme of the section is God's righteousness. The words "righteous," "upright," and "righteousness" appear six times in the eight verses.

Our God is a righteous God; therefore, His Word is righteous (v. 137). Our God is a faithful God; therefore His Word is faithful (v. 138). Our God is a pure God; therefore, His Word is pure (v. 140). Our God is a God of truth; therefore, His Word is truth (v. 142). Our God is an eternal God; therefore, His Word is eternal (vv.142-144). All of the above is sufficient cause for the psalmist to be consumed with zeal and love for the Word. The trouble and anguish that have taken hold of him are overridden by his delight in the Word and its promises.

"Give me understanding that I may learn" (v. 73). "Give me understanding that I may know" (v. 125). "Give me understanding that I may live" (v. 144). Instruction, knowledge and understanding are pre-requisites for the psalmist if he is to live. Throughout the entire psalm, the psalmist continues to cry out for more learning, more knowledge, and more understanding. Since he knows the Word is the source of understanding (v. 130), his zeal and love for the Word becomes evermore intense.

Application_____

As I read verse after verse about the psalmist's zeal and love for the Word and his delight in it, something should be happening inside of me. I should be measuring my zeal, love and delight by his.

Psalm 119:145-152

KOPH.

145. I cried with *my* whole heart; hear me, O LORD: I will keep thy statutes.
146. I cried unto thee; save me, and I shall keep thy testimonies.
147. I prevented the dawning of the morning, and cried: I hoped in thy word.
148. Mine eyes prevent the *night* watches, that I might meditate in thy word.
149. Hear my voice according unto thy lovingkindness: O LORD, quicken me according to thy judgment.
150. They draw nigh that follow after mischief: they are far from thy law.
151. Thou *art* near, O LORD; and all thy commandments *are* truth.
152. Concerning thy testimonies, I have known of old that thou hast founded them for ever.

Commentary

In section KOPH, we consider again the subject of meditation. We have previously noted that meditation upon God's Word is a major theme of Psalm 119. We have learned of the many benefits promised by God to those who take time for meditation. At this point, we might well ask, "When could I possibly find the time such meditation would involve?"

In modern English, verse 148 reads, "My eyes anticipate the night watches, that I might meditate in Your Word." The psalmist looks forward to the times he awakes during the night so that he will have the opportunity to meditate upon the Word. Following this thought through the book of Psalms, we discover the following passages: "Commune with your own heart upon your bed, and be still" (4:4); "My reins (heart) also instruct me in the night seasons" (16:7); "In the night his song shall be with me, and my prayer unto the God of my life" (42:8); "My soul shall be satisfied as with marrow and fatness, and my mouth shall praise Thee with joyful lips, when I remember Thee upon my bed, and meditate on Thee in the night watches" (63:5,6); and "I have remembered Thy name, O LORD, in the night, and have kept Thy law" (119:55). Meditation is a blessed cure for insomnia! God, Himself, will faithfully transform your meditation into restful sleep when He foresees that you need sleep for tomorrow's tasks more than you need meditation on His Word. Trust Him.

Application

Let's remember that effectual meditation first requires the memorization of God's Word. Several Christian organizations have produced memory packs to be carried and consulted throughout the day. Better still, during your daily quiet time, ask the Lord for verses that should be written on cards so that you can memorize them.

Psalm 119:153-160

RESH.

153. Consider mine affliction, and deliver me: for I do not forget thy law.
154. Plead my cause, and deliver me: quicken me according to thy word.
155. Salvation *is* far from the wicked: for they seek not thy statutes.
156. Great *are* thy tender mercies, O LORD: quicken me according to thy judgments.
157. Many *are* my persecutors and mine enemies; *yet* do I not decline from thy testimonies.
158. I beheld the transgressors, and was grieved; because they kept not thy word.
159. Consider how I love thy precepts: quicken me, O LORD, according to thy lovingkindness.
160. Thy word *is* true *from* the beginning: and every one of thy righteous judgments *endureth* for ever.

Commentary_____

There is a Hebrew word that is used three times here in the RESH section and a total of sixteen times in Psalm 119. Nine of those times the psalmist uses the word in petitioning the LORD. The King James Version renders the petition "quicken me." Some other English language Bibles translate it "revive me." Just what is the psalmist asking the LORD to do for him when he urgently cries, "quicken me"?

In verses 154 and 156 he adds, "according to Thy Word" (judgments). He expects to receive what he asks because he is beseeching a God who is merciful and kind to those who love His precepts. When he makes the plea in verses 37 and 40, the context implies that he is asking for spiritual renewal and spiritual fervor. In verses 88 and 107, he seems to have his physical wellbeing in mind. His thought appears to be, "My enemies are after me; keep me alive so that I can praise You." Considering the use of the same word in verses 50, 93, and 144, we conclude that the psalmist is primarily concerned about his spiritual attunement to the LORD. His heart's desire is for God to use His Word to do whatever is necessary to infuse and maintain vibrancy in his relationship with the LORD.

The psalmist grieves for those who transgress because they don't observe the Word; in contrast, he is sustained by placing his confidence in that which is both true and everlasting.

Application_____

Nothing in this world is everlasting but the Word of God and the souls of human beings. In what, then, should we invest our time and other resources? Human society places much emphasis upon preparation for the future. For what future should we be preparing?

Psalm 119:161-168

SCHIN.

161. Princes have persecuted me without a cause: but my heart standeth in awe of thy word.

162. I rejoice at thy word, as one that findeth great spoil.

163. I hate and abhor lying: *but* thy law do I love.

164. Seven times a day do I praise thee because of thy righteous judgments.

165. Great peace have they which love thy law: and nothing shall offend them.

166. LORD, I have hoped for thy salvation, and done thy commandments.

167. My soul hath kept thy testimonies; and I love them exceedingly.

168. I have kept thy precepts and thy testimonies: for all my ways *are* before thee.

Commentary

Although there are more than one hundred petitions in Psalm 119, there are none in section SCHIN. When a heart is filled with awe, rejoicing, and love by the Word, there is no room left for fear of persecutors. The liars are still there, but they do not rule the heart. The treasures found in the Word possess the thoughts.

"Seven times a day" is a poetic way of saying "all day long" or "constantly." Inner peace overflowing into praise is the product of love for the Word. That dispels all of the offenses that cause stumbling stones in the pathway of life. Love for the Word brings love to all who regard the Word. "He that loveth his brother abideth in the light, and there is no occasion of stumbling in him" (1 John 2:10).

The psalmist's occupation with the Word has brought him to a point of expressing his love for the Word three times in this eight verse section. Not only that, he now expresses that love with superlatives such as "exceedingly." It has brought him a hope of salvation "as an anchor of the soul, both sure and steadfast" (Heb. 6:19). He has acquired "a strong consolation" because he has "fled for refuge to lay hold upon the hope set before him" (Heb. 6:18). He is "in hope of eternal life, which God, who cannot lie, promised before the world began" (Titus 1:2).

All the ways in which he should conduct himself are before him because he determined to observe the precepts and testimonies of the LORD.

Application

Oh, that I might reach the point in my relationship with God, through His Word, that His peace and my praise would override my concern for circumstances! Then I could confidently say, "All my ways are before Thee" (v.168).

Psalm 119:169-176

TAU.

169. Let my cry come near before thee, O LORD: give me understanding according to thy word.
170. Let my supplication come before thee: deliver me according to thy word.
171. My lips shall utter praise, when thou hast taught me thy statutes.
172. My tongue shall speak of thy word: for all thy commandments *are* righteousness.
173. Let thine hand help me; for I have chosen thy precepts.
174. I have longed for thy salvation, O LORD; and thy law *is* my delight.
175. Let my soul live, and it shall praise thee; and let thy judgments help me.
176. I have gone astray like a lost sheep; seek thy servant; for I do not forget thy commandments.

Commentary_____

At first reading, section TAU appears to be a step downward from the lofty spiritual attainments of section SCHIN. Actually, the psalmist is summarizing the spiritual journey he has taken. He has come from "my soul cleaveth unto the dust" (v. 25), "my soul melteth for heaviness" (v. 28), and "I went astray" (v. 67) to "I rejoice at Thy Word" (v. 162), "seven times a day I praise Thee" (v. 164), "great peace have they who love thy law" (v. 165), and "I love [Thy testimonies] exceedingly" (v. 167). In Psalm 119, he hasn't related his journey in precise chronological order, but he has reflected upon the peaks and valleys of his spiritual growth.

Here in the final section, he relates those reflections to his desire for a continued spiritual relationship to the LORD through His Word. The Word has had an effect upon his desires (vv. 169, 170), his speech (vv. 171, 172), his choices (v. 173), and his emotions (v. 174)—his entire life (v. 175).

Late in his ministry, after a life of dedicated service, the apostle Paul stated that he had not yet attained. He continued to press forward (Phil. 3:12-14). The psalmist acknowledges that he has not yet attained. In his desperate condition, having "gone astray like a lost sheep" (v.176), he needed a seeking shepherd. He continues to need a shepherd lest he forget the LORD's commandments.

Application_____

"All we like sheep have gone astray; we have turned every one to his own way, and the LORD hath laid on Him the iniquity of us all" (Isa. 53:6). I am included in the "all" at the beginning of this verse. Therefore, how glad I am that I am also included in the "all" at the end of the verse. "For you were like sheep going astray" (1 Pet. 2:25).

Psalm 120

A Song of degrees.

1. IN MY distress I cried unto the LORD, and he heard me.
2. Deliver my soul, O LORD, from lying lips, *and* from a deceitful tongue.
3. What shall be given unto thee? or what shall be done unto thee, thou false tongue?
4. Sharp arrows of the mighty, with coals of juniper.
5. Woe is me, that I sojourn in Mesech, *that* I dwell in the tents of Kedar!
6. My soul hath long dwelt with him that hateth peace.
7. I *am for* peace: but when I speak, they *are* for war.

Commentary_____

The fifteen psalms from 120-134 are a distinct collection. Each is entitled "A Song of degrees" (ascents), which probably indicates "songs to be sung while ascending step by step." Four are ascribed to David and one to Solomon. Some of the anonymous ones may be the songs of King Hezekiah mentioned in Isaiah 38:20. Written over many years, they were compiled after the captivities and were to be used in connection with the worshippers attending the three great annual festivities as ordained in Deuteronomy 16:16.

The "lying lips" and "deceitful tongue[s]" that wreak the most havoc upon God's people are those which pervert the worship due the one true God. From the beginning of Jesus' earthly ministry (Mt. 7:15) to the end (Mt. 24:4, 5, 11), He warned of false spokesmen. Such warnings are a chief topic of both Old and New Testament writers. "What shall be done unto thee, thou false tongue?" (2 Pet. 2:17). Jude 6 answers this question—"the blackness of darkness forever." The doom of the hearer is the same as that of the deceiver (Ezk. 14:10).

Mesheck and Kedar (v. 5) are heathen people living to the north and to the south of Israel. Verses 5-7 mourn the plight of Israelites living in enemy nations throughout the world who are not privileged to observe the annual feasts of the Lord.

Application_____

Verses 5-7 certainly portray the mournful state of the Jews as we begin the twenty-first century. Those who have returned to the land have no temple in which to worship. Many others have dwelt all their lives in lands where they are hated and oppressed. They cry for peace but are accused of being instigators of war.

Psalm 121

A Song of degrees.

1. I WILL lift up mine eyes unto the hills, from whence cometh my help.
2. My help *cometh* from the LORD, which made heaven and earth.
3. He will not suffer thy foot to be moved: he that keepeth thee will not slumber.
4. Behold, he that keepeth Israel shall neither slumber nor sleep.
5. The LORD *is* thy keeper: the LORD *is* thy shade upon thy right hand.
6. The sun shall not smite thee by day, nor the moon by night.
7. The LORD shall preserve thee from all evil: he shall preserve thy soul.
8. The LORD shall preserve thy going out and thy coming in from this time forth, and even for evermore.

Commentary

The first half of verse 1 is a statement of purpose ending with the word "hills." The second half poses a question which is answered in verse 2 and expounded upon throughout the rest of the psalm.

First, read the psalm from a weary traveler's perspective as the various groups of pilgrims approach Jerusalem to observe the "feasts of the LORD" (Lev. 23:4). The traveler sees the mountains upon which the city is built, where the LORD has established His place of presence on Earth (Ps. 48:1-3; 87:1-3). However, his eye of faith sees beyond the physical mountains to behold the maker of those mountains.

The psalm is structured to be sung antiphonally. Leaders sound out the first part of each verse, and others follow with the second part (Ezra 3:11).

Next, read the psalm from every believing sojourner's perspective, of every generation including your own (Rom. 15:4).

"The LORD, who made heaven and earth"(v.2)—this phrase emphasizes the distinction between "the true, living God" and "the gods that have not made the heavens and the earth" (Jer. 10:10,11). He is the One who does not "slumber nor sleep" (v. 4) and therefore is able to "preserve thy going out and thy coming in from this time forth, and even forevermore" (v. 8).

Application

God has more than one purpose for preserving these ancient writings through all these centuries. Romans 15:4 points out that they were written for our learning, comfort and hope. The principle purpose is that we might be kept aware that our God is worthy of constant praise, adoration and glorification. "By Him, therefore, let us offer the sacrifice of praise to God continually, that is, the fruit of our lips, giving thanks to His name" (Heb. 13:15).

Psalm 122

A Song of degrees of David.

1. I WAS glad when they said unto me, Let us go into the house of the LORD.
2. Our feet shall stand within thy gates, O Jerusalem.
3. Jerusalem is builded as a city that is compact together:
4. Whither the tribes go up, the tribes of the LORD, unto the testimony of Israel, to give thanks unto the name of the LORD.
5. For there are set thrones of judgment, the throne of the house of David.
6. Pray for the peace of Jerusalem: they shall prosper that love thee.
7. Peace be within thy walls, *and* prosperity within thy palaces.
8. For my brethren and companions' sakes, I will now say, Peace *be* within thee.
9. Because of the house of the LORD our God I will seek thy good.

Commentary_____

The psalmist writes from a dedicated worshipper's perspective—a worshipper who is joyously anticipating his pilgrimage to Jerusalem. Fifteen days before the "Feast of Tabernacles," the trumpets sounded throughout the land announcing the beginning of the end of the year convocations (Lev. 23:24, 34).

The "testimony of Israel" (v. 4) refers to the Ark of the Covenant, which was the LORD's witness of His presence among His people (Ex. 25:21, 22). Both the tables of stone on which the ten commandments were written and the golden chest containing them were called "the testimony" (Ex. 32:15; 40:20, 21).

The men of the tribes of Israel were required to assemble before the presence of the LORD three times a year (Ex. 23:14-17). Usually, the entire family went to the Feast of Tabernacles, and they dwelt in booths (tents) around Jerusalem.

Hundreds of years after the psalmist's call for prayer for "the peace of Jerusalem" (v. 6), Jesus Christ came, bringing peace from Heaven (Lk. 19:38). He wept over the city because His reign of righteousness and peace was rejected (Lk. 19:41, 42). Two thousand years after that rejection, the faithful are still praying the psalmist's prayer of verses 7-9. It will be answered! The time will come when the tribes of Israel and also all the nations of the world will come to the "Prince of Peace" at Jerusalem to worship Him (Zech. 8:20-23).

Application_____

When you pray for peace, remember that peace is the product of righteousness: "[t]he work of righteousness shall be peace; and the effect of righteousness, quietness and assurance forever" (Isa. 32:17). There will be neither peace for Jerusalem nor this world until Israel receives the righteous rule of Jesus the Messiah. Only then will strife and war cease.

Psalm 123

A Song of degrees.

1. UNTO THEE lift I up mine eyes, O thou that dwellest in the heavens.
2. Behold, as the eyes of servants *look* unto the hand of their masters, *and* as the eyes of a maiden unto the hand of her mistress; so our eyes *wait* upon the LORD our God, until that he have mercy upon us.
3. Have mercy upon us, O LORD, have mercy upon us: for we are exceedingly filled with contempt.
4. Our soul is exceedingly filled with the scorning of those that are at ease, *and* with the contempt of the proud.

Commentary_____

The LORD knew that His people would need Him when they were far from Jerusalem. He also foresaw the time when Jerusalem and the temple would be destroyed and there would be no opportunity to "go up to Jerusalem and worship the LORD." Therefore, He supplied this psalm for all of His people who would experience distressful situations at any time.

The psalmist begins by letting the reader know that he has his eyes fixed upon the One enthroned in the heavens. In verse 2, he includes all who take their places as God's servants. (He does this by changing the pronoun from singular to plural.) True servants look only to the LORD for sustenance, protection, and direction.

God possesses an attribute which causes Him to supply the needs of His people whether or not they deserve His beneficence. The Hebrew word for this attribute is translated "*mercy*" or "lovingkindness" throughout the psalms. However, the word *mercy* in verses 2 and 3 is a different Hebrew word with a somewhat different connotation. Here the psalmist is beseeching the LORD to deliver His people from their present distress in recognition of their entire dependence upon Him as the only One who can help them. This plea will be answered for the nation of Israel only when its people receive as Messiah the only One who has shed His blood to deliver them from the penalty of sin.

Application_____

Every fully dedicated servant of the LORD has been, and will be, the object of scorn and contempt in this world (Jn. 15:20). This psalmist has the answer for that problem: our master's throne is in Heaven. In His time, He will fully manifest His power to reign over this world. He has already made provision for scoffers and persecutors (Mt. 25:41; Rev. 21:8).

Psalm 124

A Song of degrees of David.

1. IF *IT had not been* the LORD who was on our side, now may Israel say;
2. If *it had not been* the LORD who was on our side, when men rose up against us:
3. Then they had swallowed us up quick, when their wrath was kindled against us:
4. Then the waters had overwhelmed us, the stream had gone over our soul:
5. Then the proud waters had gone over our soul.
6. Blessed *be* the LORD, who hath not given us *as* a prey to their teeth.
7. Our soul is escaped as a bird out of the snare of the fowlers: the snare is broken, and we are escaped.
8. Our help *is* in the name of the LORD, who made heaven and earth.

Commentary_____

"When I cry unto Thee, then shall mine enemies turn back: This I know; for God is for me" (Ps. 56:9). David was delivered from a number of "impossible" situations which would prompt him to write the words of Psalm 124:1, 2. If, as suggested previously, this psalm was written by King Hezekiah, he was using David's words to glorify the LORD for his miraculous deliverance from the Assyrians (2 Ki. 19:35). Isaiah uses the same symbol as the author of Psalm 124:4, 5 does when he predicts in Isaiah 8: 7, 8 that the Assyrians will besiege and conquer Judah. This use of overflowing waters as a symbol for conquering nations is developed throughout the Psalms (18:16, 17; 32:6; 69:1, 2; 144:7). The prophets continue to use this symbol (e.g., Isa. 59:19 and Jer. 46:7, 8). The symbolic use of flood waters reaches its culmination in Revelation 12:15.

In prophetic Scripture, predatory animals are also symbols of nations that want to "swallow" (v. 3) God's people (Dan. 7:3-5; Hos. 13:7, 8; Rev. 13:2). Ezekiel 38 and Daniel 10 let us know that the one who motivates these nations' leaders is Satan, whom Jesus called "the prince of this world" (Jn. 12:31). He is the one who "like a roaring lion walketh about seeking whom he may devour" (1 Pet. 5:8).

Every saved person experiences the deliverance of verse 7 at conversion. However, this liberation will not be fully realized by Israel as a nation until Messiah comes.

Application_____

"Our help is in the name of the LORD, who made Heaven and Earth" (v. 8). "The LORD is on my side; I will not fear. What can man do unto me?"(Ps. 118:6). "If God be for us, who can be against us?" (Rom 8:31).

Psalm 125

A Song of degrees.

1. THEY THAT trust in the LORD *shall be* as mount Zion, *which* cannot be removed, *but* abideth for ever.
2. *As* the mountains *are* round about Jerusalem, so the LORD *is* round about his people from henceforth even for ever.
3. For the rod of the wicked shall not rest upon the lot of the righteous; lest the righteous put forth their hands unto iniquity.
4. Do good, O LORD, unto *those that be* good, and to *them that are* upright in their hearts.
5. As for such as turn aside unto their crooked ways, the LORD shall lead them forth with the workers of iniquity: *but* peace *shall be* upon Israel.

Commentary

Zion is named seven times in the "Songs of Degrees." It is mentioned more than 150 times in the Old Testament and 7 times in the New Testament. Originally, Zion was the rocky promontory extending southward along the west side of the Valley of Kidron. The escarpment on either side was steep. Because it was a natural fortress, David chose it as the location for his palace and seat of government (2 Sam. 5:7). Later, Zion became a designation for the entire seven mountain complex upon which Old Jerusalem was built. When used figuratively, Zion means "that place from which God's government emanates." This psalmist bases his trust in the permanency of Zion upon the Lord's promise to David in 2 Samuel 7:12-16 (the Davidic Covenant)—"thy throne shall be established forever."

The Hebrew word in verse 3 is variously translated "rod" or "scepter." For a better understanding of its scriptural usage, see Psalm 45:6 and Isaiah 14:5. At coronations, an ornate rod is held out to the new sovereign. His acceptance of that rod indicates that he is undertaking the responsibility and authority of rule. Placing a crown on his head pronounces the privilege and prerogative of his reign. The psalmist is proclaiming that the rule of the wicked is temporary and that the righteous will ultimately prevail. He is beseeching the LORD to set these matters right so that Israel will have peace.

Application

"So the LORD is round about His people from henceforth forever" (v. 2). "And I will pray the Father, and he shall give you another comforter, that He may abide with you forever" (Jn. 14:16). At the moment of conversion, the Holy Spirit comes to dwell among us for unity and fellowship, alongside us for comfort and guidance, and within us for worship, instruction, fruitfulness and power.

Psalm 126

A Song of degrees.

1. WHEN THE LORD turned again the captivity of Zion, we were like them that dream.
2. Then was our mouth filled with laughter, and our tongue with singing: then said they among the heathen, The LORD hath done great things for them.
3. The LORD hath done great things for us; *whereof* we are glad.
4. Turn again our captivity, O LORD, as the streams in the south.
5. They that sow in tears shall reap in joy.
6. He that goeth forth and weepeth, bearing precious seed, shall doubtless come again with rejoicing, bringing his sheaves *with him.*

Commentary

The psalmist recounts the singing and thanksgiving joyfully expressed by the remnant that returned to Jerusalem after the seventy years of captivity in Babylon. At the completion of the laying of the foundation of the restored temple, there was singing, praising, giving thanks, and shouting (Ezra 3:11). When worship was restored at the completion of the temple, the people "kept the feast of unleavened bread seven days with joy" (Ezra 6:22). At the celebration after the completion of the walls of Jerusalem, they "rejoiced with great joy and the women and children rejoiced, so that the joy of Jerusalem was heard afar off" (Neh. 12:43). Even the heathen nations, who had vigorously opposed rebuilding, acknowledged, "The LORD hath done great things for them." (Compare verse 6 with Neh. 6:16.)

The streams in the southern part of Israel are dry most of the year. The early winter rains bring forth just a trickle of water. The latter rains fill the streams. As the psalmist wrote, only a small remnant had returned to the Land. In verse 4, he prays for the full restoration of the nation. Many tears were shed during the captivity (Ps. 137:1). Many more have been shed (Lk. 19:41) and will yet be shed (Zech. 12:10) before Israel "shall reap in joy" (v. 4) as they receive Jesus as their Messiah.

Application

"The seed is the word of God" (Lk. 8:11). In His parable of the sower of the seed, Jesus applies the truth of Psalm 126:5, 6. Paul further develops the theme in 1 Corinthians 3:6-8 and 2 Corinthians 9:10. As Fanny Crosby wrote in the beloved hymn "Rescue the Perishing," God's faithful witnesses in every age "weep o'er the erring ones" and "tell them of Jesus, the mighty to save." However, "the harvest truly is plenteous, but the laborers are few. Pray ye, therefore, the Lord of the harvest, that He will send forth laborers into His harvest" (Mt. 9:37, 38).

Psalm 127

A Song of degrees for Solomon.

1. EXCEPT THE LORD build the house, they labour in vain that build it: except the LORD keep the city, the watchman waketh *but* in *vain*.
2. *It is* vain for you to rise up early, to sit up late, to eat the bread of sorrows: *for* so he giveth his beloved sleep.
3. Lo, children *are* an heritage of the LORD *and* the fruit of the womb *is* his reward.
4. As arrows *are* in the hand of a mighty man; so *are* children of the youth.
5. Happy *is* the man that hath his quiver full of them: they shall not be ashamed, but they shall speak with the enemies in the gate.

Commentary_____

Psalm 127 and Psalm 72 are the only two psalms in the psalter ascribed to Solomon. Some scholars say the superscriptions indicate they were written for Solomon rather than by Solomon and that the author was Solomon's father, David. Those who hold to Solomon's authorship see verses 1 and 2 echoing the language of Ecclesiastes. Verses 3-5 stress an important theme of Proverbs. Verse 1 points out that the only security in this world is complete reliance upon the Lord. Houses, no matter how well fortified, eventually are destroyed by fire, wind, flood, adversary, or time. Cities, walled or unwalled, are laid waste by natural disasters or conquest. Only the LORD possesses the power of preservation.

Verse 2 teaches that no degree of diligence is sufficient to withstand the sorrows of life. Rest and security are gifts from the LORD (Ps. 3:5), appropriated through faith. The family is God's idea (Gen. 1:28, 2:24, 9:1). He has designed it as the foundation of society. Satan has devised a world system purposed to destroy the family. He knows that the disintegration of the family perverts God's purpose for humanity. Children bring purpose and stability into the earthly life of parents. They are the only assets of this life we can enjoy eternally.

Application_____

There have always been adults who have not been privileged to rear children. Thankfully, through the church of the Lord Jesus Christ, He has broadened our family to include all blood-bought children. All individuals in God's spiritual family are privileged to be a part of "bringing many sons unto glory" (Heb. 2:10). Our eternal heritage is our eternal progeny.

Psalm 128

A Song of degrees.

1. *BLESSED IS* every one that feareth the LORD; that walketh in his ways.
2. For thou shall eat the labour of thine hands: happy *shalt* thou *be,* and *it shall be* well with thee.
3. Thy wife *shall be* as a fruitful vine by the sides of thine house: thy children like olive plants round about thy table.
4. Behold, that thus shall the man be blessed that feareth the LORD.
5. The LORD shall bless thee out of Zion: and thou shalt see the good of Jerusalem all the days of thy life.
6. Yea, thou shalt see thy children's children, *and* peace upon Israel.

Commentary_____

Psalm 127 began by pointing out the folly of attempting to "build" one's life without regard to the LORD and His purposes (v. 1). Psalm 128 begins by presenting two requirements for a "blessed" life. Both psalms continue by describing how God intends us to experience blessedness based upon living within a God-centered family. A blessed person is one who finds serenity and purpose during his earthly sojourn.

"The fear of the LORD is the beginning of wisdom" (Pr. 9:10). Continuing in "the fear LORD tendeth to life; and he who hath it shall abide satisfied" (Pr. 19:23). The evidence of godly wisdom is seeking to know the ways of the LORD that one might walk therein. Verse 2 teaches that there is a satisfaction in "the labor of thine hands." A task well-done results in a sense of well being and purpose. The vine and the olive tree are emblematic of prosperity and fruitfulness throughout Scriptures. It is a wondrous privilege to be a part of a joyous family. Satan and sin disrupt serenity and purpose. The blessedness God intends for the family will not be fully experienced in this world until "the LORD shall bless thee out of Zion." When Messiah establishes His throne at Jerusalem, the promises of verses 5 and 6 will be realized in full.

Application_____

The guidance of the indwelling Holy Spirit, through His illumination of the Scriptures, permits Christians to enjoy the blessings of Psalm 127 and 128 (Jn. 16:13). The condition is "walking in His ways"; "for as many as are led by the Spirit of God, they are the sons of God" (Rom. 8:14).

Psalm 129

A Song of degrees.

1. MANY A time have they afflicted me from my youth, may Israel now say:
2. Many a time have they afflicted me from my youth: yet they have not prevailed against me.
3. The plowers plowed upon my back: they made long their furrows.
4. The LORD *is* righteous: he hath cut asunder the cords of the wicked.
5. Let them all be confounded and turned back that hate Zion.
6. Let them be as the grass *upon* the housetops, which withereth afore it groweth up:
7. Wherewith the mower filleth not his hand; nor he that bindeth sheaves his bosom.
8. Neither do they which go by say, The blessing of the LORD *be* upon you: we bless you in the name of the LORD.

Commentary

This psalm is one of several structured to be sung antiphonally. The leader sounded out verse 1. The group responded with verse 2, and this responsive pattern continued through the psalm.

The days of Israel's youth were the days "when she came up out of Egypt" (Hos. 2:15, 11:1). The singers were looking back upon 1,000 or so years of conflict and oppression by conquering nations. "[H]ave not prevailed"(v. 2) and "shall not prevail" (Jer. 1:19)—the perseverance of Israel has now lasted for more than 3,000 years. The desire of surrounding nations to destroy Israel is still unfulfilled, and she still prevails. One of the sure proofs of Bible authenticity is the durability and resiliency of this nation.

Verse 3 is a graphic description of the deliberately cruel treatment of Israel by her oppressors. Yet the people of Israel have hope! The LORD is both righteous and sovereign. He will cut the cords with which nations have bound Israel. To "hate Zion" (v. 4) is to oppose the reign of Messiah and the preservation of Israel.

Grass growing on a sod roof is of no value to man or beast. It flourishes for a few days then withers away. So will the oppressors of Israel. They will be destroyed by the heat of God's judgment. Such will never have the joy of singing, "Blessed is He who cometh in the name of the LORD" (Ps. 118:26; Lk. 13:35).

Application

The LORD made the following promise to Israel: "the LORD thy God, He it is who doth go with thee; He will not fail thee, nor forsake thee" (Dt. 31:6,8). Jesus gave His followers a similar promise: "[l]o, I am with you always, even unto the end of the world. Amen!" (Mt. 28:20) To us, he confirms, "I will never leave thee, nor forsake thee" (Heb. 13:5).

Psalms 130

A Song of degrees.

1. OUT OF the depths have I cried unto thee, O LORD.
2. Lord, hear my voice: let thine ears be attentive to the voice of my supplications.
3. If thou, LORD, shouldest mark iniquities, O Lord, who shall stand?
4. But *there is* forgiveness with thee, that thou mayest be feared.
5. I wait for the LORD, my soul doth wait, and in his word do I hope.
6. My soul *waiteth* for the Lord more than they that watch for the morning: *I say, more than* they that watch for the morning.
7. Let Israel hope in the LORD: for with the LORD *there is* mercy, and with him *is* plenteous redemption.
8. And he shall redeem Israel from all his iniquities.

Psalm 131

A Song of degrees of David.

1. LORD, MY heart is not haughty, nor mine eyes lofty: neither do I exercise myself in great matters, or in things too high for me.
2. Surely I have behaved and quieted myself, as a child that is weaned of his mother: my soul *is* even as a weaned child.
3. Let Israel hope in the LORD from henceforth and for ever.

Commentary_____

It is good to study these two psalms together because 131 compliments and completes 130. The two psalms invoke the name *Yahweh* (LORD) seven times. *Yahweh* is the omnipotent One who, in love and mercy, deigns to reach down and supply sinful man's need for redemption. *Adonai* is the same God acknowledged to be Lord and master by the supplicant.

Psalm 130 demonstrates how one appropriates redemption. First, from the depths of his lost condition, he calls upon the true God (v. 1). He trusts that the Lord hears him (v. 2). Next, he confesses his utter inability to solve his sin problem (v. 3). He believes the God to whom he calls is both able and willing to forgive and redeem (v. 4). He now has assurance of redemption because he has gained a holy regard for the God who saved him (v. 4) and looks only to His Word in expectant hope (vv. 5, 6). The evidence that he possesses redemption is that he exhorts others to come to the LORD of mercy for redemption.

In Psalm 131, the psalmist demonstrates the correct attitude of one who takes the message of eternal redemption to others. He has a lowly heart, that is, he is neither proud nor high-minded. He is not ambitious for personal recognition or gain. His soul is at rest in the bosom of his God.

Application_____

In delivering the message of redemption, we have a great advantage over the psalmist. The power is in the Gospel of Christ (Rom. 1:16). We deliver that which we received—"that Christ died for our sins according to the Scriptures; and that He was buried, and that He rose again the third day according to the Scriptures; and that He was seen. . ."(1 Cor.15:3-8).

Psalm 132:1-9

A Song of degrees.

1. LORD, REMEMBER David, *and* all his afflictions:
2. How he sware unto the LORD, *and* vowed unto the mighty *God* of Jacob;
3. Surely I will not come into the tabernacle of my house, nor go up into my bed;
4. I will not give sleep to mine eyes, *or* slumber to mine eyelids,
5. Until I find out a place for the LORD, an habitation for the mighty *God* of Jacob.
6. Lo, we heard of it at Ephratah: we found it in the fields of the wood.
7. We will go into his tabernacles: we will worship at his footstool.
8. Arise, O LORD, into thy rest; thou, and the ark of thy strength.
9. Let thy priests be clothed with righteousness; and let thy saints shout for joy.

Commentary_____

In verses 1-6, the psalmist asks the LORD to remember the zeal-
ousness of King David to find the Ark of the Covenant and bring it to
Jerusalem. That was essential in order for the nation to worship the
LORD in conformity to the prescribed ordinances. The Ark represented
the presence of God dwelling among His people (v. 5). A description of
the Ark and the LORD's use for it are recorded in Exodus 25:10-22.
When King Saul slaughtered the priests (1 Sam. 22:18, 19), he ended
any semblance of worshipping the LORD. David found the Ark in a
secluded wooded area where it had been for twenty years (2 Sam. 7:2).
Centuries later, when Stephen recounted the history of Israel in his sermon, he quoted from verse 5 of this psalm (Acts 7:46).

After David established Jerusalem as the center for worship, he
addressed the people in a great convocation to announce his desire to
build a temple as a suitable "house of rest for the Ark of the Covenant
of the LORD, and for the footstool of our God" (1 Chr. 28:1,2). Verse 7
refers to that announcement.

After David's death, his son, King Solomon built the temple. The
Ark was brought into the temple, and the LORD manifested His presence among the people (2 Chr. 5:14). Verses 8 and 9 are a quotation
from Solomon's prayer of dedication (2 Chr. 6:41).

Application_____

This psalmist was very zealous for the proper worship of the Lord.
As an example of dedication, he presents David's complete absorption
in the task of establishing proper worship for his people. He faced great
difficulties and ridicule in his endeavor. (The story is recorded in 2
Samuel 6). We should be asking ourselves about our own dedication to
worshipping His way instead of our way (Jn 4:24).

Psalm 132:10-18

10. For thy servant David's sake turn not away the face of thine anointed.

11. The LORD hath sworn *in* truth unto David; he will not turn from it; Of the fruit of thy body will I set upon thy throne.

12. If thy children will keep my covenant and my testimony that I shall teach them, their children shall also sit upon thy throne for evermore.

13. For the LORD hath chosen Zion; he hath desired *it* for his habitation.

14. This *is* my rest for ever: here will I dwell; for I have desired it.

15. I will abundantly bless her provision: I will satisfy her poor with bread.

16. I will also clothe her priests with salvation: and her saints shall shout aloud for joy.

17. There will I make the horn of David to bud: I have ordained a lamp for mine anointed.

18. His enemies will I clothe with shame: but upon himself shall his crown flourish.

Commentary_____

In the Davidic Covenant (2 Sam. 7:12-16), the LORD unconditionally promised to establish David's throne forever. He also promised that every king anointed to sit upon that throne would be David's "seed" and of his "house," that is, his descendant. Conditional promises were made to each succeeding son. In his prayer dedicating the temple, Solomon, as the anointed son of David, said, "O LORD God, turn not away the face of thine anointed; remember the mercies of David, thy servant" (2 Chr. 6:42). In Psalm 132:10-12, a later anointed "son of David" reminds the LORD of the promises made to David. For this and other reasons, we deduce that the author of this psalm was King Hezekiah and that this is one of his songs to be sung "all the days of our life in the house of the LORD" (Isa. 38:20).

The biblical record of Hezekiah's accomplishments and the commendation God gave him in 2 Chronicles 31:20, 21, show the high regard Hezekiah had for Zion as the earthly habitation for the LORD (v. 13).

Verses 14-18 look forward to the future reign of "The Greater Son of David," the Messiah. He is the "horn of David" prophesied in the prayer of Hannah "to give strength unto His king, and exalt the horn of His anointed" (1 Sam. 2:10). ". . .I have ordained a lamp for mine anointed" (v. 17). That's God's promise that David's dynasty would never be snuffed out (1 Ki. 11:36, 15:4).

Application_____

Jerusalem is not God's" habitation"(v. 5) on Earth during the Church Age. God's present "habitation" is made of living stones "built up [as] a spiritual house, an holy priesthood, to offer up spiritual sacrifices, acceptable to God by Jesus Christ (1 Pet. 2:5). "In whom ye also are built together for an habitation of God through the Spirit" (Eph. 2:22).

Psalms 133

A Song of degrees of David.

1. BEHOLD, HOW good and how pleasant *it is* for brethren to dwell together in unity!
2. *It is* like the precious ointment upon the head, that ran down upon the beard, *even* Aaron's beard: that went down to the skirts of his garments;
3. As the dew of Hermon, *and as the dew* that descended upon the mountains of Zion: for there the LORD commanded the blessing, *even* life for evermore.

Psalm 134

1. BEHOLD, BLESS ye the LORD, all *ye* servants of the LORD, which by night stand in the house of the LORD.
2. Lift up your hands *in* the sanctuary, and bless the LORD.
3. The LORD that made heaven and earth bless thee out of Zion.

Commentary

Psalm 133 speaks of the blessedness of brethren dwelling in unity. Psalm 134 is a call to worship in unity. First, the psalmist likens dwelling in brotherly unity to the anointing of Aaron for service (Ex. 29:7). When used figuratively, oil represents empowering by the Holy Spirit. The anointing of kings, priests, and prophets acknowledged that their authority came from God. The oil with which Aaron was anointed was holy, precious, and very fragrant (Ex. 30:22-31). The portrayal the psalmist makes in 133:2 is that the empowering by the Spirit is without measure (Jn 3:34) and is designed for the benefit and enjoyment of the brethren.

Mt. Herman is a snow-capped mountain at the northern border of the Promised Land. Its 9000 ft. height dwarfs the other mountains of Israel. The descending cold air causes copious dew essential for survival of both plant and animal life during the dry season. The blessings that fall upon those worshipping in unity at Zion refresh and sustain like the dews of Mt. Hermon.

Psalm 134 is a doxology serving as a benediction at the close of worship each day of the Holy Convocations. It also serves as a benediction for the "Songs of Degrees" sung before and during the festivals. The closing emphasis is upon the worship of the true God, maker of Heaven and Earth (Ps. 121:2, Jer. 10:10, 11).

Application

Division among God's people impedes His work. We are to "be perfectly joined together in the same mind and in the same judgment" (1 Cor. 1:10). "[U]nity in the Spirit in the bond of peace" comes "[w]ith all lowliness and meekness, with longsuffering, forbearing one another in love" (Eph. 4:2, 3).

Psalm 135:1-12

1. PRAISE YE the LORD. Praise ye the name of the LORD; praise *him*, O ye servants of the LORD.
2. Ye that stand in the house of the LORD, in the courts of the house of our God,
3. Praise the LORD; for the LORD *is* good: sing praises unto his name; for *it is* pleasant.
4. For the LORD hath chosen Jacob unto himself, *and* Israel for his peculiar treasure.
5. For I know that the LORD *is* great, and *that* our Lord *is* above all gods.
6. Whatsoever the LORD pleased, *that* did he in heaven, and in earth, in the seas, and all deep places.
7. He causeth the vapours to ascend from the ends of the earth; he maketh lightnings for the rain; he bringeth the wind out of his treasures.
8. Who smote the firstborn of Egypt, both of man and beast.
9. *Who* sent tokens and wonders into the midst of thee, O Egypt, upon Pharaoh, and upon all his servants.
10. Who smote great nations, and slew mighty kings;
11. Sihon king of the Amorites, and Og king of Bashan; and all the kingdoms of Canaan:
12. And gave their land *for* an heritage, an heritage unto Israel his people.

Commentary_____

This song of praise is an expansion of Psalm 134. The psalmist has added words and thoughts from other scriptures and thereby crafted an anthology of adoration to the One who is truly worthy to be praised.

Verses 1 and 2 call upon those who serve in the temple to continue the worship that has prevailed during the annual Holy Convocations. Verses 3 and 5 extol the LORD for His goodness to His specially chosen people whom He redeemed out of bondage for His own purposes.

Verse 5 announces the superiority of the LORD over the non-gods worshipped by the heathen. The psalm expands upon that theme by contrasting what the true God can do (vv. 6-12) with what the idols of the other nations cannot do (vv. 15-18).

Because the LORD made both Heaven and Earth (134:3), He is able to do whatever He pleases in both Heaven and Earth (v. 6). Verse 7 extols the LORD as creator. Verses 8-12 extol Him for that which He did historically for His people. First, the psalmist summarizes the account in Exodus of the LORD's mighty hand in that redemption. Then the psalmist remembers the LORD's mighty hand in providing a place for His people to learn His ways and serve Him. The kingdoms of Sihon and Og were the first to be conquered by the Israelites after they left Egypt.

Application_____

Psalm 135 teaches us the meaning of worship, which is the act of attributing worthiness to someone or something. True worship wells up from a heart filled with love and gratitude. It is manifested by praise and thanksgiving. Hebrews 13:15 calls the manifestation of worship "the fruit of our lips giving thanks to His name." Jesus said that the Father is seeking individuals who will worship Him "in spirit and in truth" (Jn. 4:23).

Psalm 135:13-21

13. Thy name, O LORD, *endureth* for ever; *and* thy memorial, O LORD, throughout all generations.
14. For the LORD will judge his people, and he will repent himself concerning his servants.
15. The idols of the heathen *are* silver and gold, the work of men's hands.
16. They have mouths, but they speak not; eyes have they, but they see not;
17. They have ears, but they hear not; neither is there *any* breath in their mouths.
18. They that make them are like unto them: *so is* every one that trusteth in them.
19. Bless the LORD, O house of Israel: bless the LORD, O house of Aaron:
20. Bless the LORD, O house of Levi: ye that fear the LORD, bless the LORD.
21. Blessed be the LORD out of Zion, which dwelleth at Jerusalem. Praise ye the LORD.

Commentary_____

Verses 4-12 proclaimed that the LORD, as creator of Heaven and Earth, is able to do His good pleasure in both Heaven and Earth. This included choosing and redeeming a special people and then providing for them. Because the LORD is eternal, He is able to preserve and perpetuate His people in the time of judgment. (Verse 14 is a direct quote from Deuteronomy 32:36. The context of that verse enables us to better understand this verse in Psalm 135.)

On the other hand, the idols of other nations, the work of men's hands, have no power to choose, redeem, or provide for those who worship them. These idols cannot speak, see, or hear. (Verses 15-18 are a shorter version of Psalm 115:4-8 which states that the idols also cannot smell, handle or walk.) Since they are both inanimate and temporal, they cannot save their worshippers from judgment that ends in damnation. For other satirical denunciations of idols, see Isaiah 44:9-20 and Jeremiah 10:2-11.

The psalm began with four exhortations to praise the LORD. It ends with four calls to bless the LORD. In praising and blessing we are voicing our understanding of all that the LORD is, and we are gratefully acknowledging all that He has done for us. We fulfill our desire to praise when we gather together "speaking in psalms and hymns and spiritual songs, singing and making melody in [our hearts] to the LORD, [g]iving thanks always for all things unto God and the Father in the name of our Lord Jesus Christ" (Eph. 5:19,20).

Application_____

A good time to "bless the LORD" is during our daily quiet time. Out of a grateful heart, we tell Him how much we appreciate all that He is and all that He has done. We express our trust in His promises. It blesses His heart to hear us speak of His greatness and goodness and of our love for Him.

Psalm 136:1-9

1. O GIVE thanks unto the LORD; for *he is* good: for his mercy *endureth* for ever.
2. O give thanks unto the God of gods: for his mercy endureth for ever.
3. O give thanks to the Lord of lords: for his mercy *endureth* for ever.
4. To him who alone doeth great wonders: for his mercy *endureth* for ever.
5. To him that by wisdom made the heavens: for his mercy *endureth* for ever.
6. To him that stretched out the earth above the waters: for his mercy *endureth* for ever.
7. To him that made great lights: for his mercy *endureth* for ever:
8. The sun to rule by day: for his mercy *endureth* for ever:
9. The moon and stars to rule by night: for his mercy *endureth* for ever.

Commentary

This, the climactic song of the Jewish Passover, has been designated the "Great Hallel (Praise)." It is the most obvious of those psalms structured for antiphonal singing. The leader (or leaders) loudly proclaims the first line of each verse. Then the group responds with the same refrain in all twenty-six verses.

The psalm begins and ends with thanksgiving. The gratitude in the first three verses is directed to the LORD (*Yahweh*), to God (*Elohim*), and to the Lord (*Adonai*). These are the three most prominent Old Testament names for God in order of their scriptural usage.

The "great wonders" of verse 4 are enumerated in the rest of the psalm. Only the wisdom of an infinite God is sufficient for the wonder of creation (Pr. 3:19; Jer. 10:11, 12). Jesus Christ, our Savior, is the pre-eminent One in creation (Col. 1:15-19; Heb. 1:3-10). He is wisdom personified (Pr. 8:1, 22-36; Col. 2:3).

Verses 6-9 come directly from the creation story of Genesis 1. Verse 9 clarifies Genesis 1:16. In most English language Bibles, "he made" is italicized, indicating the translator added this to the Hebrew text. When those two words are omitted, Genesis 1:16 and Psalm 136:9 both say, "the moon and stars to rule by night." That is important for understanding how stars are used figuratively in the Bible (Dan. 12:3; 2 Pet. 1:19; Rev. 1:16). Stars are individual servants lighting up the night (Phil. 2:15).

Application

Translators must sometimes supply words in order to convey the meaning of the original text. The word *endureth* in Psalm 136 is an example. It is good to use a Bible that in some way identifies these additional words so you can read the text both with and without the supplied words. Seek the wisdom of the Holy Spirit in choosing the best translation (Jn. 16:13).

Psalm 136:10-26

10. To him that smote Egypt in their firstborn: for his mercy *endureth* for ever:

11. And brought out Israel from among them: for his mercy *endureth* for ever:

12. With a strong hand, and with a stretched out arm: for his mercy *edureth* for ever.

13. To him which divided the Red sea into parts: for his mercy *endureth* for ever:

14. And made Israel to pass through the midst of it: for his mercy *endureth* for ever:

15. But overthrew Pharaoh and his host in the Red sea: for his mercy *endureth* for ever.

16. To him which led his people through the wilderness: for his mercy *endureth* for ever.

17. To him which smote great kings: for his mercy *endureth* for ever:

18. And slew famous kings: for his mercy *endureth* for ever:

19. Sihon king of the Amorites: for his mercy *endureth* for ever:

20. And Og the king of Bashan: for his mercy *endureth* for ever:

21. And gave their land for an heritage: for his mercy *endureth* for ever:

22. *Even* an heritage unto Israel his servant: for his mercy *endureth* for ever.

23. Who remembered us in our low estate: for his mercy *endureth* for ever:

24. And hath redeemed us from our enemies: for his mercy *endureth* for ever.

25. Who giveth food to all flesh: for his mercy *endureth* for ever.

26. O give thanks unto the God of heaven: for his mercy *endureth* for ever.

Commentary_____

The word translated "mercy" in Psalm 136 denotes the outward manifestation of God's attribute of love. It is often translated "lov-ingkindness." The translator supplied the word *endureth* to emphasize that God's love is steadfast—not dependent in any way on the conduct of the recipient. The word translated "mercy" in Exodus 33:19 and used frequently in the prophetic books is a different word meaning "the manifestation of God's attribute of compassion."

Verses 10-15 recount God's manifestation of love to Israel by the performance of "great wonders" (v. 4) in their deliverance from bondage, as recorded in Exodus 12-14. Verse 16 refers to the "great wonders" the LORD performed in guiding, providing, and protecting the Israelites after their redemption (Exodus 15-17).

Verses 17-22 expand Psalm 135:10-12, summarizing Numbers 21:21-35. Verses 23 and 24 reflect upon all the "great wonders" the LORD performed for Israel in faithfully manifesting His steadfast love for them in the face of their disloyalty to Him.

Verse 25 looks forward to God's provision for all people. "For the bread of God is He who cometh down from Heaven, and giveth life unto the world" (Jn 6:33). "And Jesus said unto them, I am the bread of life; he that cometh to me shall never hunger, and he that believeth on me shall never thirst" (Jn. 6:35).

Application_____

Jesus said that "things . . . were written . . . in the psalms, concerning me" (Lk. 24:44). These references come alive for us when we look for Him in each psalm, especially when we place ourselves in the psalm with Him. This psalm expresses gratitude for who God is and for what He has done in redemption and provision. It reminds us of the truth of 1 Corinthians 10:11.

Psalm 137

1. BY THE rivers of Babylon, there we sat down, yea, we wept, when we remembered Zion.

2. We hanged our harps upon the willows in the midst therof.

3. For there they that carried us away captive required of us a song; and they that wasted us *required of us* mirth, *saying*, Sing us *one* of the songs of Zion.

4. How shall we sing the LORD'S song in a strange land?

5. If I forget thee, O Jerusalem, let my right hand forget *her cunning*.

6. If I do not remember thee, let my tongue cleave to the roof of my mouth; if I prefer not Jerusalem above my chief joy.

7. Remember, O LORD, the children of Edom in the day of Jerusalem; who said, Rase *it*, rase *it*, *even* to the foundation thereof.

8. O daughter of Babylon, who art to be destroyed; happy *shall he be*, that rewardeth thee as thou hast served us.

9. Happy *shall he be*, that taketh and dasheth thy little ones against the stones.

Commentary

We deduce that this psalm was written by a temple musician who was taken captive by the Babylonians when they destroyed Jerusalem in 586 BC. In verses 1-4, the psalmist is reflecting upon the early days of his captivity. By hanging his harp on a tree (v. 2), he is demonstrating to his captors that the worshipful songs of Zion can only be sung in Zion. The tears mentioned in verse 1 convey his intense sorrow over this situation.

In verses 5 and 6, the psalmist vows never to forget to exalt Jerusalem, the place dedicated to the worship of the One True God.

When Jerusalem was taken by the Babylonian army, the Edomites rejoiced, blocking the escape of the Israelites and delivering them to the Babylonians. Then the Edomites ransacked Jerusalem (Obad. 10-14). Ezekiel 25:12-14 lets us know the LORD answered the psalmist's prayer of verse 7.

In verses 8 and 9, the psalmist is invoking the prophecy the LORD made against Babylon two hundred years previously (Isa. 13:16). The LORD also said concerning Babylon, "I will repay them according to their deeds and according to the works of their own hands" (Jer. 25:14). See also Jeremiah 51:24. The one who "rewardeth" Babylon in verse 8 is God's chosen instrument of retribution. The word *happy* in verses 8 and 9 is translated "blessed" in Psalm 1:1 and Psalm 128:1. It means "to be blessed with prosperity." When the LORD brings judgment upon Babylon, the Israelite captives will return to their own land. The psalmist longs for that day.

Application

Since Jesus came and conquered Satan (Jn. 12:31; Heb. 2:14), we do not concern ourselves with retribution. We leave that to the Lord (Heb. 10:30). We concern ourselves with that which the Lord has given us to do—reach a lost world with the saving Gospel message.

Psalm 138

A *Psalm* of David.

1. I will praise thee with my whole heart: before the gods will I sing praise unto thee.
2. I will worship toward thy holy temple, and praise thy name for thy lovingkindness and for thy truth: for thou hast magnified thy word above all thy name.
3. In the day when I cried thou answeredst me, *and* strengthenedst me *with* strength in my soul.
4. All the kings of the earth shall praise thee, O LORD, when they hear the words of thy mouth.
5. Yea, they shall sing in the ways of the LORD: for great *is* the glory of the LORD.
6. Though the LORD *be* high, yet hath he respect unto the lowly: but the proud he knoweth afar off.
7. Though I walk in the midst of trouble, thou wilt revive me: thou shalt stretch forth thine hand against the wrath of mine enemies, and thy right hand shall save me.
8. The Lord will perfect *that which* concerneth me: thy mercy, O LORD, *endureth* for ever: forsake not the works of thine own hands.

Commentary_____

The word *gods* in verse 1 may refer to idols. More likely it refers to rulers and judges whom King David encountered. It is used in this way in Psalm 82:6 which is quoted and interpreted by Jesus in John 10:34-36. When a human being judges (rules), he is exercising a prerogative of deity and acting on behalf of God.

Praise is worship when it is offered to God with the "whole heart" (v. 1). A temple is a place in which the LORD manifests His glory (Jn. 2:21; 1 Cor. 6:19, 20). Before Solomon's temple was built, the LORD manifested His glory through the Ark of the Covenant (1 Sam. 1:9, 3:3). Praise is the exaltation of the name, the attributes, and the word of God. His name and His attributes are magnified through His word. "Though the LORD be high, yet hath He respect unto the lowly" (v. 6). Verses 4 and 5 look forward to Messiah's future earthly reign when all the kings of the Earth pay homage to His magnificence. Yet One so high deigns to hear the cry of the lowly and to give them strength when they call upon Him. Verse 3 is true because verse 6 is true!

The word *revive* in verse 7 means "to give life to." In the Psalms this word is used in reference both to preserving physical life and to spiritual enlivening.

Philippians 1:6 gives the New Testament application of verse 8 for Christians of our time.

Application_____

"Now the God of peace, that brought again from the dead our Lord Jesus, that great Shepherd of the sheep, through the blood of the everlasting covenant, make you perfect in every good work to do His will, working in you that which is well-pleasing in His sight, through Jesus Christ, to whom be glory forever and ever. Amen" (Heb. 13:20, 21).

Psalm 139:1-12

To the chief Musician, A Psalm of David.

1. O LORD, thou hast searched me, and known *me.*
2. Thou knowest my downsitting and mine uprising, thou understandest my thought afar off.
3. Thou compassest my path and my lying down, and art acquainted *with* all my ways.
4. For *there is* not a word in my tongue, *but,* lo, O LORD, thou knowest it altogether.
5. Thou hast beset me behind and before, and laid thine hand upon me.
6. *Such* knowledge *is* too wonderful for me; it is high, I cannot *attain* unto it.
7. Whither shall I go from thy spirit? or whither shall I flee from thy presence?
8. If I ascend up into heaven, thou *art* there: if I make my bed in hell, behold, thou *art there.*
9. *If* I take the wings of the morning, *and* dwell in the uttermost parts of the sea;
10. Even there shall thy hand lead me, and thy right hand shall hold me.
11. If I say, Surely the darkness shall cover me; even the night shall be light about me.
12. Yea, the darkness hideth not from thee; but the night shineth as the day: the darkness and the light *are* both alike *to thee.*

Commentary

Psalm 139 is presented in four stanzas of six verses each. The first stanza focuses on a very personal, omniscient God and me. As I read verses 1-4, it is as though I am watching with rapt attention while the psalmist paints a word picture of what a God who knows everything knows about me. He has an intimate awareness of my thoughts, my walk, my ways, and my words. He knows before I do what action my thoughts will take.

In verses 5 and 6, I contemplate the word picture before me. How can my finite mind possibly grasp the implications of that which I behold? I can benefit by pondering, but I cannot absorb the totality.

The second stanza (vv. 7-12) presents another word portrait. It pictures the omnipresent God and me. Again, the first four verses of the stanza paint the picture, and the last two are my musings about what I see. My sinfulness causes me to want to flee from the presence of such a God (Gen. 3:8). But whether my pathway leads to Heaven or Hell, He is ever-present. As each day dawns, He is there. As the morning light races across the sky, even to the setting of the sun, He offers to hold my hand. The journey is arduous; the night is dark and fraught with danger. I need Him; I'll take His hand.

Application

Jesus said, "I will not leave you comfortless: I will come to you" (Jn. 14:18). He also said, "lo, I am with you always, even unto the end of the world. Amen" (Mt. 28:20). Paul reiterates this promise in Hebrews 13:5, 6—". . . for He hath said, I will never leave thee nor forsake thee. So that we may boldly say, the Lord is my helper, and I will not fear what man shall do unto me."

Psalm 139:13-24

13. For thou hast possessed my reins: thou hast covered me in my mother's womb.

14. I will praise thee; for I am fearfully *and* wonderfully made: marvellous *are* thy works; and *that* my soul knoweth right well.

15. My substance was not hid from thee, when I was made in secret, *and* curiously wrought in the lowest parts of the earth.

16. Thine eyes did see my substance, yet being unperfect; and in thy book all *my members* were written, *which* in continuance were fashioned, when *as yet there was* none of them.

17. How precious also are thy thoughts unto me, O God! how great is the sum of them!

18. *If* I should count them, they are more in number than the sand: when I awake, I am still with thee.

19. Surely thou wilt slay the wicked, O God: depart from me therefore, ye bloody men.

20. For they speak against thee wickedly, *and* thine enemies take *thy name* in vain.

21. Do not I hate them O LORD, that hate thee? and am not I grieved with those that rise up against thee?

22. I hate them with perfect hatred: I count them mine enemies.

23. Search me, O God, and know my heart: try me, and know my thoughts:

24. And see if *there be any* wicked way in me, and lead me in the way everlasting.

Commentary

Stanza one of this psalm depicted The Omniscient God and Me; stanza two portrayed The Omnipresent God and Me. Now in stanza three the psalmist paints a word picture of The Omnipotent God and Me. When I was hidden away from human eyes in my mother's womb, the Creator of all things carefully crafted every element of my being. He watched over every intricate detail of the formation of that which He had planned for me before the world existed. He thought it all through to completion.

God has many thoughts (vv. 17, 18). His thoughts are very deep (Ps. 92:5). They are also much "higher" than mine (Isa. 55:9). He has "heart" thoughts about the generation in which I live (Ps. 33:11). His thoughts are directed toward us. Marvel of marvels, "the Lord thinketh upon me" (Ps. 40:5, 17). His thoughts toward me are good thoughts (Jer. 29:11). Therefore, His thoughts are precious to me.

Stanza four (vv. 19-24) sets forth The Holy God and Me. God defines "the wicked" as those who speak against Him, blaspheme His Holy Name, and rise up against Him—His enemies and my enemies. I take my stand with Him and against wickedness. If my thoughts about holiness and wickedness are to be perfected, that is, like His, I need to pray the prayer of verses 23 and 24.

Application

"Search me." Dear Lord, I beseech you to uncover for me the thoughts of my heart. When you see wickedness there (Jer. 17:9, 10), please show me. I want to think like you do so that I can walk in your ways. "O Lord, I know that the way of man is not in himself; it is not in man that walketh to direct his steps" (Jer. 10:23). Therefore, "[o]rder my steps in thy word and let not any iniquity have dominion over me" (Ps. 119:133).

Psalm 140

To the chief Musician, A Psalm of David.

1. DELIVER ME, O LORD, from the evil man: preserve me from the violent man;
2. Which imagine mischiefs in *their* heart; continually are they gathered together *for* war.
3. They have sharpened their tongues like a serpent; adders' poison *is* under their lips. Selah.
4. Keep me, O LORD, from the hands of the wicked; preserve me from the violent man; who have purposed to overthrow my goings.
5. The proud have hid a snare for me, and cords; they have spread a net by the wayside; they have set gins for me. Selah.
6. I said unto the LORD, Thou *art* my God: hear the voice of my supplications, O LORD.
7. O GOD the LORD, the strength of my salvation, thou hast covered my head in the day of battle.
8. Grant not, O LORD, the desires of the wicked: further not his wicked device; *lest* they exalt themselves. Selah.
9. *As for* the head of those that compass me about, let the mischief of their own lips cover them.
10. Let burning coals fall upon them: let them be cast into the fire; into deep pits, that they rise not up again.
11. Let not an evil speaker be established in the earth: evil shall hunt the violent man to overthrow *him*.
12. I know that the LORD will maintain the cause of the afflicted, *and* the right of the poor.
13. Surely the righteous shall give thanks unto thy name: the upright shall dwell in thy presence.

Commentary_____

The compiler of Book V of Psalms attributes Psalms 138-145 to David. Some students of the Psalms deduce that these were written later and that the writers simply drew material from the Davidic psalms. But no textual reasons exist that would disprove Davidic authorship. In fact, a number of situations in the biblical record (1 and 2 Samuel) could have prompted David to write Psalm 140. In this psalm he is petitioning the LORD to deliver him and then protect him from the devices of evil men.

In Psalm 58:3-5, David likens the liars who beset him to poisonous snakes. In Romans 3:12-18, the apostle cites Psalm 140:3 as well as several other scriptures as he describes the depravity of the human heart.

Verse 4 rewords verses 1 and 2. In verse 5, David sees himself as a hunted deer and as the prey of a fowler.

"Thou art my God" (v. 6). In Scripture, God often refers to His people as His possession. That is awesome! Beyond awesome is His desire for me to proclaim to Him that He is mine! In this psalm, David invokes the name *Yahweh* (Jehovah) seven times. This is proper because *Yahweh* is God's name as He acts toward man. David is praying for action. As he frequently does, David uses all three of the prominent names of God in one psalm (*Yahweh*, *Adonai*, and *Elohim*).

In verse 7, David recounts the LORD's past protection. Verse 8 gives reasons God should deal with the wicked. Verses 9 and 10 implore God to judge evil. In verse 11, he tells why God should judge and suggests a course of action. He closes by expressing assurance that God will vindicate the afflicted and that they will then render thankful praise as they dwell in His presence.

Application_____

When we petition God, it is good to call Him our God, to speak of past deliverance, and to declare our trust in Him. In Psalm 140, David did this. He also acknowledges that the proper response to God is praise and thanksgiving. We believe our Righteous God will judge sinfulness and reward righteousness.

Psalm 141

A Psalm of David.

1. LORD, I cry unto thee: make haste unto me; give ear unto my voice, when I cry unto thee.
2. Let my prayer be set forth before thee *as* incense; *and* the lifting up of my hands *as* the evening sacrifice.
3. Set a watch, O LORD, before my mouth; keep the door of my lips.
4. Incline not my heart to *any* evil thing, to practise wicked works with men that work iniquity: and let me not eat of their dainties.
5. Let the righteous smite me; *it shall be* a kindness: and let him reprove me; *it shall be* an excellent oil, *which* shall not break my head: for yet my prayer also *shall be* in their calamities.
6. When their judges are overthrown in stony places, they shall hear my words; for they are sweet.
7. Our bones are scattered at the grave's mouth, as when one cutteth and cleaveth *wood* upon the earth.
8. But mine eyes *are* unto thee, O GOD the Lord: in thee is my trust; leave not my soul destitute.
9. Keep me from the snares *which* they have laid for me, and the gins of the workers of iniquity.
10. Let the wicked fall into their own nets, whilst that I withal escape.

Commentary_____

This Davidic prayer is a close follow-up to the one recorded in Psalm 140. He is beset by violent enemies who purpose to overthrow him (cf. 140:4) by "wicked devices" (cf. 140:8). He urgently beseeches the LORD to give immediate and active attention to the situation.

The making and use of incense for worship is described in Exodus 30:34-38. Using it for any other purpose was punishable by death. In Scripture, incense is emblematic of effectual spiritual prayer (Jn. 4:24; Rev. 5:8, 8:3, 4). Just as incense and sacrifices were governed by strict regulations, David wants his prayer to be proper in all aspects. In verse 3, he asks the LORD to "set a watch" over his mouth, his heart, and his actions. He is willing to accept reproof when he needs it, for "open rebuke is better than secret love." "Faithful are the wounds of a friend" (Pr. 27: 5, 6).

Through his prayer, David trusts that the judges (rulers) oppressing him will be overthrown and will hear his words. Many of his people have been slain and left unburied. He knows that God's favorite way of bringing retribution is to use the perpetrator's own devices to destroy him. One of the best scriptural examples is Haman who was hanged on the gallows that he had prepared for Mordecai (Est. 7:10). See also Psalm 7:15, 16 and Psalm 9:16.

Application_____

David knew and confessed that he was unrighteous (2 Sam. 12:13; also Rom. 3:10, Ps. 14:3). He also knew that when he confessed his sinfulness, asking God to search out his heart, God would count him to be righteous (Ps. 32:1, 2). "If we confess our sins, He is faithful and just to forgive us our sins, and to cleanse us from all unrighteousness" (1 Jn. 1:9).

Psalm 142

Maschil of David; A Prayer when he was in the cave.

1. I CRIED unto the LORD with my voice; with my voice unto the LORD did I make my supplication.
2. I poured out my complaint before him; I shewed before him my trouble.
3. When my spirit was overwhelmed within me, then thou knewest my path. In the way wherein I walked have they privily laid a snare for me.
4. I looked on *my* right hand, and beheld, but *there was* no man that would know me: refuge failed me; no man cared for my soul.
5. I cried unto thee, O LORD: I said, Thou *art* my refuge *and* my portion in the land of the living.
6. Attend unto my cry; for I am brought very low: deliver me from my persecutors; for they are stronger than I.
7. Bring my soul out of prison, that I may praise thy name: the righteous shall compass me about; for thou shalt deal bountifully with me.

Commentary_____

Psalm 142 is best understood as a combination of two Davidic prayers. The first prayer (vv. 1-4) is from an individual completely over-whelmed by his circumstances. He had fled alone from King Saul who was set upon killing him. The king of Gath denied David refuge (1 Sam. 21:10-15), and thus he was hiding in a cave (1 Sam. 22:1). See also the superscriptions above this psalm and Psalm 57.

Hiding in a dark cave, pursued and rejected even though he had been anointed king and acclaimed as a national hero, soon brought David to the depths of despair.

The LORD heard his plea. In the second prayer (vv. 5-7), David has mentally triumphed over his circumstances. Complaining to the LORD and showing the LORD his troubles (v. 2) has changed to prais-ing His name (v. 7). "There was no man that would know me" (v. 4) is now "the righteous shall compass me about" (v. 7). "Refuge failed me" (v. 4) has become "[t]hou art my refuge" (v. 5). "[N]o man cared for my soul" (v. 4) becomes "for thou shalt deal bountifully with me" (v. 7).

The immediate fulfillment of verse 7 came when David's family joined him in the cave; then David's four hundred mighty men arrived (1 Sam. 22:1, 2). Many of these men are named along with their mighty deeds in 2 Samuel 23 and 1 Chronicles 11. More complete fulfillment came during David's forty year reign as king. Ultimately, this verse may refer to David's role in the Millenium.

Application_____

David's prayer didn't motivate God to action. God had already pre-pared the way. David's prayer brought his own thinking into alignment with God's promise to him. When we call upon the Lord in faith, he for-tifies us with His promises. We must know His promises in order to rely upon them. They are recorded in His Book.

Psalm 143

A Psalm of David.

1. HEAR MY prayer, O LORD, give ear to my supplications: in thy faithfulness answer me, *and* in thy righteousness.
2. And enter not into judgment with thy servant: for in thy sight shall no man living be justified.
3. For the enemy hath persecuted my soul; he hath smitten my life down to the ground; he hath made me to dwell in darkness, as those that have been long dead.
4. Therefore is my spirit overwhelmed within me; my heart within me is desolate.
5. I remember the days of old; I meditate on all thy works; I muse on the work of thy hands.
6. I stretch forth my hands unto thee: my soul *thirsteth* after thee, as a thirsty land. Selah.
7. Hear me speedily, O LORD: my spirit faileth: hide not thy face from me, lest I be like unto them that go down into the pit.
8. Cause me to hear thy lovingkindness in the morning; for in thee do I trust: cause me to know the way wherein I should walk; for I lift up my soul unto thee.
9. Deliver me, O LORD, from mine enemies: I flee unto thee to hide me.
10. Teach me to do thy will; for thou *art* my God: thy spirit *is* good; lead me into the land of uprightness.
11. Quicken me, O LORD, for thy name's sake: for thy righteousness' sake bring my soul out of trouble.
12. And of thy mercy cut off mine enemies, and destroy all them that afflict my soul: for I *am* thy servant.

Commentary_____

Years before David encountered the circumstances that evoked this psalm, the LORD had anointed him to serve his LORD as king over His people. David finds himself pursued, persecuted, smitten to the ground, dwelling in darkness, and desolate. He is overwhelmed by his plight and petitions the LORD on the basis of His faithfulness and righteousness, not on the basis of His judicial right to pass sentence on David's sinfulness.

David had spent time meditating upon the ways in which the LORD had used him in the past to perform mighty acts. Now he is wasting away, yearning to have his thirst quenched by the hand of God. He is saying, "Please hurry—I am perishing. Let me awake in the morning experiencing your lovingkindness. I am trusting in you."

David is pleading for direction and deliverance. He declares God to be his only refuge from his enemies (see Ps. 142: 4, 5). He expresses a need for instruction in order to do God's will. He is asking that the Spirit of God lead him in the pathway of righteousness.

In this psalm, David declares God to be faithful, righteous, loving, kind, good, and merciful. All of that is included in God's name—that is how He is known. Thus David asks that his soul be brought "out of trouble" to a life of productive service "for thy name's sake" (v. 11). He perceives that this deliverance will require the destruction of his enemies (v. 12).

Application_____

God ordains that the pathway of His servants pass through deep valleys as well as over mountaintops. On the peaks we learn of His power. In the depths we experience His heart. Both are required so that we may "be conformed to the image of His Son, that He might be the firstborn among many brethren" (Rom. 8:29), "bringing many sons unto glory" (Heb. 2:10).

Psalm 144

A *Psalm* of David

1. BLESSED *BE* the LORD my strength, which teacheth my hands to war, *and* my fingers to fight:
2. My goodness, and my fortress: my high tower, and my deliverer; my shield, and *he* in whom I trust; who subdueth my people under me.
3. LORD, what *is* man, that thou takest knowledge of him! *or* the son of man, that thou makest account of him!
4. Man is like to vanity: his days *are* as a shadow that passeth away.
5. Bow thy heavens, O LORD, and come down: touch the mountains, and they shall smoke.
6. Cast forth lightning, and scatter them: shoot out thine arrows, and destroy them.
7. Send thine hand from above; rid me, and deliver me out of great waters, from the hand of strange children;
8. Whose mouth speaketh vanity, and their right hand *is* a right hand of falsehood.
9. I will sing a new song unto thee, O God: upon a psaltery *and* an instrument of ten strings will I sing praises unto thee.
10. *It is he* that giveth salvation unto kings: who delivereth David his servant from the hurtful sword.
11. Rid me, and deliver me from the hand of strange children, whose mouth speaketh vanity, and their right hand *is* a right hand of falsehood:
12. That our sons *may be* as plants grown up in their youth; *that* our daughters *may be* as corner stones, polished *after* the similitude of a palace:
13. *That* our garners *may be* full, affording all manner of store: *that* our sheep may bring forth thousands and ten thousands in our streets:
14. *That* our oxen *may be* strong to labour; *that there be* no breaking in, nor going out; that *there be* no complaining in our streets.
15. Happy *is that* people, that is in such a case: *yea*, happy *is that* people, whose God *is* the LORD.

Commentary

We will examine Psalm 144 from the viewpoint that King David formulated it for worship purposes as he led his army into battle. The historical setting would be the conquests described in 2 Samuel 8. David draws heavily from previously written psalms, particularly Psalm 18 which duplicates 2 Samuel 22. Compare 144:1, 2 with 18:1, 2, 34, and 47. Also compare verse 3 with 8:4, verse 4 with 39:5, and verse 9 with 33:3.

This form is ideal for a proper petition. Verses 1 and 2 extol the LORD by proclaiming the petitioner's comprehension of the capabilities of the One being petitioned. Verses 3 and 4 confess what the petitioner is in the presence of his awesome God. Verses 5-7 present the request. Having announced his utter dependence upon his God and his trust in his God, David remembers scriptural ways in which the LORD has used His creation to subdue the enemies of His people. In verses 8 and 11, he presents reasons the enemy deserves to be vanquished. In verses 9 and 10, he sings a song of trust in anticipation of victory.

Verses 12-15 look forward to the fruit of victory. People whose God is the LORD dwell in peace and prosperity. All is right within the family structure ordained by God from the beginning. This happy existence on Earth was attained to an extent under the forty year reign of Solomon, but it will reach its complete fulfillment only under the coming Messiah's reign in His future kingdom on Earth.

Application

As Christ's servants today, our goal is not material prosperity on Earth. We received peace *with* God at conversion because of Calvary (Rom. 5:1). We appropriate the peace *of* God day to day as we avail ourselves of the ministry of the resurrected Christ (Phil. 4: 7, 9). As Fanny J. Crosby wrote, our goal as His servants is to "rescue the perishing" from the sinking ship of society through the saving gospel message.

Psalm 145:1-9

Daivd's *Psalm* of Praise.

1. I WILL extol thee, my God, O king; and I will bless thy name for ever and ever.
2. Every day will I bless thee; and I will praise thy name for ever and ever.
3. Great *is* the LORD, and greatly to be praised; and his greatness *is* unsearchable.
4. One generation shall praise thy works to another, and shall declare thy mighty acts.
5. I will speak of the glorious honour of thy majesty, and of thy wondrous works.
6. And *men* shall speak of the might of thy terrible acts: and I will declare thy greatness.
7. They shall abundantly utter the memory of thy great goodness, and shall sing of thy righteousness.
8. The LORD *is* gracious, and full of compassion; slow to anger, and of great mercy.
9. The LORD *is* good to all: and his tender mercies *are* over all his works.

Commentary

". . . I will bless thy name forever and ever. Every day will I bless thee . . ." (vv. 1, 2). How do I bless the name of the LORD? I must do what the psalmist does in verses 3-9. Although there are no words sufficient to express God's greatness, which is beyond human comprehension, I will search for words to express the degree of the comprehension I have. In addition, I will surely inform the next generation and make certain it understand its obligation to extol His greatness and the greatness of His mighty acts to following generations (Ps. 78:1-7).

In a world that dishonors His name by using it in vain, I will speak words that honor His glorious majesty. In a world that gives the honor due to Him to "science falsely so called" (1 Tim. 6:20), I will extol His wondrous works.

My reason for declaring the greatness of my God is that others shall speak of His awe-inspiring acts. They shall remember how the greatness of His goodness to them caused them to sing of His righteousness. The LORD desires to demonstrate His graciousness to others. He has not exhausted His storehouse of compassion for lost humanity. While He withholds His anger over sin, He wants to bestow His great supply of mercy. All humans, both saved and lost, are the product of His works. In His goodness, He has provided a way to shower His tender mercies on all who will receive.

Application

Our younger generation must know of its place in the relay race of dispensing the saving gospel message. How else will future generations know? "Thou, therefore, my son, be strong in the grace that is in Christ Jesus. And the things that thou has heard from me among many witnesses, the same commit thou to faithful men, who shall be able to teach others also" (2 Tim. 2:1, 2).

Psalm 145:10-21

10. All thy works shall praise thee, O LORD; and thy saints shall bless thee.

11. They shall speak of the glory of thy kingdom, and talk of thy power;

12. To make known to the sons of men his mighty acts, and the glorious majesty of his kingdom.

13. Thy kingdom *is* an everlasting kingdom, and thy dominion *endureth* throughout all generations.

14. The LORD upholdeth all that fall, and raiseth up all *those that be* bowed down.

15. The eyes of all wait upon thee; and thou givest them their meat in due season.

16. Thou openest thine hand, and satisfiest the desire of every living thing.

17. The LORD *is* righteous in all his ways, and holy in all his works.

18. The LORD *is* nigh unto all them that call upon him, to all that call upon him in truth.

19. He will fulfil the desire of them that fear him: he also will hear their cry, and will save them.

20. The LORD preserveth all them that love him: but all the wicked will he destroy.

21. My mouth shall speak the praise of the LORD: and let all flesh bless his holy name for ever and ever.

Commentary

This is the last of the nine acrostic psalms. The first verse begins with *Aleph*, the first letter of the Hebrew alphabet. The second begins with *Beth*, and so on through the twenty-two letters. However, the verse for the fourteenth letter, *Nun*, is missing. That is the reason the psalm has twenty-one verses instead of twenty-two. One ancient manuscript supplied "[f]aithful is the LORD in His words and holy in all His works" as verse 14. Translators deduced it to be a scribe's attempt to fix the problem until the discovery of the Dead Sea scrolls prompted many to accept the verse's authenticity.

Verses 10-13 look forward to Messiah's future earthly kingdom. Only then will all the LORD's works be universally praised for "the glorious majesty of His kingdom" (v. 12).

The promises of verses 14-19 apply to those who "call upon Him in truth" (v. 18) and "fear Him" (v. 19). These individuals include both the people of the psalmist's day and those of our day who bow to the LORD and wait for Him. He upholds, raises up, gives food, opens His hand, satisfies, hears, and saves.

Because He is faithful, "the LORD preserveth all those who love Him" (v. 20). Because He is holy, "all the wicked will He destroy" (v. 20). Because of all that is proclaimed in this psalm about His greatness (v. 3), His majesty (vv. 5, 12), His wondrous works (v. 5), His goodness (vv. 7, 9), His righteousness (vv. 7, 17), His graciousness, compassion and mercy (v. 8), and His glory and power (v.11), the psalmist concludes with the words of verse 21!

Application

When we read the promise of verse 18, we are thankful that "in Christ Jesus we who once were far off are made nigh by the blood of Jesus Christ" (Eph. 2:13). As Cleland B. McAfee wrote, "There is a place of quiet rest, Near to the heart of God; A place where sin cannot molest, near to the heart of God. There is a place of full release, Near to the heart of God; A place where all is joy and peace, Near to the heart of God."

Psalm 146

1. PRAISE YE the LORD. Praise the LORD, O my soul.

2. While I live will I praise the LORD: I will sing praises unto my God while I have any being.

3. Put not your trust in princes, *nor* in the son of man, in whom *there is* no help.

4. His breath goeth forth, he returneth to his earth; in that very day his thoughts perish.

5. Happy *is he* that *hath* the God of Jacob for his help, whose hope *is* in the LORD his God:

6. Which made heaven, and earth, the sea, and all that therein *is:* which keepeth truth for ever:

7. Which executeth judgment for the oppressed: which giveth food to the hungry. The LORD looseth the prisoners:

8. The LORD openeth *the eyes of* the blind: the LORD raiseth them that are bowed down: the LORD loveth the righteous:

9. The LORD preserveth the strangers; he relieveth the fatherless and widow: but the way of the wicked he turneth upside down.

10. The LORD shall reign for ever, *even* thy God, O Zion, unto all generations. Praise ye the LORD.

Commentary_____

The last five psalms all begin and end with the Hebrew word *Hallelujah*, meaning "Praise the LORD!" The King James Version renders it, "praise <u>ye</u> the LORD" in order to indicate the imperative mood. The five psalms together present a veritable tidal wave of praise, culminating in the crescendo of Psalm 150.

Verse 2 stresses the resolve of Psalm 104:33 and Psalm 116:2. Verse 3 repeats the advice given in Psalm 118:9. Verse 4 gives the reason for the advice. Jeremiah 17:6 tells the consequences of trusting in princes (prominent people). Every individual is impotent because every one is transitory. Every moment he is one breath from death. The One to trust is He "who made heaven, and earth, the sea, and all that therein is" (v. 6). He is omnipotent and eternal.

The One who keeps those who trust Him is not only the Creator (v. 6) but also the righteous Judge, providing Father, and able Deliverer (v. 7). He opens blinded eyes and causes those who are bowed down to walk upright. He is especially cognizant of all who are destitute for any reason.

The "wicked" include all who disregard the one true God. "Fret not thyself because of him who prospereth in his way, because of the man who bringeth wicked devices to pass . . . [f]or evildoers shall be cut off. . ." (Ps. 37:7, 9).

Therefore, praise ye the LORD, "for the LORD shall reign forever" (v. 10).

Application_____

Some concerned church leaders see that praise to God in the churches does not measure up to scriptural exhortations to praise. There is a tendency to call in specialists to teach congregations how to praise. Though it is possible to generate motions and words of praise, true praise wells up from a thankful heart that comprehends, from scriptural teaching, who God is, what He has done, and what He will do.

Psalm 147:1-11

1. PRAISE YE the LORD: for *it is* good to sing praises unto our God; for *it is* pleasant; *and* praise is comely.

2. The LORD doth build up Jerusalem: he gathereth together the outcasts of Israel.

3. He healeth the broken in heart, and bindeth up their wounds.

4. He telleth the number of the stars; he calleth them all by *their* names.

5. Great *is* our LORD, and of great power: his understanding *is* infinite.

6. The LORD lifteth up the meek: he casteth the wicked down to the ground.

7. Sing unto the LORD with thanksgiving; sing praise upon the harp unto our God:

8. Who covereth the heaven with clouds, who prepareth rain for the earth, who maketh grass to grow upon the mountains.

9. He giveth to the beast his food, *and* to the young ravens which cry.

10. He delighteth not in the strength of the horse: he taketh not pleasure in the legs of a man.

11. The LORD taketh pleasure in them that fear him, in those that hope in his mercy.

Commentary_____

The psalmist begins with a call to sing praises to our God because it is good (Ps. 92:1), pleasant (Ps. 135:3), and comely (Ps. 33:1) to do so. He continues (vv. 2-6) by presenting ten reasons it is good, pleasant, and comely (befitting) to sing praises unto God. Each verse is a couplet in which the second reason (phrase) complements the first. The LORD rebuilt Jerusalem so that He could re-gather His people in the Promised Land after the seventy year Babylonian captivity. That historical event looks forward to the final re-gathering prophesied in Deuteronomy 30:3.

Verse 3 had fulfillment in the ministry of Jesus Christ (Lk. 4:18) at His first coming and will be consummated in His millennial reign (Isa. 61: 1-3).

1 Corinthians 15:41, 42 makes a spiritual application to verse 4 in comparing the diversity of the stars to our resurrection bodies. Verse 5 glorifies the LORD as creator by rewording Jeremiah 10:12. Verse 6 rewords Ps. 145:20.

Verse 7 exhorts us to include thanksgiving in singing His praises and to use musical instruments to enhance the singing. Notice that the singing is "unto our God"—not for the aggrandizement of the performer or the hilarity of the human audience!

Verses 8 and 9 praise God as the provider for all His creatures. Reliance upon military and physical strength displeases the LORD. Reliance upon Him brings Him pleasure.

Application_____

This psalm emphasizes the truth of the saying—"The New (Testament) is in the Old concealed; the Old is in the New revealed." As we look for Jesus in each psalm, He opens to us the Scriptures in such a way that "our hearts burn within us" (Lk. 24: 32, 44). He does this through the ministry of the indwelling Holy Spirit (Jn. 16:13), as He applies New Testament light to the Old Testament.

Psalm 147:12-20

12. Praise the LORD, O Jerusalem; praise thy God, O Zion.
13. For he hath strengthened the bars of thy gates; he hath blessed thy children within thee.
14. He maketh peace *in* thy borders, *and* filleth thee with the finest of the wheat.
15. He sendeth forth his commandment *upon* earth: his word runneth very swiftly.
16. He giveth snow like wool: he scattereth the hoarfrost like ashes.
17. He casteth forth his ice like morsels: who can stand before his cold?
18. He sendeth out his word, and melteth them: he causeth his wind to blow, *and* the waters flow.
19. He sheweth his word unto Jacob, his statutes and his judgments unto Israel.
20. He hath not dealt so with any nation: and as *for his* judgments, they have not known them. Praise ye the LORD.

Commentary

Considering verses 12-14 together with verse 2, we conclude that this psalm was written soon after the completion of the rebuilt wall of Jerusalem in 443 BC. This was 143 years after the destruction of Jerusalem by the Babylonians in 586 BC. It was seventy-two years after the completion of the rebuilt Temple (Ezra 6:15).

All during the rebuilding of the temple and the city walls, the returned Jews faced fierce opposition from those who inhabited the Promised Land while the Jews were in captivity. The opposition's ridicule, conspiracy, intrigue, and threat of military force is related in the books of Ezra and Nehemiah.

When the enemy saw the completed walls, realizing it was the work of God, they ceased overt opposition. With great celebration, the walls were dedicated as recorded in Nehemiah 12:27-43. Likely, these final five psalms of praise were written for that occasion.

Compare verse 15 with the apostle Paul's request for prayer in 2 Thessalonians 3:1. "Have free course" in the KJV means "run swiftly without impediment."

Verses 16-18 extol the Creator's continual participation in all that He created. Verses 19 and 20 point out the privilege God bestowed upon Israel by transmitting His Holy Word through that nation. The apostle Paul comments upon this privilege in Romans 3:2.

Application

Find time today to read about the festive procession in Nehemiah 12. Verse 43 tells us the women and children took part in the celebration which "was heard even afar off." You can decide for yourself whether or not these five psalms of praise were written for that occasion.

Psalm 148

1. PRAISE YE the LORD. Praise ye the LORD from the heavens: praise him in the heights.
2. Praise ye him, all his angels: praise ye him, all his hosts.
3. Praise ye him, sun and moon: praise him, all ye stars of light.
4. Praise him, ye heavens of heavens, and ye waters that *be* above the heavens.
5. Let them praise the name of the LORD: for he commanded, and they were created.
6. He hath also stablished them for ever and ever; he hath made a decree which shall not pass.
7. Praise the LORD from the earth, ye dragons, and all deeps:
8. Fire, and hail; snow, and vapour; stormy wind fulfilling his word:
9. Mountains, and all hills; fruitful trees, and all cedars:
10. Beasts, and all cattle; creeping things, and flying fowl:
11. Kings of the earth, and all people; princes, and all judges of the earth:
12. Both young men, and maidens; old men, and children:
13. Let them praise the name of the LORD: for his name alone is excellent; his glory *is* above the earth and heaven.
14. He also exalteth the horn of his people, the praise of all his saints; *even* of the children of Israel, a people near unto him. Praise ye the LORD.

Commentary

"Praise ye the LORD from the heavens" (vv. 1-6).

What do the angelic hosts say when they praise the LORD? They say, "Glory to God in the highest" (Lk. 2:14). They say, "Holy, holy, holy Lord God Almighty who was, and is, and is to come" (Rev. 4:8). They say with a loud voice, "Worthy is the Lamb that was slain to receive power, and riches, and wisdom, and strength, and honor, and glory, and blessing" (Rev. 5:12).

How do the sun, moon, and stars praise Him? By showing His handiwork, they speak of His knowledge day and night in every language "to the end of the world" (Ps. 19:1-4). They do it because "[h]e commanded, and they were created" (Ps. 148:5). They perform according to His decree, and they do not digress from it.

"Praise the LORD from the earth" (vv. 7-12).

How do the creatures of the sea and the elements of the weather fulfill His word? They do His bidding even against their nature (Jon. 2:10; Mk. 4:39). Mountains quake at His presence (Ps. 68:8). Animals speak at His behest (Num. 22:28). Birds perform His work (Gen. 8:8; 1 Ki. 17:4), according to His command. The time will come when the kings of the earth will worship Him (Isa. 49:7: 60:3).

When rulers and the redeemed of every ilk join the angels in praising the LORD, what will they say? They will all say, "Amen! Blessing, and glory, and wisdom, and thanksgiving, and honor, and power, and might be unto our God forever and ever. Amen" (Rev. 7:12).

Application

How should we now be praising our Lord? ". . .be filled with the Spirit, [s]peaking to yourselves in psalms and hymns and spiritual songs, singing and making melody in your heart to the Lord, [g]iving thanks always for all things unto God and the Father in the name of our Lord Jesus Christ" (Eph. 5:18-20). See also Colossians 3:16.

Psalm 149

1. PRAISE YE the LORD. Sing unto the LORD a new song, *and* his praise in the congregation of saints.
2. Let Israel rejoice in him that made him: let the children of Zion be joyful in their King.
3. Let them praise his name in the dance: let them sing praises unto him with the timbrel and harp.
4. For the LORD taketh pleasure in his people: he will beautify the meek with salvation.
5. Let the saints be joyful in glory: let them sing aloud upon their beds.
6. Let the high *praises* of God *be* in their mouth, and a two-edged sword in their hand;
7. To execute vengeance upon the heathen, *and* punishments upon the people;
8. To bind their kings with chains, and their nobles with fetters of iron;
9. To execute upon them the judgment written: this honour have all his saints. Praise ye the LORD.

Commentary

"He hath put a new song in my mouth, praise unto our God; many shall see, and fear, and shall trust in the LORD" (Ps. 40:3). Here are two other reasons given in the Psalms for singing a new song: "For the word of the LORD is right, and all His works are done in truth" (Ps. 33:4); ". . . for He hath done marvelous things. . ."(Ps. 98:1). Some of those "marvelous things" are enumerated in Ps. 98:1-3. Isaiah says the Lord keeps declaring "new things" before "they spring forth," and thus we should sing new songs (Isa. 42: 9, 10). There will be more new songs in the future (Rev. 5:9, 14:3).

Proper scriptural dancing is an outward expression of joy before the LORD. It is always performed in groups (Ex. 15:20; 1 Sam. 21:11) or by individuals (2 Sam. 6:14)—never by couples. It is never a display of one's talents before an audience.

King David's warfare was undertaken with "the high praises of God in their mouth, and a two-edged sword in their hand" (v. 6). Our warfare is undertaken with the "shield of faith" and "the sword of the Spirit, which is the word of God" (Eph. 6:16, 17). "For we wrestle not against flesh and blood, but against . . . spiritual wickedness in high places" (Eph. 6:12). When our Lord comes in power to reign, "out of his mouth goeth a sharp sword, that with it He should smite the nations" (Rev. 19:15). Then Psalm 149:7-9 will be fulfilled.

Application

It is good to sing "his praise in the congregation of saints" (v. 1). The psalmist also recommended singing alone at night (v. 5). Psalm 42:8 reads, ". . . in the night His song shall be with me. . . ." Also Psalm 77:6 declares, "I call to remembrance my song in the night; I commune with mine own heart. . . ." Aloud or in quiet meditation, "Praise ye the LORD!"

Psalm 150

1. PRAISE YE the LORD. Praise God in his sanctuary: praise him in the firmament of his power.
2. Praise him for his mighty acts; praise him according to his excellent greatness.
3. Praise him with the sound of the trumpet: praise him with the psaltery and harp.
4. Praise him with the timbrel and dance: praise him with stringed instruments and organs.
5. Praise him upon the loud cymbals: praise him upon the high sounding cymbals.
6. Let every thing that hath breath praise the LORD. Praise ye the LORD.

Commentary

The book of Psalms is a river of praise, flowing into a cataract of praise in Psalms 146-149 and culminating into a veritable cascade of praise in Psalm 150. After the "praise ye the LORD" which character- izes each of the five final psalms, this psalm exhorts us to praise twice in each of its six verses. It tells where, why, to whom, with what, and by whom praise should be offered.

Under the old covenant, God's sanctuary on Earth was that place He set apart for communion with His people (Ex. 25:8, 22). The word *firmament* can mean the first heaven (Gen. 1:15-17). "The firmament of his power" may extend the term to include God's heavenly abode as well. God is to be praised everywhere.

"[H]is mighty acts" arise from "his excellent greatness" (v. 2). We praise that which God does because His awesome work manifests the awesomeness of His being!

Book I of Psalms ends with a benediction upon the everlasting God followed by a double "Amen" (41:13). Book II ends with a benediction upon His wondrous works, His glorious name and an ascription to His glory (doxology), again adding the double "Amen" (72:18, 19). Book III repeats the benediction of Book I (89:52). Book IV repeats the benedic- tion of Books I and III. Psalm 150 serves as a doxology for the entire psalter.

Application

Since the birth of the church at Pentecost, God's sanctuary on Earth is within each believer in the person of the Holy Spirit (Jn. 14:16, 17). He binds us together in one accord for worship, edifica- tion, and fruitfulness. "And let us consider one another to provoke unto love and to good works, [n]ot forsaking the assembling of ourselves together. . ." (Heb. 10:24, 25).